The Great C

The Bible and Literature

Books by Northrop Frye

Books by Northrop Frye

FEARFUL SYMMETRY: A STUDY OF WILLIAM BLAKE

ANATOMY OF CRITICISM: FOUR ESSAYS

FABLES OF IDENTITY

THE WELL-TEMPERED CRITIC

THE STUBBORN STRUCTURE

FOOLS OF TIME

A NATURAL PERSPECTIVE

THE CRITICAL PATH

THE SECULAR SCRIPTURE

CREATION AND RECREATION

T.S. ELIOT: AN INTRODUCTION

THE GREAT CODE

THE MYTH OF DELIVERANCE

THE EDUCATED IMAGINATION

WORDS WITH POWER

Northrop Frye

The Great Code

The Bible and Literature

A HARVEST BOOK • HARCOURT, INC.

San Diego   New York   London

For information about permission to reproduce
selections from this book, write to Permissions,
Houghton Mifflin Harcourt Publishing Company,
215 Park Avenue South NY, NY 10003

www.hmhco.com

Library of Congress Cataloguing-in-Publication Data

Frye, Northrop.

The great code.

"A Harvest book."

Includes bibliographical references and indexes.

PN56.B547   1983   809'.93522   83-8377

ISBN 0-15-602780-1

First Harvest edition 1983

DOH   10 9

4500550900

Contents

Introduction
xi

Contents

PREFACE AND
ACKNOWLEDGMENTS

This book (with its successor) has been on my mind for a long time, during which I have given lectures on Biblical topics at various places, including McGill (Divinity School), Minnesota, Cincinnati, Cornell, and several universities in Scandinavia. I am grateful for the patience and attention of audiences who listened to early versions of some of the ideas propounded here, some versions too crude in retrospect to bear thinking about. I owe even more to my students, as I trust my Introduction makes clear.

A scholar in an area not his own feels like a knight errant who finds himself in the middle of a tournament and has unaccountably left his lance at home. In such a situation he needs encouragement as well as help. Encouragement has come from many quarters: from Professor William Blissett and Barker Fairley, the two friends referred to in the Introduction; from Professor Cyrus Hamlin, who read the whole manuscript; and from many other colleagues, along with much timely help from my research assistants, among whom I may mention Willard McCarty and Michael Dolzani. Bob Sandler, and also Bill Somerville and his colleagues at the University of Toronto Media Centre, have worked wonders in transferring much of the material of this book to the very different format of television.

Two of my obligations extend beyond the orbit of words altogether. One is to my secretary, Mrs. Jane Widdicombe, for her

unfailing patience and good humor in coping with the whims of two
unpredictable word processors, one of them the author. The other is
to my wife Helen, who has quietly watched over the coming and
going of so many books.

N.F.

Introduction

This book attempts a study of the Bible from the point of view of a literary critic. Originally I wanted to make a fairly thorough inductive survey of Biblical imagery and narrative, followed by some explanation of how these elements of the Bible had set up an imaginative framework—a mythological universe, as I call it—within which Western literature had operated down to the eighteenth century and is to a large extent still operating. I have not lost sight of this aim, but it has receded through a process I had experienced before, when its result was the *Anatomy of Criticism* (1957). Certain preliminary questions, which I had thought would be confined within an introductory chapter or two, expanded, first into an enormous Hegelian preface, and finally into a volume in its own right. After considerable thought, I have decided to remove the ominous heading "Volume One" from the title page, because I should want any book I publish to be a complete unit in itself. But a second volume is in active preparation nonetheless, and this introduction is partly to it as well.

The present book is not a work of Biblical scholarship, much less of theology: it expresses only my own personal encounter with the Bible, and at no point does it speak with the authority of a scholarly consensus. To the question why it should exist at all I have no direct answer, only an explanation of how it came into being. My interest in the subject began in my earliest days as a junior instructor, when I found myself teaching Milton and writing about Blake, two authors who were exceptionally Biblical even by the standards of English literature. I soon realized that a student of English literature who does not know the Bible does not understand a good deal of what is going on in what he reads: the most conscientious student will be continually misconstruing the implications, even the meaning. So I offered a course in the English Bible as a guide to the study of English literature, and as the most efficient way of learning about it myself.

My first aim was only to provide students with enough information about the Bible to enable them to see what kind of literary influence it has had. This would have resulted in, essentially, a "footnote" course, concerned with allusion and texture. Blake's line "O Earth, O Earth return," for example, though it contains only five words and only three different words, contains also about seven direct allusions to the Bible. And in many nineteenth-century authors the cadences of the 1611 translation are constantly echoed, giving an effect rather like that of the echoes of popular proverbs in writings of other cultures. But allusion and texture were not a satisfactory basis for a teaching course, and I had to move to more solid ground.

I examined similar courses in other universities, and found that many of them were called something like "The Bible as Literature," which the reader will have noted is not quite the subtitle of this book. They were based mainly on materials in the Bible that resembled the student's other literary experiences, such as the Book of Job or the parables of Jesus. Naturally these parts of the Bible were important to me as well, but the assumption seemed to be that the Bible was, or could be treated as, a kind of anthology of ancient Near Eastern literature, and such an approach violated all my instincts as a critic. Those instincts told me that the critical operation begins with reading a work straight through, as many times as may be necessary to possess it in totality. At that point the critic can begin to formulate a conceptual unity corresponding to the imaginative unity of his text. But the Bible is a very long and miscellaneous book, and many of those who have tried to read it straight through have bogged down very soon, generally around the middle of Leviticus. One reason for this is that the Bible is more like a small library than a real book: it almost seems that it has come to be thought of as *a* book only because it is contained for convenience within two covers. In fact what the word "Bible" itself primarily means is *ta biblia*, the little books. Perhaps, then, there is no such entity as "the Bible," and what is called "the Bible" may be only a confused and inconsistent jumble of badly established texts.

However, all this, even if true, does not matter. What matters is that "the Bible" has traditionally been read as a unity, and has influenced Western imagination as a unity. It exists if only because it has been compelled to exist. Yet, whatever the external reasons, there has to be some internal basis even for a compulsory existence. Those who do succeed in reading the Bible from beginning to end will discover that at least it has a beginning and an end, and some traces of a total structure. It begins where time begins, with the creation of the world; it ends where time ends, with the Apocalypse, and it surveys human history in between, or the aspect of history it is interested in, under the symbolic names of Adam and Israel. There is also a body of concrete images: city, mountain, river, garden, tree, oil, fountain, bread, wine, bride, sheep, and many others, which recur so often that they clearly indicate some kind of unifying principle. That unifying principle, for a critic, would have to be one of shape rather than meaning; or, more accurately, no book can have a coherent meaning unless there is some coherence in its shape. So the course turned into a presentation of a unified structure of narrative and imagery in the Bible, and this forms the core of the present book.

For my purposes the only possible form of the Bible that I can deal with is the Christian Bible, with its polemically named "Old" and "New" Testaments. I know that Jewish and Islamic conceptions of the Bible are very different, but that is practically all that I do know about them, and it is the Christian Bible that is important for English literature and the Western cultural tradition generally. For quotations I use the "Authorized Version" of 1611, abbreviated as AV, except where it is wrong or inadequate. I use it not because of the beauty of its cadences: conventional aesthetic canons of that sort I wanted to get rid of at the start. Nor is it only because of its central place as the most familiar and accessible version. Most copies of the AV in general circulation not only omit the Apocrypha, which was part of the 1611 enterprise, but, while they include the dedication to King James, which is only a perfunctory piece of rhetoric, they also omit the "Address to the Reader," where the translators set forth very honestly what they were trying to do and what their translating policy was. I use their version because, as they explain in that Address, they were not trying to make a new translation but a traditional one. In other words the AV is a translation centrally in the Vulgate tradition, and so comes very close to the Bible familiar to writers in Europe from the fifth century on. The differences between Protestant and Roman Catholic versions of the Bible, which have been greatly exaggerated in any case, are of very little importance for a book like this. I am not concerned with the true meaning of such words as *episcopos* or *ecclesia*, but, for the most part, with nouns so concrete that it is practically impossible for any translator to get them wrong.

The course proved useful (I am still teaching it), and it was obvious that a book along the lines of the course was badly needed. This suggested a kind of handbook or introductory study, and the present volume still retains its original aim of introducing the general reader to a knowledge of the Bible and to some of the applications he can make of such knowledge in the rest of his reading. But the original aim has become overlaid with other issues. In a sense all my critical work, beginning with a study of Blake published in 1947, and formulated ten years later in *Anatomy of Criticism*, has revolved around the Bible. Hence the total project is, among other things, a restatement of the critical outlook I have been expounding in various ways for years. I feel that it is now very far from being what I was afraid at first it would turn into, a rewritten version of the *Anatomy*, but I apologize in advance to readers who may often feel that they have been here before. All I can say is that I am aware of the dangers of restating what I have said elsewhere in a different context, and that the repetitions unavoidable here are not wholly that. In this volume such features as the categories of metaphor, the ladder of "polysemous sense," the conception of literal meaning, and the identification of mythology and literature are presented in what I hope is a new framework.

Two very good friends and colleagues of mine on the Toronto campus understood my situation, and made a point of reminding me whenever they saw me that I had still to write "a big book on the Bible," as one of them called it. The immediate obstacle there was my lack of scholarly competence in the primary fields. I am not a Biblical scholar, and anyone who was one could say of my Hebrew and Greek what Samuel Johnson said, with far less justice, of Milton's two Tetrachordon sonnets, that the first is contemptible, and the second not excellent. Yet even these were only the shallow waters. A scholarly book was out of the question: too many scholarly fields were relevant.

I have begun with a reference to my teaching because the present book has grown directly out of my teaching interests rather than out of scholarly ones. But then all my books have really been teachers' manuals, concerned more with establishing perspectives than with adding specifically to knowledge. Certainly this book shows all the tactics of teaching, including the use of paradox and the pretense of naïveté. By that I mean that simplifying and oversimplifying are much the same thing from two points of view, the student's and the scholar's, and this book is addressed to the student's position. The ideal of the scholar is to convey what he knows as clearly and fully as he can: he lays down his hand and remains dummy, so to speak, while the reader plays it. The teacher may do some of his work as a scholar on a popularizing level, retailing established information to less advanced students. This conception of teaching as secondhand scholarship is common among academics, but I regard it as inadequate.

The teacher, as has been recognized at least since Plato's *Meno*, is not primarily someone who knows instructing someone who does not know. He is rather someone who attempts to re-create the subject in the student's mind, and his strategy in doing this is first of all to get the student to recognize what he already potentially knows, which includes breaking up the powers of repression in his mind that keep him from knowing what he knows. That is why it is the teacher, rather than the student, who asks most of the questions. The teaching element in my own books has caused some resentment among my readers, a resentment often motivated by loyalty to different teachers. This is connected with a feeling of deliberate elusiveness on my part, prompted mainly by the fact that I am not dispensing with the quality of irony that all teachers from Socrates on have found essential. Not all elusiveness, however, is merely that. Even the parables of Jesus were *ainoi*, fables with a riddling quality. In other areas, such as Zen Buddhism, the teacher is often a man who shows his qualifications to teach by refusing to answer questions, or by brushing them off with a paradox. To answer a question (a point we shall return to later in the book) is to consolidate the mental level on which the question is asked. Unless something is kept in reserve, suggesting the possibility of better and fuller questions, the student's mental advance is blocked.

And just as the "scholarly/unscholarly" antithesis had somehow to be got over, whether evaded or transcended, so the "personal/impersonal" antithesis had to be got over too. Academics, like other people, start with a personality that is afflicted by ignorance and prejudice, and try to escape from that personality, in Eliot's phrase, through absorption in impersonal scholarship. One emerges on the other side of this realizing once again that all knowledge is personal knowledge, but with some hope that the person may have been, to whatever degree, transformed in the meantime. I was attracted to the

Bible, not because I thought it reinforced any "position" of mine, but because it suggested a way of getting past some of the limitations inherent in all positions.

A literary approach to the Bible is not in itself illegitimate: no book could have had so specific a literary influence without itself possessing literary qualities. But the Bible is just as obviously "more" than a work of literature, whatever "more" means—I could not feel that a quantitative metaphor was much help. I have spoken of my wish to get clear of conventional aesthetic canons, but "unity" is one of those canons, and the Bible's disregard of unity is quite as impressive as its exhibition of it. Ultimately, as we should expect, the Bible evades all literary criteria. As Kierkegaard said, an apostle is not a genius—not that I ever found "genius" a very useful word either. My experience in secular literature had shown me how the formal principles of literature had been contained within literature, as the formal principles of music, embodied in sonata, fugue, or rondo, have no existence outside music. But here is a book that has had a continuously fertilizing influence on English literature from Anglo-Saxon writers to poets younger than I, and yet no one would say that the Bible "is" a work of literature. Even Blake, who went much farther than anyone else in his day in identifying religion and human creativity, did not call it that: he said "The Old and New Testaments are the Great Code of Art," a phrase I have used for my title after pondering its implications for many years.

I realized early in my critical life that evaluation was a minor and subordinate function of the critical process, at best an incidental by-product, which should never be allowed to take priority over scholarship. It is often said that choosing one poet to talk about rather than another implies a value judgment; this is true, and indicates where value judgments belong: in the area of tentative working assumptions, where they can be subject to revision. They are not the beginning of the critical operation properly speaking. Accepting the usual value judgment on Shakespeare, and finding that value judgment confirmed by experience, may prompt one to continue studying Shakespeare; but the resulting scholarship will never be founded on the value judgment. Still less are they the end of it: the answer to the question Why is *A* more rewarding to talk about than *B*?, so far as there is an answer, can be found only in the further study of *A*. Further study of *A* could eventually lead us through literature into the broader question of the social function of words. Evaluation, which stops of necessity with the category of literature, blocks that expansion. The Bible by-passed this obstruction, mainly because all questions of value in its regard were so palpably futile. Thus it began to lead me outside literature into the larger verbal context of which literature forms a part.

There have always been two directions in Biblical scholarship, the critical and the traditional, though often they have merged. The critical approach establishes the text and studies the historical and cultural background; the traditional interprets it in accordance with what a consensus of theological and ecclesiastical authorities have declared the meaning to be. I could not find the clues I wanted in critical Biblical scholarship, so far as I was acquainted with it. The analytical and historical approach that has dominated Biblical criticism for over a century was of relatively little use to me, however incidentally I may depend on it. At no point does it throw any real light on how or why a poet might read the Bible. I have suggested elsewhere that textual scholarship has never really developed the "higher" criticism that made such a noise in the nineteenth century. Instead of emerging from lower criticism, or textual study, most of it dug itself into a still lower, or sub-basement, criticism in which disintegrating the text became an end in itself. As a result its essential discoveries were made quite early, and were followed by a good deal of straw-thrashing.

There are any number of books, for example, telling us that the account of creation with which the Book of Genesis opens comes from the Priestly narrative, much the latest of the four or five documents that make up the book. A genuine higher criticism, I should think, would observe that this account of creation stands at the beginning of Genesis, despite its late date, because it belongs at the beginning of Genesis. That would lead to an integrated study of the Book of Genesis, and eventually of the whole Bible, as it now stands, concerning itself with the question of why the Bible as we know it emerged in that particular form. The Bible does not, for all its miscellaneous content, present the appearance of having come into existence through an improbable series of accidents; and, while it is certainly the end product of a long and complex editorial process, the end product needs to be examined in its own right.

There remained the more traditional approaches of medieval typology and of certain forms of Reformation commentary. These were more congenial to me because they accepted the unity of the Bible as a postulate. They do tell us how the Bible can be intelligible to poets, and we can understand from them why, for example,

Claudel would have turned to the Victorine typological school and made it a seminal influence on his poetry. But again, as a twentieth-century writer addressing twentieth-century readers, there seemed to me a need for a fresh and contemporary look at the Bible as an element in our present literary and critical concerns.

In my *Anatomy of Criticism* I remarked that literary criticism was approaching the area of the social sciences. The statement was strongly resisted, as it cut across the conditioned reflexes of most humanists at the time, but language since then has been taken to be a model of investigation in so many fields, and the theory of language has revolutionized so many approaches in psychology, anthropology, and political theory, to say nothing of literary criticism itself, that no one can any longer regard the humanistic concern with language as separable or even distinguishable from other concerns. In many respects this simply opens up a new field of ignorance for me, and in any case many seminal questions in contemporary criticism would overcomplicate this introduction and must be left for later discussion. Some current critical issues seem to me to be temporary, leading only to some kind of paradoxical or irrational dead end. But the genuine issues are, I think, closely related to the study of the Bible, and in fact are hampered by not being related more closely to it.

Man lives, not directly or nakedly in nature like the animals, but within a mythological universe, a body of assumptions and beliefs developed from his existential concerns. Most of this is held unconsciously, which means that our imaginations may recognize elements of it, when presented in art or literature, without consciously understanding what it is that we recognize. Practically all that we can see of this body of concern is socially conditioned and culturally inherited. Below the cultural inheritance there must be a common psychological inheritance, otherwise forms of culture and imagination outside our own traditions would not be intelligible to us. But I doubt if we can reach this common inheritance directly, by-passing the distinctive qualities in our specific culture. One of the practical functions of criticism, by which I mean the conscious organizing of a cultural tradition, is, I think, to make us more aware of our mythological conditioning.

The Bible is clearly a major element in our own imaginative tradition, whatever we may think we believe about it. It insistently raises the question: Why does this huge, sprawling, tactless book sit there inscrutably in the middle of our cultural heritage like the "great Boyg" or sphinx in *Peer Gynt*, frustrating all our efforts to walk around it? Giambattista Vico, a thinker to whom I will refer again in a moment, worked out an elaborate theory of culture as he saw it, confining himself to secular history and avoiding the whole of the Bible. This was doubtless for prudential reasons, but there is no such excuse today for scholars who, in discussing cultural issues originally raised by the Bible and still largely informed by it, proceed as though the Bible did not exist. It seems to me that someone not a specialist in the Biblical field needs to call attention to the Bible's existence and relevance. Some of my suggestions may be based on nothing more than a *post hoc propter hoc* fallacy, but until the *post hocs* have been looked at more closely we cannot know how many of them are only that.

Many issues in critical theory today had their origin in the hermeneutic study of the Bible; many contemporary approaches to criticism are obscurely motivated by a God-is-dead syndrome that also developed out of Biblical criticism; many formulations of critical theory seem to me more defensible when applied to the Bible than they are when applied elsewhere. Naturally, if such statements are true now, they must have had counterparts in the past. In English literature the canons of criticism were established mainly by Samuel Johnson, who followed the normal Protestant practice of keeping the poetic aspect of the Bible in a separate compartment from secular literature. It was the Romantics who realized that such a separation was irrational. Coleridge's brilliant insights into Biblical typology make it clear that he would have made things much easier for his students, and more productive for his influence, if he had provided an interconnected statement of his views on that subject. Such a statement would not have had to be the massive encyclopedic treatise on the Logos which he meditated, and which perhaps no single scholar could have completed. Ruskin's work, too, would surely have been far less diffuse if his conceptions of Biblical typology had been more systematically worked out. There was a misguided vogue fifty years ago for attacking the Romantics on this point, asserting that they confused literature and religion; but critical theory is coming back into focus, and many contemporary critics are well aware of the relevance of Biblical criticism to secular literature. Of these, three in particular, Hans-Georg Gadamer, Paul Ricoeur, and Walter Ong, have been influential on this book, if not necessarily always in ways that they would endorse.

In the last two decades a great many books have been written on the relevance of Oriental religion to contemporary Western modes of thought, in psychology, philosophy, even in physics. Meanwhile a good deal of the Orient is committed to Marxism, which is the direct heir of the revolutionary and socially organized forms of religion derived from the Bible. Recently a Chinese student, a teacher in his own country and about to return there, asked me how he could explain the cultural importance of Christianity for the West to his students in a way that would be intelligible to them. I suggested that they would have some understanding of Marxism, that Marx's spiritual father was Hegel, and that therefore his spiritual grandfather was Martin Luther. As for the other half of this cultural exchange, one naturally welcomes the increased interest in Buddhist and Hindu and Taoist modes of thought in the West, but perhaps these would be even more illuminating for us if we understood better what kind of counterparts they have in our own tradition. No serious treatment of this subject can be attempted here, but a book on the imaginative aspect of the Bible may suggest some leads to it.

As a teacher I know how emotionally explosive the material I am dealing with is, and how constantly it is the anxieties of the reader that make the primary response to whatever is being said. There are fewer mental blocks in studying religious traditions outside our own. Naturally, in teaching a course under the rubrics of academic freedom and professional ethics, one has to avoid any suggestion of leading the student toward or away from any position of what is called belief. The academic aim is to see what the subject means, not to accept or reject it. The great majority of my students understood this principle at once: those who had difficulty with it showed an invariable pattern of resistance. If they felt already committed to a position of acceptance, they were afraid of being led away from it; if they were antagonistic to such a position, they were afraid of being led toward it.

This raised the question in my mind: Why are belief and disbelief, as ordinarily understood, so often and so intensely anxious and insecure? The immediate answer is that they are closely connected with the powers of repression I referred to earlier as being the teacher's first point of attack. What we usually think of as acceptance or rejection of belief does not in either case involve any disturbance in our habitual mental processes. It seems to me that trying to think within the categories of myth, metaphor, and typology—all of them exceedingly "primitive" categories from most points of view—does involve a good deal of such disturbance. The result, however, I hope and have reason to think, is an increased lucidity, an instinct for cutting through a jungle of rationalizing verbiage to the cleared area of insight.

Information does have to be conveyed in teaching, of course, but for the teacher the imparting of information is again in a context of irony, which means that it often looks like a kind of game. When the subject to be taught is literature, this element of game takes on a special appearance. Literature continues in society the tradition of myth-making, and myth-making has a quality that Lévi-Strauss calls *bricolage*, a putting together of bits and pieces out of whatever comes to hand. Long before Lévi-Strauss, T. S. Eliot in an essay on Blake used practically the same image, speaking of Blake's resourceful Robinson Crusoe method of scrambling together a system of thought out of the odds and ends of his reading. I owe a great deal to this essay, somewhat negatively, because I soon realized that Blake was a typical poet in this regard: he differed from Dante only in that Dante's *bricolage* was more widely accepted, and differed from Eliot himself, in this respect, hardly at all.

In a way I have tried to look at the Bible as a work of *bricolage*, in a book which is also that. I retain my special affection for the literary genre I have called the anatomy, especially for Burton's *Anatomy of Melancholy*, with its schematic arrangements that are hardly those of any systematic medical treatment of melancholy, and yet correspond to something in the mind that yields a perhaps even deeper kind of comprehension. Such books as Burton's have an extraordinary pulling power: I understand very well what Samuel Johnson meant by saying that Burton's was the only book that got him out of bed earlier than he wanted to. If I cannot match that, I have at least been more liberal with charts and diagrams than usual.

What follows attempts to extract the introductory and prefatory part of what I have to say about the Bible's relation to Western literature. A book concerned with the impact of the Bible on the creative imagination has to by-pass the much more fully cultivated areas of faith, reason, and scholarly knowledge, though it must show some awareness of their existence. As a result, issues that the reader may feel are entitled to much fuller treatment often have to be cut to a sentence or two. The first chapter is concerned with language—not the language of the Bible itself, but the language that people use in talking about the Bible and questions connected with it, such as the existence of God. Kenneth Burke calls such language the rhetoric of religion. This opening chapter establishes a context for discussing the Bible as an imaginative influence, and seems to me a necessary introduction for that reason, even though its direct contact with the Bible may seem slight at first reading.

There follow two chapters on myth and metaphor, defining those terms within the area of criticism, and concerned mainly to establish the point that myth and metaphor answer the question: What is the literal meaning of the Bible? The general thesis is that the Bible comes to us as a written book, an absence invoking a historical presence "behind" it, as Derrida would say, and that the background presence gradually shifts to a foreground, the re-creation of that reality in the reader's mind. The fourth chapter on typology concludes the first part by adding a temporal dimension to the argument, and connects it with the traditional way in which Christianity has always read its Bible.

The book fell accidentally into the "double mirror" pattern it describes as existing in the Christian Bible itself, and the second part deals with a more direct application of its critical principles to the structure of the Bible, but in reverse order. We start with what I isolate as seven phases of what is traditionally called revelation: creation, exodus, law, wisdom, prophecy, gospel, and apocalypse. Two forms of apocalyptic vision are postulated, making eight in all, the eighth bringing us back to the central thesis of the role of the reader. Then comes an inductive survey of, first, the imagery, and then the narrative structures of the Bible, which is the point from which the book took its origin. The final chapter makes a second approach to the "rhetoric of religion," and includes a brief sketch of a "polysemous" or multileveled conception of meaning as applied to the Bible. The latter attempts to suggest some answers to questions about the direction in which we go from the "literal" meaning.

I should hope that a further study would bring us closer to commentary in more detail on the text of the Bible. Ruth, the Song of Songs, and the folktale material in the Apocrypha have a particularly obvious literary reference and yet get very short shrift here. Most readers of this book are assumed either to have relatively little familiarity with the Bible, or, if they are familiar with it, to be unaccustomed to relating it to imaginative rather than doctrinal or historical criteria. I am not, of course, claiming that imaginative criteria have a monopoly of truth or relevance, only that they are the only ones consistent with my specific assumptions.

At one end of the spectrum of possible readers for this book are those so deeply committed to the existential and the religious issues of the Bible that they would regard such a book as this as a mere exercise in sterile dilettantism. At the other end are those who assume that the Bible must be some kind of "establishment" symbol, bound up with sexual inhibitions and a primitive view of biology, and that any interest in it must be a sign of some authoritarian or infantile malaise. This book is addressed to readers of good will who are somewhere in between. Some even of these may well feel that to attempt a fresh and firsthand look at the Bible is mere foolhardiness, and of course they may be right, but the years have brought me an elastic conscience and a tenure appointment. Besides, I know of no other book that covers the same ground. Nevertheless, I have often felt during its writing like Milton's Satan journeying through chaos, where every step, which may be not a step but burrowing or flying or swimming, is surrounded by endless vistas of unknown territory. What I have to say may often seem stupefyingly obvious—this derives partly from the "handbook" nature of what I originally wanted to do—but even the obvious, in this field, is seldom put together in a connected form. For moments of discouragement I have adopted a motto, a haunting and deeply moving phrase from Giordano Bruno: "Est aliquid prodisse tenus." It may still be something to have made a statement, if only to stimulate the writing of better books.

THE
ORDER
OF
WORDS

CHAPTER ONE

LANGUAGE I

A sacred book is normally written with at least the concentration of poetry, so that, like poetry, it is closely involved with the conditions of its language. The Koran, for instance, is so interwoven with the special characteristics of the Arabic language that in practice Arabic has had to go everywhere the Islamic religion has gone. Jewish commentary and scholarship, whether Talmudic or Kabbalistic in direction, have always, inevitably, dealt with the purely linguistic features of the Hebrew text of the Old Testament. In contrast, while Christian scholarship is naturally no less aware of the importance of language, Christianity as a religion has been from the beginning dependent on translation. The New Testament was written in a *koine* Greek unlikely to have been the native language of its authors, and, whatever the degree of familiarity of those authors with Hebrew, they tended to make more use of the Septuagint Greek translation in referring to the Old Testament. The Jews, on the evidence of the Letter of Aristeas, at first greeted the Septuagint with great enthusiasm, but the use made of it by Christianity tended to push them back to a renewed emphasis on the Hebrew original.

St. Jerome's Latin, or Vulgate, translation of the Bible, if it did not exactly establish a new text, certainly established a new perspective on the text; and the Vulgate, in Western Europe, *was* the Bible for a thousand years. The revival of Greek and Hebrew studies at the end of the Middle Ages coincided with the Reformation and the issue of vernacular translations, of which the German and English were the most important from a literary and cultural point of view. From the first Pentecost, when, according to Acts 2, a "gift of tongues" descended on the original disciples, down to the missionary societies of the nineteenth century, with their ideal of eventually translating the Bible into every language spoken, the emphasis on translation has been consistent. Sometimes this activity has created written languages where there were none before, with new alphabets devised for the purpose.

Yet everyone concerned with language is aware of the extent to which reading a translation is a settling for the second best. This is particularly true of major poetry, where translation has to be a miracle of tact, and even then does not claim to replace its original. On the other hand, abstracts of articles in scientific or mathematical journals can easily be translated or even read in the original by those with limited command of the language, because there is a third underlying language of subject matter which is international. The Bible, however, seems much closer to the poetic area than to the scientific-journal area. Clearly, then, one of our first problems is to determine the positive reality of translation, the essential thing or force or process that translation translates.

This question normally starts with a rough-and-ready distinction between sound and sense. The sound-associations within a language cannot usually be translated adequately, although they are of immense importance in building up linguistic responses. This fact has nothing to do with whether philology recognizes the associations as genuine within its own area. The assonances between words of similar reference (e.g., "God" and "good" in English), the standard rhymes, the words of multiple meanings that allow for puns, are all accidents, or, as philologists like to say, "pure" coincidences; yet they make up a texture that enters into the mental processes of all native speakers of the language, whether they are writers or not. Such a texture, extending as it does to a dense mass of idioms that can often be translated only by a complete rephrasing of the original, helps to make language one of the most fragmented of all human phenomena.

What can be translated, we assume, is that particular relation between different signifiers to a common signified that is known as "sense." To use a convenient French distinction: there is, in addition to the *langue* that separates English and French and German, also a *langage* that makes it possible to express similar things in all three languages. This is true even of poetry or drama. If we enter a Chinese or Japanese theater we are instantly aware, even if we know nothing of the language, that a dramatic experience recognizably like those we are familiar with is being presented. If we take the next step and learn something of the language, we discover that, for all the difference in linguistic and cultural reference, there is still a common sense that can, up to a point, be translated. It is not necessary to invoke any more subtle entities, such as Jung's collective unconscious, to explain the fact that human creative expression all over the world has some degree of mutual intelligibility and communicating power. We note further that Luther's German Bible, and the sequence of English Bibles culminating in the AV, were powerful generators of imagery, narrative, allusion, and other forms of verbal articulateness in their cultures; the same could be said of many Classical and other translations. What we call *langage*, then, is a very positive linguistic force. One wonders whether it is substantial enough for there to be such a thing as a history of *langage*, a sequence of modes of more or less translatable structures in words, cutting across the variety of *langues* employed, affected and conditioned but not wholly determined by them. Such a possibility, if it could become anything more than that, would provide a historical context for the Bible of a type that I do not think has yet been examined.

This question took me to Vico, the first person in the modern world to think seriously about such matters. According to Vico, there are three ages in a cycle of history: a mythical age, or age of gods; a heroic age, or age of an aristocracy; and an age of the people, after which there comes a *ricorso* or return that starts the whole process over again. Each age produces its own kind of *langage*, giving us three types of verbal expression that Vico calls, respectively, the poetic, the heroic or noble, and the vulgar, and which I shall call the hieroglyphic, the hieratic, and the demotic. These terms refer primarily to three modes of writing, because Vico believed that men communicated by signs before they could talk. The hieroglyphic phase, for Vico, is a "poetic" use of language; the hieratic phase is mainly allegorical; and the demotic phase is descriptive. Vico's three terms, apart from their identification with writing, are extremely suggestive as providing a starting point for thinking about the place of the Bible in the history of language as *langage*, though in what finally emerged for me very little of Vico was left. The sequence of literary modes in my *Anatomy of Criticism* is much closer to Vico, but that relates to a different set of phenomena, as I shall try to show.

I think we can see in most Greek literature before Plato, more especially in Homer, in the pre-Biblical cultures of the Near East, and in much of the Old Testament itself, a conception of language that is poetic and "hieroglyphic," not in the sense of sign-writing, but in the sense of using words as particular kinds of signs. In this period there is relatively little emphasis on a clear separation of subject and object: the emphasis falls rather on the feeling that subject and object are linked by a common power or energy. Many "primitive" societies have words expressing this common energy of human personality and natural environment, which are untranslatable into our normal categories of thought but are very pervasive in theirs: the best known is the Melanesian word *mana*. The articulating of words may bring this common power into being; hence a magic develops in which verbal elements, "spell," and "charm," and the like, play a central role. A corollary of this principle is that there may be a potential magic in any use of words. Words in such a context are words of power or dynamic forces.

Thus knowing the name of a god or elemental spirit may give the knower some control over it; puns and popular etymologies involved in the naming of people and places affect the character of whatever thing or person is given the name. Warriors begin battles with boasts that may be words of power for them: boasting is most objectionable to the gods for a corresponding reason: the possibility of man's acquiring through his words the power that he clearly wants. The vow that cannot be broken, including the rash vows that begin so many folktales, as in Jephthah's "I have opened my mouth unto the Lord, and I cannot go back" (Judges 11:35), again expresses the sense of quasi-physical power released by the utterance of words. When a sacrosanct myth is read at a religious ritual, as, say, the Babylonian creation myth *Enuma elish* was read at the New Year, some kind of magical energy is clearly being released. It would perhaps be overconceptualizing to say that it was thought to encourage the natural cycle to keep turning for another year; but where the subject and the object are not clearly separated, and there are forms of energy common to both, a controlled and articulated expression of words may have repercussions in the natural order.

All words in this phase of language are concrete: there are no true verbal abstractions. Onians' monumental study of Homer's vocabulary, *Origins of European Thought*, shows how intensely physical are such conceptions as soul, mind, time, courage, emotion, or thought, in the Homeric poems. They are solidly anchored in physical images connected with bodily processes or with specific objects. Similarly the word *kairos,* which came to mean a crucial moment in time, originally meant the notch of an arrow. What this means from the critical point of view is that while Homer's conceptions would not have been metaphorical to him (when he uses a figure of speech it is usually a simile), they have to be metaphorical to us. As we think of words, it is only metaphor that can express in language the sense of an energy common to subject and object. The central expression of metaphor is the "god," the being who, as sun-god, war-god, sea-god, or whatever, identifies a form of personality with an aspect of nature.

The operations of the human mind are also controlled by words of power, formulas that become a focus of mental activity. Prose in this phase is discontinuous, a series of gnarled epigrammatic and oracular statements that are not to be argued about but must be accepted and pondered, their power absorbed by a disciple or reader. Pre-Socratic philosophers such as Heraclitus or Pythagoras seem to have been essentially oral teachers or gurus; and what has survived from them consists mainly of discontinuous aphorisms with a cosmological reference, like the "all things flow" of Heraclitus. We shall return to this feature of discontinuity at the end of the book.

With Plato we enter a different phase of language, one that is "hieratic," partly in the sense of being produced by an intellectual elite. I am speaking here not of ordinary language but of the culturally ascendant language, a language that, at the time or later, is accorded a special authority by its society. In this second phase language is more individualized, and words become primarily the outward expression of inner thoughts or ideas. Subject and object are becoming more consistently separated, and "reflection," with its overtones of looking into a mirror, moves into the verbal foreground. The intellectual operations of the mind become distinguishable from the emotional operations; hence abstraction becomes possible, and the sense that there are valid and invalid ways of thinking, a sense which is to a degree independent of our feelings, develops into the conception of logic. What Homeric heroes revolve in their bosoms is an inseparable mixture of thought and feeling; what Socrates demonstrates, more especially in his death, is the superior penetration of thought when it is in command of feeling.

The basis of expression here is moving from the metaphorical, with its sense of identity of life or power or energy between man and nature ("this is that"), to a relationship that is rather metonymic ("this is put for that"). Specifically, words are "put for" thoughts, and are the outward expressions of an inner reality. But this reality is not merely "inside." Thoughts indicate the existence of a transcendent order "above," which only thinking can communicate with and which only words can express. Thus metonymic language is, or tends to become, analogical language, a verbal imitation of a reality beyond itself that can be conveyed most directly by words.

The basis of Plato's use of language is the teaching method of Socrates; and Socrates, unlike his predecessors in Greek philosophy, professed not to know anything but only to be looking for something. His celebrated "irony" was a momentous step in transforming the use of language: it implied renouncing the personal possession of wisdom in favor of an ability to observe it. Wisdom so observed emerges from a dialogue or group discussion, typically the symposium, but, with Socrates usually acting as a guide, it seems to take on a direction and purpose of its own, and eventually enters its real home, a world of ideas, where it can be followed only by the intellectual soul within the body of the seeker. Plato is a very great literary artist, but his greatness has much to do with the break that he made from typically literary forms of expression. The first phase of language, being founded on the metaphor, is inherently, as Vico says, "poetic"; the second phase, which is Plato's, retreats from the poetic into the dialectical, a world of thought separate from and in some respects superior to the physical world of nature.

Socrates does not, like Heraclitus, utter discontinuous aphorisms to be pondered and assimilated, though he quotes one or two from oracles, but orders his discussion in a sequacious argument. The argument, like the argument of the epic in a different way, starts in the middle and moves both backward and forward: backward to definitions of the terms used, forward to the consequences and implications of adopting these definitions. Eric Havelock, in *A Preface to Plato*, associates the Platonic revolution in language with the development of writing, which was originally confined mainly to commercial transactions but was now extending itself into culturally ascendant areas. For my purposes, however, it will be more useful to associate the Platonic revolution with the development of continuous prose. Continuous prose, though often regarded, with Molière's Jourdain, as the language of ordinary speech, is a late and far from "natural" stylistic development, and is much less direct and primitive than verse, which invariably precedes it in the history of literature. The language of ordinary speech, as I have tried to show elsewhere, has a loose associative rhythm quite different from actual prose.

Plato's interest in mathematics is consistent with his use of language, for there are obvious metonymic features in mathematics. In Euclidean geometry, for example, the drawn line, which necessarily has some breadth, is "put for" the ideal or conceptual line that is length without breadth; similarly with the conception of abstract number apart from a number of things. One feels that some of the pre-Socratics and atomic philosophers, such as Anaxagoras or Democritus, were moving more directly from metaphor toward what we should think of as science, from gods to the operations of nature, and that Plato turns away from this direction, toward a transcendent world rather than an objective one. The *Timaeus* seems to be involved primarily with the degree to which nature conforms to conceptual models, and in the *Phaedo* this sense of aesthetic conformity seems to be linked to matters of faith. But what may seem in hindsight to be a retrograde tendency may be less so in the perspective we are trying to attain here.

In Raphael's *School of Athens* Plato points to heaven and Aristotle to the earth, but as far as his main historical influence goes Aristotle points straight ahead. He worked out the organon of a deductive logic based on a theory of multiple causation, and provided a technique for arranging words to make a conquering march across reality, subjects pursuing objects through all the obstacles of predicates, as the Macedonian phalanxes of his pupil Alexander marched across Asia. But it was a long time before his techniques could really be absorbed by later thinkers. In the later Classical period Plato's sense of a superior order that only language, in both its verbal and mathematical forms, can approach merges with the conception generally identified as *logos*. This is a conception of a unity of consciousness or reason, suggested by the fact that properly constructed verbal sequences seem to have an inherent power of compelling assent. In Stoicism, and in Christianity in a different way from the beginning, the conception of *logos* acquires both a religious and a political dimension: it is seen as a possible means of uniting human society both spiritually and temporally.

In metaphorical language the central conception which unifies human thought and imagination is the conception of a plurality of gods, or embodiments of the identity of personality and nature. In metonymic language this unifying conception becomes a monotheistic "God," a transcendent reality or perfect being that all verbal analogy points to. Such conceptions as the Form of the Good in Plato or the Unmoved Mover in Aristotle are not difficult to absorb into this idea of God, but the Zeus of Homer is more recalcitrant. A monotheism in which one god is supreme over all other gods exists in a different linguistic context from a monotheism in which "other gods" do not and cannot exist at all, at least as fully divine beings. In Homer, however, there is sometimes the suggestion that Zeus is not merely the king of gods but contains all the other gods, as in the passage in the *Iliad* (viii) where he tells the squabbling subordinate deities that he holds heaven and earth, including them, on a gigantic chain that he can at any time pull up into himself. This form of metaphor, which unites the group and the individual, will be of great importance in our argument later, and the passage is also a portent of the great metonymic conception of the chain of being, of which also more later. In any case the word "God," however great its number of referents, is practically a linguistic requisite for metonymic thinking. There is no point in making analogical constructs out of words unless we have something to relate the analogy to.

As Christian theology gained cultural ascendancy, thought began to take on a deductive shape in which everything followed from the perfection of God, because of the need for irrefutable premises. In this process certain tensions were bound to arise with the more metaphorical constructs of earlier ages, when metonymic thinkers were compelled to take them seriously. The tension expresses itself in a moralizing and rationalizing approach to them: if God says or does A, then he cannot also say or do B, if B is inconsistent with A. There are some tendencies in this direction within the Bible itself: compare, for example, II Samuel 24:1 and I Chronicles 21:1. Paganism had similar difficulties, and the metaphorical element in "indecent" or morally paradoxical stories about the gods, found in Homer and elsewhere, had to be deconstructed and assimilated to other linguistic procedures. This was normally done through allegory, which is a special form of analogy, a technique of paralleling metaphorical with conceptual language in which the latter has the primary authority. Allegory smooths out the discrepancies in a metaphorical structure by making it conform to a conceptual standard.

What makes this possible is the development of continuous prose, the main instrument of thought in the metonymic period. In continuous prose, if A and B seem to be inconsistent, one can always insert intermediary verbal formulas, or rephrase them in a commentary, in a way that will "reconcile" them: if only we write enough of such intermediate sentences, any statement whatever can eventually be reconciled with any other statement. Commentary thus becomes one of the leading metonymic genres, and the traditional metaphorical images are used as illustrations of a conceptual argument.

In Christian theology the principle of analogy can readily be invoked without recourse to allegory. In the *Summa contra Gentiles* (I, 96) we read "That God hates nothing." In St. Thomas's metonymic context, such a proposition is practically self-evident: no perfect being could hate anyone or anything without ceasing to be a perfect being. Faced with the list of things in the far more metaphorical Bible that God is explicitly said to hate, St. Thomas has to fall back on the general principle of analogy. What is interesting here is that when a metaphorical tradition conflicts with the metonymic need for conceptual and moral models, it is the tradition that has to give way.

Again, the AV represents Jesus as saying to Nicodemus in John 3:8, "The wind bloweth where it listeth . . . so is everyone that is born of the Spirit." This is a metonymic translation: "Spirit" is a conception, identified with the Holy Spirit of Christian doctrine, and "wind" is a concrete illustration of it. But in the Greek text the same word, *pneuma*, is used for both wind and spirit. Hence a purely metaphorical translation is also possible: "The wind blows where it likes . . . that's what everyone is like who is born of the wind." We may find this rendering a trifle unsettling, and so, apparently, did Nicodemus, who heard only the word *pneuma*. But the example shows how deeply the history of language, and of thought in relation to language, is involved in translation.

We spoke of a verbal magic in the metaphorical phase, arising from a sense of an energy common to words and things, though embodied and controlled in words. In the metonymic phase this sense of verbal magic is sublimated into a quasi-magic inherent in sequence or linear ordering. Hence the medieval fascination with the syllogism and the great medieval dream of deducing all knowledge from the premises of revelation. Later we have the "I think, therefore I am" of Descartes, where the operative word is "therefore," because before we can accept the proposition we must accept the cogency and reality of therefores. The Cartesian formula is close to being a restatement of the old ontological argument for God, which is reducible to "I think, therefore God exists." Beliefs of this period that may seem to us perverse—about, for example, predestination or the divine right of kings—may be stubbornly clung to because of the strength of the feeling: if you accept this, then you must, etc. During the Christian centuries, too, the fear of "heresy," or logical deviation from Christian premises, amounted to what was perhaps the deadliest social psychosis in history.

Analogical language thus came to be thought of as sacramental language, a verbal response to God's own verbal revelation. Some form of analogy was essential, otherwise there would be no reality that human language is "put for," and no one would maintain that human language was fully adequate to conveying such a reality. The other extreme, represented by the tradition that runs through the pseudo-Dionysius, Erigena, and Eckhart, emphasized the inadequacies of analogy. For some of them no word, such as "Being," is strictly applicable to God, because words are finite and God is not: the real God is "hidden," beyond all thought, and *a fortiori* beyond words. This tendency in thought seems to point in the direction of a non-verbal mysticism, like that of some Oriental religions, notably Tao and Zen, and was also regarded as dangerous.

The rise of a new European culture on the ruins of Roman power, during the early Christian centuries, saw something of a Viconian *ricorso* in literature. This was mainly because the new vernacular languages, bringing in the new poetic features of rhyme, alliteration, and heavy accentual rhythm, were making themselves felt. When Latin continued as the poetic medium, it was forced into vernacular-dominated patterns very unlike those of Classical Latin. But in the culturally ascendant forms of writing, particularly philosophy and theology, there is no *ricorso*, but a continuity of metonymic and dialectical language. Its transcendental perspective remained a cultural and political necessity for preserving authority, even after the Renaissance and Reformation. Hence the metonymic phase of language retained a great deal of cultural ascendancy down to the time of Kant and Hegel, after which it became increasingly specialized and academic. One of its culminating points is the metonymic universe of Kant, where the phenomenal world is "put for" the world of things in themselves.

It was much earlier, however, that a third phase of language had begun to develop out of a dissatisfaction with certain elements in second-phase language, two in particular. Syllogistic reasoning, it was felt, led to nothing genuinely new, because its conclusions were already contained within its premises, and so its march across reality seemed increasingly to be a verbal illusion. Then again, an analogical approach to language appeared to have no criteria for distinguishing existents from non-existents. Grammatically, logically, and syntactically, there is no difference between a lion and a unicorn: the question of actual existence does not enter the ordering of words as such. And if it does not, there can be no real difference between reasoning and rationalizing, as both procedures order words in the same way. The difference can be established only by criteria external to words, and the first of these criteria has to be that of "things," or objects in nature.

This third phase of language begins roughly in the sixteenth century, where it accompanies certain tendencies in the Renaissance and Reformation, and attains cultural ascendancy in the eighteenth. In English literature it begins theoretically with Francis Bacon, and effectively with Locke. Here we start with a clear separation of subject and object, in which the subject exposes itself, in sense experience, to the impact of an objective world. The objective world is the order of nature; thinking or reflection follows the suggestions of sense experience, and words are the servomechanisms of reflection. Continuous prose is still employed, but all deductive procedures are increasingly subordinated to a primary inductive and fact-gathering process. The seventeenth-century poet Cowley, hailing Bacon as the Moses who had led modern thought out of the Egypt of superstition, says:

> From words, which are but pictures of the thought,
> (Though we our thoughts from them perversely drew)
> To things, the mind's right object, he it brought.

Hence this approach treats language as primarily descriptive of an objective natural order. The ideal to be achieved by words is framed on the model of truth by correspondence. A verbal structure is set up beside what it describes, and is called "true" if it seems to provide a satisfactory correspondence to it. The criterion of truth is related to the external source of the description rather than to the inner consistency of the argument. Its controlling figure, then, is a kind of simile: a true verbal structure is one that is *like* what it describes. In this phase we return to a direct relation between the order of nature and the order of words, as in the metaphorical phase, but with a sharp and consistent distinction between the two. This involves a reaction against the transcendental perspective of the second phase, and extreme forms of third-phase thinking demonstrate the "impossibility of metaphysics," or declare that all religious questions are unmeaning.

The descriptive phase of language corresponds to Vico's "vulgar" or demotic, which implies that it is close to what had always been accessible and extensively used, but used more particularly in the ordinary language that does not become culturally ascendant. A Sumerian or Egyptian of 3000 B.C., if he were ordering stone for a building, or dickering with his in-laws about the finances of his marriage, or assessing the amount of tax owed by a farmer, would doubtless use much the same demotic categories of true and false, reasonable and fanciful, that we should use now. And in Aristotle, to give one very obvious example, observation continually intertwines with and supplements deductive logic. The central principle of Locke, that nothing exists in the intellect that has not previously existed in the senses, had been an established axiom for many centuries before him. But considerable social changes have to take place before this use of language becomes culturally dominant, and separable from other modes.

One of these changes is the growth of science on a basis of inductive observation. Science assumes two levels of sense perception: a particular accidental level that is largely illusion, and an ideal level that is our real source of knowledge. The notion that the earth is flat, fixed, and at the center of the universe is an illusion of accident. Educated people had known for centuries before Columbus that the earth must be a sphere, but the fact did not become "demotic," or penetrate the popular consciousness, until the circumnavigations began, which suggested a more comprehensive form of sense perception. The rational arguments that finally convinced people that the earth went around the sun instead of the other way were formulated long before astronauts and spaceships. Nevertheless such arguments contained an implicit appeal to a possible ideal sense perception: if we were in the right place to do so, we could see a spherical earth revolving around the sun. The two questions: What is really there? and What are we really seeing? thus tend to become the same "phenomenological" question.

The problem of illusion and reality therefore becomes a central one in third-phase language. Copernicus is the great symbol for a new realization that such words as "sunrise" and "sunset," though metaphorically efficient, had become "only" metaphors, and that, so far as they were descriptive, what they described was illusory. Darwin is the great symbol for a new realization that divine creation, as generally conceived, was an illusion projected from the evolutionary operations within nature. Einstein is the great symbol for a new realization that matter, which up to the twentieth century had been the great bastion of the objectivity of the world, was an illusion of energy. With this, however, the sense of the clear separation of subject and object, which was so marked a feature of the scientific attitude up to that point, overreached itself and began to come to an end. It was no longer possible to separate the observer from what he observes: the observer had to become an observed object too.

The thought suggests itself that we may have completed a gigantic cycle of language from Homer's time, where the word evokes the thing, to our own day, where the thing evokes the word, and are now about to go around the cycle again, as we seem now to be confronted once again with an energy common to subject and object which can be expressed verbally only through some form of metaphor. It is true that many metaphorical elements are reappearing in our language, but it is rather the positive aspect of the same process—that we may be entering a new phase altogether in our understanding of language—that has to be kept in mind. Certainly it is interesting and rather reassuring that there should be so heavy an emphasis on language and linguistic models in contemporary thought, apart from whatever embodies the emphasis.

It is primarily to Roman Jakobson that we owe the distinction between the metaphorical and the metonymic, and I apologize for adding one more ingredient to what very quickly became a considerably overspiced stew. It seems to me that there are three major senses in which the word "metonymic" can be used. First, it is a figure of speech in which an image is "put for" another image: this is really a species of metaphor. Second, it is a mode of analogical thinking and writing in which the verbal expression is "put for" something that by definition transcends adequate verbal expression: this is roughly the sense in which I use it. Third, it is a mode of thought and speech in which the word is "put for" the object it describes: this corresponds more or less to my "descriptive" phase. There are no rights and wrongs in such matters, but it seems to me useful to separate both the language of immanence, which is founded on metaphor, and the language of transcendence, which is founded on metonymy in my sense, from descriptive language.

In the first, or metaphorical, phase of language, the unifying element of verbal expression is the "god," or personal nature-spirit. In the second phase the conception of a transcendent "God" moves into the center of the order of words. In the third phase the criterion of reality is the source of sense experience in the order of nature, where "God" is not to be found, and where "gods" are no longer believed in. Hence for the third phase of language the word "God" becomes linguistically unfunctional, except when confined to special areas outside its jurisdiction. Mythological space became separated from scientific space with the new astronomy of the seventeenth century, and mythological time from scientific time with nineteenth-century geology and biology. Both developments helped to push the conception of God out of the world of time and space, even as a hypothesis. The charge of "God-building" is a most damaging one to a third-phase writer, and the subject that used to be called natural theology does not now make much cultural impact, with the remarkable exception of Teilhard de Chardin.

In the nineteenth century there were many thinkers, mainly of the idealistic school, who adhered to the metonymic tradition with its God. But some even of them give an impression of having said to themselves: Here's this word "God"; what am I to do with it? What they did was often ingenious, but frequently confirmed the feeling that the conception of God, like Biblical metaphors in metonymic theology, was becoming, however unconsciously, a cumbersome piece of traditional baggage. In a conception of language where no premises are beyond scrutiny, there is nothing to stop anyone from returning to square one and the question: Is there a God? What is significant about this is that the answer, if it is to remain within the framework of third-phase language, can only be no, because any question beginning with "is there" is, so to speak, already an ungodly question, and "a god" is for all practical purposes no God. Nietzsche's formula "God is dead," despite the amount of attention it has attracted, was incidental to his more important aim of de-deifying the natural environment, and in particular of removing the metaphor of "law" from ordinary consciousness to describe the operations of nature. There are no laws in nature, Nietzsche says, only necessities; but the metaphor "law of nature" carries with it a vestigial sense of a personality who commands and other personalities (ourselves) who have the option of obeying or disobeying; and this vestigial metaphor, for Nietzsche, is a superstition in the most exact sense of an inorganic survival of tradition.

The political and psychological aspects of third-phase writing led to similar positions. One of the earliest of third-phase writers, Machiavelli, attempted to distinguish and isolate the tactical use of illusion in the art of ruling. For Rousseau civilization was largely an illusion concealing a society of nature and reason; for Marx the whole second-phase approach to language had become an ideology, or façade of ascendant-class authority; for Freud the language of consciousness was largely a screen concealing other motives for speech. To conservative thinkers, including Burke, the façade of authority in society revealed the real structure of that society. There is no social contract, Burke maintained, except the contract that a society shows it has accepted by its structure. A radical opponent of Burke, such as Paine, would think rather of the façade of authority as concealing its real structure, and would regard the difference between his attitude and Burke's as precisely the difference between a rational attitude and a rationalizing one. And while religious issues are not directly involved here, it is clear that the rational attitude would regard "God" as a symbol of traditional authority, or, as Blake says, the ghost of the priest and king.

What I am concerned with at present is not the question whether God is dead or obsolete, but with the question of what resources of language may be dead or obsolete. The metaphorical and metonymic phases of language have been in large measure outgrown because of the obvious limitations that they imposed on the human mind. But it seems clear that the descriptive phase also has limitations, in a world where its distinction of subject and object so often does not work. There is no question of giving up descriptive language, only of relating it to a broader spectrum of verbal expression. The word "God" is a noun, and so falls into the category of things and objects. For metonymic writing this is not an insuperable problem: what is beyond all things and objects can still be a noun, or at any rate have a name. For most writers of the second phase, God represents an immutable being, set over against the dissolving flow of the world of becoming in which we are; and practically the only grammatical device for conveying this sense of the immutable is the abstract noun. For third-phase writing, founded as it is on a sense-apprehended distinction between objects that are there and objects that are not, "God" can go only into the illusory class. But perhaps this kind of noun-thinking is, at least here, a fallacy of the type that Whitehead calls a fallacy of misplaced concreteness.

In Exodus 3:14, though God also gives himself a name, he defines himself (according to the AV) as "I am that I am," which scholars say is more accurately rendered "I will be what I will be." That is, we might come closer to what is meant in the Bible by the word "God" if we understood it as a verb, and not a verb of simple asserted existence but a verb implying a process accomplishing itself. This would involve trying to think our way back to a conception of language in which words were words of power, conveying primarily the sense of forces and energies rather than analogues of physical bodies. To some extent this would be a reversion to the metaphorical language of primitive communities, as our earlier references to a cycle of language and the "primitive" word *mana* suggested. But it would also be oddly contemporary with post-Einsteinian physics, where atoms and electrons are no longer thought of as things but rather as traces of processes. God may have lost his function as the subject or object of a predicate, but may not be so much dead as entombed in a dead language.

The Biblical terms usually rendered "word," including the *logos* of the Gospel of John, are solidly rooted in the metaphorical phase of language, where the word was an element of creative power. According to Genesis 1:4, "God said, Let there be light; and there was light." That is, the word was the creative agent that brought the thing into being. This is usually thought of as characteristically Hebrew in approach, although in Heraclitus the term *logos* is also essentially metaphorical, and still expresses a unity of human consciousness and physical phenomena. In the metonymic phase *logos* takes on rather the meaning of an analogical use of words to convey the sense of a rational order. This order is thought of as antecedent to both consciousness and nature. Philo and the author of John combine the two traditions, and John's "In the beginning was the *logos*" is a New Testament commentary on the opening of Genesis, identifying the original creative word with Christ.

Erasmus, in the Latin translation appended to his edition of the Greek New Testament, renders "In the beginning was the Word" as "In principio erat sermo." This is a purely metonymic translation: in the beginning, Erasmus assumes, was the infinite mind, with its interlocking thoughts and ideas out of which the creative words emerged. Erasmus is clearly more influenced than Jerome by the later Greek history of the word. It would be cheap parody to say that Erasmus really means "In the beginning was continuous prose," but the link between his "sermo" and the development of continuous prose is there nonetheless. At the beginning of the third phase we have Goethe's Faust, who claims to have studied theology but seems not to understand it very well, struggling with the same phrase. He rejects "das Wort," and traverses the whole cycle of language as outlined above, passing through the second-phase "der Sinn," and emerging finally with "die That," the event or existential reality that words describe at secondhand. At that point Faust begins to fall into the power of Mephistopheles, the spirit of denial. What significance this has I am not sure, except that while it is not easy to translate "In the beginning was the Word," there seems to be no future in deliberately mistranslating it. Still, Faust makes us realize how completely we have lost the metaphorical clue to what John means by *logos*. For John goes on to say "And the *logos* became flesh." Evidently he thought of this as an intelligible statement of the type "And the boy became a man," or "And the ice became water." But within a descriptive framework of language it can be only an unintelligible statement of the type "And the apple became an orange." For descriptive language, the word has no power to be anything but a word.

Each of our three phases of language has a characteristic word for the human entity that uses the language. In the metaphorical phase, where the world is held together by a plurality of gods, there is often assumed to be a corresponding plurality of psychic forces that disintegrate or separate at death. Ancient Egypt had a *ba* and a *ka* and several other entities, besides the mummified body itself; Homer (or a later editor) speaks of Hercules as existing after death simultaneously as a god in Olympus and a shade in Hades. Even Aristotle's *De Anima* describes a complex soul. But the nearest to the purely metaphorical conception is perhaps the word "spirit," which, with its overtones of "breath," expresses the unifying principle of life that gives man a participating energy with nature.

In proportion as metonymic thinking and its monotheistic God developed, man came to be thought of as a single "soul" and a body, related by the metaphor of "in." Human consciousness feels that it is inside a body it knows next to nothing about, even such elementary facts as the circulation of the blood being relatively recent discoveries. Hence it cannot feel that the body is identical with consciousness: the body is born of nature and will return to nature, but the soul belongs to the transcendent world and will return to that world. The figures employed to describe their relation include a body in a tomb, a prisoner in a cell, a peasant in a decaying cottage, a bird in a cage, and the like. The separation of body and soul at death is thought of as a vertical one, the soul going "up" and the body "down."

In the third phase the conception associated with consciousness modulates from "soul" to "mind," and the relation with the bodily world of nature, including one's own body, becomes more horizontal. By this time the "mind" has become firmly located in the head, and consciousness is in fact often thought of as a function of the brain. The idealistic philosophers of the last century mentioned above sometimes transferred the older arguments for the immortality of the soul to the mind, but the immortality of the mind does not seem so obvious as that of the soul, mainly because the vertical and transcendent associations of "soul" are not built into the word. From Freud's time on we have tended to revert to the original metaphorical or pluralistic view of consciousness, and to think of the "psyche" as a bundle of distinguishable and often conflicting forces.

All the languages relevant to the Bible distinguish between soul and spirit: Hebrew has *nephesh* and *ruach*, Greek *psyche* and *pneuma*, Latin *anima* and *spiritus*; and there are similar distinctions in modern languages. No one would claim that there was a consistent use of either word in the Bible, but neither would anyone speak of the third person of the Trinity as the Holy Soul, and Paul's prayer for his correspondent's "spirit and soul and body" (I Thessalonians 5:23) suggests that the difference between soul and spirit means something. Jesus' resurrection was a bodily one, and Paul explains (I Corinthians 15:44) that what enters the resurrection is not the soul or abstract essence of the body but a "spiritual body." This spiritual body is contrasted with the natural body, or "flesh and blood," but the phrase still suggests that immortality must include the body, in however transfigured a form, as it did in Jesus' resurrection. Here again the New Testament adheres to older metaphorical modes of thought rather than to the more up-to-date and rational Greek ones.

Christianity placed the doctrine of the resurrection of the body in its creed, though the addition seems historically to have had little effect on the soul-body dichotomy. The people Dante meets in his visions of hell and purgatory and heaven are souls of the dead: at the Last Judgment, we are told, they go back to pick up their bodies, but what change that will make is very little emphasized, except that clearly it will make hell hurt a lot more. The term "spirit" seems to belong properly only to the Holy Spirit and, in a different context, to the angels: for man, and for discarnate beings like elemental "spirits," it seems to be a mere doublet of "soul." Yet Paul, again (I Corinthians 2:14), contrasts the *pneumatikos* or spiritual with the *psychikos*, the soul-body. The AV renders this latter term as the "natural" man: the difficulty in translation is that there is no English adjective related to "soul" corresponding to "spiritual." But Paul seems to be drawing the essential line between spirit and soul, not between soul and body.

Each phase of language has its characteristic virtues as well as its limitations. In the first phase, language can be used with an immediacy and vitality, such as we find in Homer, that later ages never consistently recapture. Yet this use of language is restricted by an identity with nature from which metonymic dialectic has freed itself. The crossing of the bridge from "gods" to "God," which has already taken place in the Bible, is felt as a release from the tyranny of nature.

The limitations of metonymic language, in its turn, have already been mentioned. Descriptive language, and the development of science that has accompanied it, have helped to reveal to us a richness and variety in the objective world far beyond even the imaginations of those who lived before it. Yet there is a curious restiveness about this kind of revelation, some feeling of what Blake calls "the same dull round, even of a universe." What is dull is not the universe but the mental operations prescribed for us in observing it. In bookshops we often find ourselves looking at rows of books about reincarnation, telepathy, astrology, out-of-body flights, unidentified flying objects, revelations through dreams, and the like, which are usually described in the blurbs as utterly shattering to orthodox notions of science. It seems as though, whatever the validity of these interests in themselves, their attraction for the public begins in some sense of imaginative holiday, of getting away to other modes and possibilities of experience not permitted in our normal linguistic classrooms.

This sense of being confined to an objective order, and feeling a constraint in being so confined despite the infinite variety in the order, has been enshrined in the language for a long time. The bigger the objective world becomes, the smaller in range and significance the subjective world seems. The basis of authority in third-phase writing is the social consensus that the writer appeals to. Hence the modern use of language has been driven increasingly to define the objective reality of the world, on the assumption that "objective" means real, because it allows of such a consensus, and that "subjective" means unreal because it does not. The word "subject" in English means the observer of the objective, and it also has the political meaning of an individual subordinated to the authority of his society or its ruler, as in "British subject." It is not really possible, however, to separate the two meanings. The "subject" is subjected to the objective world, and not only subjected but almost crushed under it, like Atlas. Perhaps something of this sense lurks also in that very curious word "understanding," along with what the understanding stands under: that is, traditionally, "substance," which sounds like another form of the same word. Demotic language, and to some extent its predecessor as well, seems to confine us to a level of reality that Paul (I Corinthians 13:12) very aptly compares to a riddle in a mirror.

But, in all this, what is not "objective"? As soon as we realize that observation is affected essentially by the observer, we have to incorporate that observer into the phenomena to be observed, and make him an object too. This fact has transformed the physical sciences, and of course the social sciences are based entirely on the sense of the need to observe the community of observers. That leaves us with nothing genuinely "subjective" except a structure of language, including as said mathematical language, which is the only thing left that can be distinguished from the objective world. Even that structure is objective to each student of it. People are "subjects," then, not as people, but only to the extent that they form a community within a linguistic structure which records some observation of the objective. In this context the word "subject" incorporates its other meaning of what is treated by language, as when we speak of the subject of a book. These are puns, but puns can give useful clues to the way we relate words to experience. It is not a difficult step from here to the feeling, often expressed in contemporary criticism and philosophy, that it is really language that uses man, and not man that uses language. This does not mean that man is being taken over by one of his own inventions, as in science-fiction stories of malignant computers and self-reproducing robots. It means rather that man is a child of the word as well as a child of nature, and that, just as he is conditioned by nature and finds his conception of necessity in it, so the first thing he finds in the community of the word is the charter of his freedom.

We have so far not spoken of literature. The first phase of language, as Vico indicates, is inherently poetic: it is contemporary with a stage of society in which the main source of culturally inherited knowledge is the poet, as Homer was for Greek culture. It has been recognized from earliest times that the primary social function of the poet is connected with something very ancient and primitive in society and in society's use of words. The Elizabethan critics, for example, tell us that in pre-Homeric times, the days of the legendary Orpheus and Hermes Trismegistus, the poet was the repository of all wisdom and knowledge, the teacher, or, in Shelley's phrase about a later era of history, the "unacknowledged legislator," of his society. There were technical reasons for this: verse, with its formulaic sound-schemes, is the easiest vehicle for an oral culture in which memory, or the keeping alive of tradition, is of primary importance. As the critics of the god Thoth, the inventor of writing, remark in Plato's *Phaedrus*, the ability to record has a lot more to do with forgetting than with remembering: with keeping the past in the past, instead of continuously recreating it in the present.

Poets and critics of English literature began to revive the sense of affinity between the poetic and the primitive in the later half of the eighteenth century, and in the Romantic period Peacock, in a paradoxical essay, *Four Ages of Poetry*, remarked that poetry originated in the flattery of barbarian conquerors. In proportion as civilization had developed, Peacock suggested, poetry had fallen behind, an increasingly atavistic survival. Shelley's reply to Peacock, *A Defence of Poetry*, was not a refutation but an attempt to express the positive side of Peacock's thesis, reversing the fallacy that Peacock pretended to take seriously: the naïve belief in progress which identifies the primitive with the outmoded. This issue, familiar to students of literature, I refer to here for two reasons. One is that the same issue will turn up in the next chapter in connection with myth; the other is that it illustrates the present stage in our argument: that it is the primary function of literature, more particularly of poetry, to keep re-creating the first or metaphorical phase of language during the domination of the later phases, to keep presenting it to us as a mode of language that we must never be allowed to underestimate, much less lose sight of.

We remarked that Homer's language is metaphorical to us, if not necessarily to him. In his poetry the distinction between figured and literal language hardly exists, apart from the special rhetorical showcase of the epic simile already mentioned. With the second phase, metaphor becomes one of the recognized figures of speech; but it is not until the coming of a different conception of language that a tension arises between figurative and what is called "literal" meaning, and poetry begins to become a conscious and deliberate use of figures. In the third phase this tension is often very sharp. A demotic descriptive writer will tend to avoid as many figures of speech as he can, on the ground that they are "merely verbal" and interfere with the transparency of description. Similarly, we speak of metaphors as being "just" or "only" metaphors when we become aware of other possible verbal formulations of what they convey, as with the "sunrise" and "sunset" mentioned above.

This last point is worth more emphasis. We suggested that demotic habits of language have always been with us, and it would be easy to assume that poetry, however ancient, is still a later development out of an original demotic speech. It is very difficult for many twentieth-century minds to believe that poetry is genuinely primitive, and not an artificial way of decorating and distorting ordinary "prose." Take the opening of the great Psalm 19, with its superb second verse: "Day unto day uttereth speech, and night unto night showeth knowledge." The third verse reads, more or less: "No speech nor language; no voice is heard." It has been suggested (I have no expertise in such matters) that this was originally a sniveling and puling gloss, stuck in by someone who was afraid, like so many of his kind, that some readers would be seduced into idolatry by reading great poetry about the sun's rising like a bridegroom. If so, the AV, by rendering the verse "There is no speech nor language *where* their voice is not heard" has baffled his foolish intention and reversed his meaning, and has therefore translated the verse correctly. But the point goes deeper than this. It is not only that the real meaning is metaphorical and that any superstitious "literal" view of it would have seemed as absurd to the original writer as it does to us. We have to eradicate from our minds the notion of confused earlier anthropomorphic views out of which such metaphors have "developed." The images are *radically* metaphorical: this is the only way in which language can convey the sense of the presence of a numinous personality in the world, and that is where we stop.

We notice that in Psalm 19 the Biblical God is to some degree being personated by *a* god, a sky-god or sun-god. This was presumably what was worrying our glossing editor, if he existed. However impressive the achievement of Christian poets, poets as a whole seem to find it easier to deal with "pagan" gods, because gods are, as explained, ready-made metaphors, and go into poetry with the minimum of adjustment. In, say, sixteenth-century painting or seventeenth-century opera, the preoccupation with Classical gods was a kind of easy-going imaginative game. With some nineteenth-century poets, notably Hölderlin, it becomes much more like a challenge to Christianity. We might express this by saying that in proportion as the God of Christianity began to look metaphorical, the metaphorical gods began to look like objects of worship again. In Blake the Classical and other gods are regarded as projections of aspects of the human imagination, and these he tries to portray, in their unprojected forms, as Orc and Urizen and the rest. In any case the Old Testament Jehovah, like Zeus, has figurative connections with the sky and the thunderbolt, along with associated social functions like the protection of strangers. In Psalm 18:10 he is said to use a "cherub" as a kind of private airplane. Such a figurative god is both God and not God, a metaphorical illustration used as an analogy.

If the first phase of *langage* is predominantly poetic, the next two are not; and naturally poets will try to adapt to the changed linguistic conditions. In the second phase, poetry normally does this by allegory, as in Dante, where a metaphorical narrative runs parallel with a conceptual one but defers to it. That is, in the metonymic period

Dante as a mere poet, even though a very great one, would not be given the authority in religious matters that would be accorded theologians and other sources of the conceptual side of his allegory. In the third phase, literature adapts itself mainly through what is usually called realism, adopting categories of probability and plausibility as rhetorical devices. As a fairly extreme example, Zola wrote novels that have an obvious relation to sociology, novels in which, again, the sociological aspect by definition is a more direct rendering of "truth" than the fictional one. The fictional mode is adopted because it presents a unity to the imagination more intense than the documentary materials: an elementary point we must keep in mind for the Bible as well.

Poetry, then, keeps alive the metaphorical use of language and its habits of thinking in the identity relations suggested by the "this is that" structure of metaphor. In this process the original sense of magic, of the possible forces released by words of power, disappears. The poet's approach to language in itself is hypothetical: in free societies he is allowed to assume anything he likes, but what he says remains detached from faith, power, or truth, as we ordinarily understand those words, even when it expresses them. And yet the release of metaphorical language from magic into poetry is an immense emancipation of that language. Magic demands prescribed formulas that cannot be varied by a syllable, whereas novelty and uniqueness are essential to poetry. Poetry does not really lose its magical power thereby, but merely transfers it from an action on nature to an action on the reader or hearer.

If we ask what form of writing re-creates the second phase of *langage* in later periods, it is perhaps the kind of writing that is often called "existential." I am not fond of the word, but I know of no other that conveys the sense of anchoring an interest in the transcendental in the seabed of human concern. The great systematic thinkers are all aware of the analogical nature of their language, but they throw the emphasis on the unifying of their thought. Unity, or rather unification, of language is for them the appropriate way of responding to a transcendental form of being. Luther, Pascal, and Kierkegaard differ from St. Thomas or Leibnitz or Hegel in stressing the negative aspect of analogy, in showing how experience in time eludes final or definitive unification in thought. "The squirming facts exceed the squamous mind," as Wallace Stevens says, though the "facts" here are rather elements of experience.

We see the connection in Plato, for example, who in the *Phaedo* puts Socrates in the limit-situation of martyrdom, which takes place at the end of the dialogue. The quiet progression of Socrates' dialectic remains within a metonymic context, the sense that the argument is being "put for" a reality accessible to experience rather than to discussion. What I am saying, Socrates says, may not be precisely true, but something like this must be true. This is metonymic writing and thinking on its very highest level, where both sides of the analogy are given equal weight. It is a level sometimes reached also by Augustine, whose systematic presentations of doctrine are balanced against the emphasis on experience in the *Confessions*. In Kant also the two aspects of metonymy are balanced, though in a different way. God's existence disappears from the context of "pure reason," where rational proofs are needed, but reappears in the context of "practical reason," where reality in experience is what is appropriate.

Elsewhere there are sharper contrasts and tensions. Kierkegaard, though very Hegelian in his habit of mind, regards the element of synthesis in Hegel's thought as a fortress or prison; and Karl Barth, a theologian contemporary with third-phase language, begins his dogmatic exposition by cutting down the great ridgepole of metonymic thought, the analogy of being (*analogia entis*). The issue seems, once more, to turn on the superiority of what Kierkegaard calls "ethical freedom" to the contemplative values afforded by a synthesis of thought. Most "existential" writing, at least in our day, carries on the transcendental perspective of religion and metaphysics in a phase of language profoundly unsympathetic to any separated realm of immutable being. A great deal of such writing is naturally not religious, but when it is not it is often explicitly antireligious, understanding the relevance of transcendental issues but renouncing them in favor of a greater human freedom. Thus we have two forms of writing descended from earlier periods of linguistic history, and these in their present form are submerged, so to speak, and have in consequence turned revolutionary. To illustrate (the additional category will be discussed in a moment):

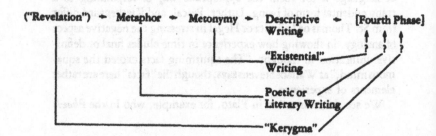

The origins of the Bible are in the first metaphorical phase of language, but much of the Bible is contemporary with the second-phase separation of the dialectical from the poetic, as its metonymic "God" in particular indicates. Its poetic use of language obviously does not confine it to the literary category, but it never falls wholly into the conventions of the second phase. There are no true rational arguments in the Bible, not even in the New Testament, which despite its late date keeps very close to the Old Testament in its attitude toward language. What may look like rational argument, such as the Epistle to the Hebrews, turns out on closer analysis to be a disguised form of exhortation. Nor is there much functional use of abstraction. Biblical Hebrew is an almost obsessively concrete language, and while there are a few abstract terms like "nature" in the New Testament, they hardly affect what is still a metaphorical structure. Still, the Bible fits rather awkwardly into our cycle of three phases, and we need another conception or two to account for it.

One of the verbal genres that are prominent throughout the second phase of language is rhetoric in the sense of oratory. Oratorical rhetoric is "hieratic" in the sense that it tries to draw its audience together in a closer unity, but is "hieroglyphic" in that it makes extensive use of figuration and devices usually associated with verse, such as antithesis and alliteration. Thus oratorical rhetoric, as we have it in the history of literature, represents a kind of transitional stage of language between first-phase metaphor and second-phase argument. Between Cicero and the Renaissance the orator became the symbol of an educational ideal of versatility and fluency in the use of language, which made the orator to some degree the successor of the poet in the earlier phase as the teacher of his society, the encyclopedic repository of its traditional knowledge. But the predominance of the oratorical ideal was still useful to poets, because the training of the orator was largely a training in the kind of rhetorical and figured language that poets also use. Hence oratory at its best is really a combination of metaphorical or poetic and "existential" idioms: it uses all the figures of speech, but within a context of concern and direct address that poetry as such does not employ.

From the beginning, philosophers and other students of language, including Plato and Aristotle, have pointed to the immense force that oratorical rhetoric can exert either for good or for evil, depending on who is in charge of it. In the metonymic period it was assumed that "good" rhetoric was, as Aristotle put it, the *antistrophos* or answering chorus of dialectic, as in the sermon that expounded true doctrine or the courtroom defense that was on the side of justice. Poetry also was justified, in Sidney's *Apology* and elsewhere, on the same ground: poetry may support, by the peculiar resonance given it by its rhetorical structure, the truths of morality, persuading the emotions to follow their intellectual guidance. On this basis many confused arguments, trying to distinguish "good" and "bad" rhetoric within literature itself, have been made, asserting that some writers merely portray evil and that others are agents of it, and that censorship should be applied to the latter group. However well meaning, it is usually these arguments themselves that show the pernicious side of rhetoric, rather than what they discuss.

The rise of third-phase writing was signaled by the ideology of humanism, with its cult of plain sense and the use of ordinary language. A genuinely specialized subject cannot avoid technical language, but it is true that clarity and lucidity of style, where the author puts all his evidence before the reader, is a feature of the best and most honestly motivated third-phase writing. Serious writing that does not attempt these qualities generally falls into the existential or the literary category. In our day the appearance of oratorical rhetoric in a genuine form seems to be confined to very exceptional circumstances of social crisis, as in the Gettysburg Address of Lincoln or the 1940 speeches of Churchill. For the most part oratorical figures in our day are a feature of advertising and propaganda. Third-phase writing, we said, is centrally concerned with distinguishing reality from illusion: advertising and propaganda are designed deliberately to create an illusion, hence they constitute for us a kind of anti-language, especially in the speeches by so-called charismatic leaders that set up a form of mass hypnosis. When such oratory pretends to be, or thinks it is, rational, it adopts a highly characteristic shuffle derived from a desire to reach certain conclusions in advance, whatever the evidence suggests. There is a good deal of this kind of anti-language in religious writing also, where it takes the tone that Hegel calls edifying, emotional resonance without content. There are also rhetorical features that express the author's social slant or bias: these can be very pervasive when the bias is unconscious.

The essential idiom of the Bible is clearly oratorical, a fact all the more necessary to recognize in an age where there is so well-founded a distrust of the wrong kind of rhetoric. The Bible is often thought to be the wrong kind too: a horrified pre-Revolutionary French lady is said to have remarked, "Quel effroyable ton!" on opening a Bible for the first time. On the other hand, the Bible has traditionally been assumed to be the rhetoric of God, accommodated to human intelligence and coming through human agents. In my diagram it appears chronologically prior to metaphorical language: it is not, and it is partly my own lack of ingenuity in such matters that so represents it. But it has been traditionally believed to come from a time out of time, so the arrangement is not too misleading from that point of view.

Oratory on the highest level of oracle, exhortation, *kerygma*, or whatever the most appropriate term is, has to be seen from both of its two aspects—metaphor and concern. In ordinary language we think of a real subject and a real object with a more tenuous interaction between them. In figurative language the reality of subject and object is what becomes tenuous, and the interaction comes into the foreground as the reality that identifies the two. In ordinary language, words are simply understood; in concerned address a much more comprehensive response from all aspects of the personality is called for.

The linguistic idiom of the Bible does not really coincide with any of our three phases of language, important as those phases have been in the history of its influence. It is not metaphorical like poetry, though it is full of metaphor, and is as poetic as it can well be without actually being a work of literature. It does not use the transcendental language of abstraction and analogy, and its use of objective and descriptive language is incidental throughout. It is really a fourth form of expression, for which I adopt the now well-established term *kerygma*, proclamation. In general usage this term is largely restricted to the Gospels, but there is not enough difference between the Gospels and the rest of the Bible in the use of language to avoid extending it to the entire book.

Kerygma is a mode of rhetoric, though it is rhetoric of a special kind. It is, like all rhetoric, a mixture of the metaphorical and the "existential" or concerned but, unlike practically all other forms of rhetoric, it is not an argument disguised by figuration. It is the vehicle of what is traditionally called revelation, a word I use because it is traditional and I can think of no better one. But if we take this word to mean the conveying of information from an objective divine source to a subjective human receptor, we are making it a form of descriptive writing. Perhaps that is not out of the question either, but it cannot be a *simple* form of descriptive writing, as in the populist view (as we might call it) which speaks of the Bible as literally true. The Bible is far too deeply rooted in all the resources of language for any simplistic approach to its language to be adequate. Then again, the word *kerygma* is associated mainly with the theology of Bultmann, and in Bultmann's view *kerygma* is to be opposed to myth, which he regards as an obstacle to it. In the next chapter I shall give my reasons for saying that myth is the linguistic vehicle of *kerygma*, and that to "demythologize" any part of the Bible would be the same thing as to obliterate it.

CHAPTER TWO

MYTH I

The first thing that confronts us in studying verbal structures is that they are arranged sequentially, and have to be read or listened to in time. I shall here use "reading" as the typical way of responding to a sequence of words. We cannot read far in the Bible without recognizing verbal structures that remind us of what are called myths, and so we have to arrive at once at some understanding of what in this book is meant by a myth. As a literary critic I want to anchor the word in its literary context; so myth to me means, first of all, *mythos*, plot, narrative, or in general the sequential ordering of words. As all verbal structures have some kind of sequence, even if, like telephone books, they are not read that way, all verbal structures are mythical in this primary sense, a sense that is really a tautology.

In the metaphorical phase of language, where there is as yet little sense of deductive inference or abstraction, most verbal narratives take some form of story. In a story the propelling force is the link between personalities and events, and this link is typically formed by the actions of gods, who, as we said, are the representative metaphors of this phase of language. In the metonymic phase, verbal structures still have narratives and have still to be read in sequence, by turning over a series of pages to the end. But the typical narrative form of this phase is conceptual, or what is normally called an argument. In the third or descriptive phase, the sequence in the narrative is suggested by the sequential features in whatever is being described. However, there is still no real sequence apart from the one given by the words. Anyone who says "the facts speak for themselves" is using another verbal figure of speech, technically known as prosopopoeia.

In our culture, some narratives dealing with personalities run parallel to a sequence of events external to themselves; others are based on a sequence of events that seems to be constructed for its own sake. This distinction is reflected in the difference between the words "history" and "story." The word "myth," for reasons we shall come to later, has tended to become attached only to the latter, and hence to mean "not really true." This is a vulgarism for many reasons, apart from the fact that it so often assumes a judgment on factuality long before we are in any position to make one. In any case, in the primary sense we have given to myth as words in sequence, the mythical or narrative structure will still be there whether there is, as we say, any "truth" in it or not. In a history the words seem to be following a corresponding procession of antecedent events, and up to a point they do, but the selection and arrangement of data involved in the verbal narrative is primary, and the notion that the shape of the sequence comes from outside the words is an illusion of projection.

Thus Gibbon's *Decline and Fall of the Roman Empire* was intended to be a history, a faithful account of the fortunes of the later Roman Empire, with all the scholarly virtues of documentation and the like attached to it. Gibbon was also essentially a third-phase descriptive writer, concerned with the difference between the reality of what was happening to Rome, as he saw it, and the illusions, whether pagan or Christian, that the Romans themselves held about their place in history. But the phrase "decline and fall" in the title indicates the narrative principle on which Gibbon selected and arranged his material: that is his *mythos*, and without such a *mythos* the book could have had no shape. The extent to which the Bible is historical in the same way is a more complicated matter, but not many would disagree with the statement that it tells a story; and for me the two statements "The Bible tells a story" and "The Bible is a myth" are essentially the same statement.

However, this primary use of the word "myth" as verbal sequence is too broad to be very useful in itself, and we generally associate the term with a more restricted context. The verbal culture of a pre-discursive society will consist largely of stories, but among those stories there grows up a specialization in social function that affects some stories more than others. Certain stories seem to have a peculiar significance: they are the stories that tell a society what is important for it to know, whether about its gods, its history, its laws, or its class structure. These stories may be called myths in a secondary sense, a sense that distinguishes them from folktales—stories told for entertainment or other less central purposes. They thus become "sacred" as distinct from "profane" stories, and form part of what the Biblical tradition calls revelation. This distinction may not exist in many "primitive" societies, but it usually gets established sooner or later, and once established it may persist for centuries. In Western Europe the Bible stories had a central mythical significance of this kind until at least the eighteenth century. Mythical, in this secondary sense, therefore means the opposite of "not really true": it means being charged with a special seriousness and importance. Sacred stories illustrate a specific social concern; profane stories are related to social concern much more distantly: sometimes, at least in their origin, not at all.

Myths in the secondary sense, however, and folktales are equally stories or verbal narratives, and so there is no consistent structural difference between them. Nor is there a consistent difference of content: stories about gods that are "believed in" or are the objects of a cult are likely to be myths, but not all myths are stories about gods. The stories about Samson in the Book of Judges were mythical for Western Europe, because they belonged to the central body of sacrosanct Biblical legend. But the structural analogues to the Samson saga are in folktales, and Samson was not a god. Similarly with, say, the story of Odysseus and Polyphemus, which was mythical for the Greeks in the secondary concerned sense because it was in Homer, but which again has folktale analogues. After the rise of metonymic language, stories are frequently used as concrete illustrations of abstract arguments, in other words as allegories. This is close to the role that myths have in Plato. We can also have myths within myths, like the parables of Jesus or Achilles' fable of the two jars of Zeus at the end of the *Iliad*, which are also illustrative but where the context is not strictly an argument. See the chart on page 34.

Secondary myths have two qualities that folktales do not, remembering that these qualities derive from their social function and authority rather than from their structure. First, some sense of a *canon* relates them to one another: a myth takes its place in a mythology, an interconnected group of myths, whereas folktales remain nomadic, traveling over the world and interchanging their themes and motifs. I speak for convenience of myths' forming a mythology, but that may

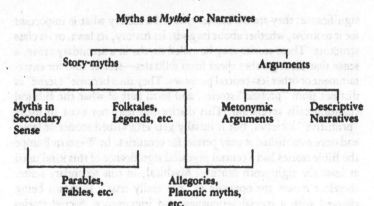

Myths as *Mythoi* or Narratives

Story-myths | Arguments

Myths in Secondary Sense | Folktales, Legends, etc. | Metonymic Arguments | Descriptive Narratives

Parables, Fables, etc. | Allegories, Platonic myths, etc.

not be the right order: perhaps a mythology may be in some sense prior to the individual myths that articulate episodes of it. In the second place, myths outline a specific area of human culture and mark it off from others. The extensive borrowing of mythical themes that seems to have gone on in the Near East does not affect this process: seeds of Sumerian mythology sprouted in Hittite culture, but grew up as an integral part of that culture. A mythology rooted in a specific society transmits a heritage of shared allusion and verbal experience in time, and so mythology helps to create a cultural history.

As a mythology contains a great deal of legendary and traditional history, it also helps to foster the growth of what we should call history. This is why historical narratives are the earliest forms of descriptive techniques in writing. But, as we remember from the previous chapter, literature, and poetry especially, has the function of re-creating the metaphorical use of language. Hence the direct descendant of mythology is literature, if we can in fact speak of it as a descendant at all. In the secondary sense we gave to myth there are societies, such as the South American tribes studied by Levi-Strauss, that have what for all practical purposes may be called a pre-literary mythology, though it is still a form of language. But myth and literature are already inextricable in the Gilgamesh epic, which is much older than any part of the Bible, as they are in Homer, who is roughly contemporary with the older parts of the Old Testament. Hence it is impossible for the present book to regard literature as a contamination of myth: it is an integral and inevitable part of a myth's development. What a myth "means" has various answers, some of which we shall consider in a moment; but what it means to a literary critic includes everything it has been made to mean in later literature.

Many fallacies result from the notion that "a" myth remains buried underneath all its later literary developments like a repressed desire. We spoke a moment ago of the Samson stories in the Book of Judges, which seem cruder and wilder than other stories, like those told of Samuel, for instance, in its general vicinity. We may notice that Samson's name resembles early Semitic words for the sun, and that his story tells of a supernaturally powerful hero associated with the burning of crops, who eventually falls into a dark prison-house in the west. That the story shows structural or narrative analogies to the kind of story that might be suggested by the passage of the sun across the sky is true, and no storyteller worth his keep would try to eliminate such analogies. But to say that the Samson stories "derive from" a solar myth or that a solar myth "lies behind" them is to say more than anyone knows. To use an example I have given elsewhere, anyone writing the life of Napoleon might speak of the "rise" of his career, the "zenith" of his fame, or the "eclipse" of his fortunes. This is the language of solar mythology, but it does not follow that the story of Napoleon evolved from a sun myth. What follows is that mythical structures continue to give shape to the metaphors and rhetoric of later types of structure. The Samson stories are of a very different type from that of any conceivable life of Napoleon, but the solar elements in them are still metaphorical and rhetorical elements.

Earlier students of myth seem to have put up a strong resistance to the fact that myth is a form of imaginative and creative thinking, and is therefore autonomous. There must have been some *cause* of myths, it was felt: we are giving up the game if we suggest that man makes myths because he makes myths, and that no deterministic explanation will work. Frazer is one such early investigator who is indispensable for a book like this, not only because his center of cultural interest is close to mine, but because he treats myths as interlocking story patterns like a literary critic, rather than in terms of their functions within their various cultures. But Frazer was a Classical and Biblical scholar who thought he was a scientist because he had read so much anthropology, and hence was subject to fits of rationalism, which seem to have attacked him like a disease. In *Folklore in the Old Testament* he collects flood stories from all over the world, in typically Frazerian fashion, and then suggests that in every case a local flood was the reason for the myth. True, there do seem to have been floods in lower Mesopotamia, though the really big ones appear to be later than the great story in the Gilgamesh epic. But why does man respond to such events by myth? There are simpler ways of talking about the year of the big water than by inventing such stories as the ones we have about Noah or Deucalion or Ut-napishtim. And if a flood in Sumeria developed a flood myth that was carried to the corners of the earth by cultural diffusion, why was this particular myth so exportable?

People have believed for centuries, on the authority of the Book of Genesis, that there was a universal or general deluge over the whole world, and that the widespread distribution of flood myths is a testimony to it. But a wide distribution of flood myths is no more evidence for such a flood than a wide distribution of creation myths is evidence for the creation. In our day the authority of the Book of Genesis has receded, but we discover that the desire to "believe in" a universal deluge is as strong as ever, though it is now frequently attached to Plato's Atlantis myth or its various occult derivations. One wonders why. Perhaps there is a collective unconscious with a flood archetype in the middle of it, as for all I know there may be. But this is not an answer: it merely restates the question. Men produce flood myths because they have a collective unconscious that makes them produce flood myths: as Molière's doctor said, opium puts people to sleep because it has a dormative faculty. If we turn from the Jungians to the Freudians, we meet the suggestion, in Geza Roheim's *Gates of the Dream*, that deluge myths originate in urethral dreams designed to prevent the sleeper from deluging his bed. But the same circularity is present here: why do flood dreams become flood myths?

It seems clear that flood myths are better understood when they are compared with other flood myths, not when they are compared with floods. An actual flood may be the occasion of a flood myth: it can hardly be its cause, because so many factors in the stories of Noah and Deucalion and Ut-napishtim are equally or more important than the flood itself. We may also get some understanding of a flood myth by examining its place in a total mythology, as we shall try to do later. What stands in the middle of the question is the extraordinarily haunting power of the myth. The traditional explanation for this is that the story of Noah is a divine revelation telling us what we should not otherwise know. On the other hand, Plato's account of Atlantis, whatever legend or historical fact may have suggested it, is usually thought of as an invention of Plato's. But the psychological effect of the myth is much the same in both contexts. Whatever Plato's conscious mind was doing when he wrote the account of Atlantis, he was not inventing a myth so much as releasing it, and the power of what he released can still nearly paralyze our faculties with its suggestion of a magical submarine kingdom where the prototypes of our own culture are still to be found.

Mythology is not a *datum* but a *factum* of human existence: it belongs to the world of culture and civilization that man has made and still inhabits. As a god is a metaphor identifying a personality and an element of nature, solar myths or star myths or vegetation myths may suggest something of a primitive form of science. But the real interest of myth is to draw a circumference around a human community and look inward toward that community, not to inquire into the operations of nature. Naturally it will draw elements from nature, just as creative design in painting or sculpture would do. But mythology is not a direct response to the natural environment; it is part of the imaginative insulation that separates us from that environment. Star myths are a good example of the creative autonomy of myth: there is no such thing in nature as a constellation, and when a group of stars is said to be a crab or a goat or something else that it does not in the least resemble, the myth-making activity that does this is clearly not dependent on anything the stars themselves suggest in their appearance or movement, however much astronomical observation may eventually form part of the myth.

In the preceding chapter we noted the controversy, if that is the word, between Peacock and Shelley over the nature of poetry. Both understand that poetry re-creates something very primitive and archaic in society. Peacock treats this satirically, pretending to adopt a view of progress in civilization as a whole that puts the poet increasingly out of touch with his own time. Shelley feels that "progress" is always a progress toward disaster at least as much as it is a progress toward improvement, and that poetry is primitive in the sense of expressing a fundamental and persisting link with reality. This issue is dead as regards poetry: no serious critic would make a serious use of Peacock's thesis, any more than Peacock did himself. In mythology the issues are more confused: it apparently takes social scientists much longer than poets or critics to realize that every mind is a primitive mind, whatever the varieties of social conditioning. It would be easy to misinterpret the metaphorical-metonymic-descriptive sequence set out in the previous chapter as a form of progress. But while progress may be a relevant conception in many areas of human life, the arts, in Hazlitt's phrase, are not progressive, and mythology belongs to the arts.

As a form of imaginative and creative thinking, myth does not improve with the growth of society or technology, much less become abolished by them. Just as African sculpture can be a highly sophisticated influence on the highly sophisticated work of Picasso, so the myths of Australian indigenes can be as profound and suggestive as their counterparts in our own culture. A century ago, many scholars, influenced partly by a naïve identifying of evolution with progress, assumed that mythological thinking was an early form of conceptual thinking. This of course led immediately to the discovery that it was very bad conceptual thinking. Thus Frazer again, in another fit of rational *tic doloureux*: "By myths I understand mistaken explanations of phenomena, whether of human life or of external nature." This was obviously part of an ideology designed to rationalize the European treatment of "natives" on darker continents, and the less attention given it now the better.

At the same time mythology, because of its sacrosanct nature, is likely to persist in a society in inorganic ways, and so come to make assertions or assumptions about the order of nature that conflict with what the actual observation of that order suggests. When this happens, the mythological explanation has to be replaced by a scientific one. We saw earlier that Copernicus now symbolizes for us the replacing of mythological by scientific conceptions of space, and Darwin the replacing of mythological by scientific conceptions of time. But the accidents of a mythological tradition are not real mythology, the central line of which is re-created in every age by the poets.

As a literature develops, "profane" or secular folktale and legend become part of its material. In Western literature Dante and Milton choose their major subjects from within the mythical area; Chaucer and Shakespeare stay with folktale and legend. This process is possible because of the structural analogy, if not identity, of sacred and profane story. When the serious and concerned nature of myth is widely accepted, a poet's freedom of treating it is conditioned by that fact. Sophocles and Milton could not tell the stories of Oedipus or Adam without respecting the concerns of their audiences, though there might be special features, as there were in Greek culture, permitting a comic poet to treat mythical themes farcically, up to a point. Here the authority of the traditional myth is partly independent of the poet. If the poet is dealing with a "profane" Classical myth in the Christian period, he is, in theory, free to do as he likes with it. Hence it is all the more interesting that in practice poets seem to show

great respect for the integrity of the myths they treat. A by-product of
the same respect for tradition accounts for the endlessly allusive
quality of poetry, the tendency of poets to keep referring to the same
familiar mythical themes, to treat all wars as clones of the siege of
Troy. Because of this, we get a strong sense of "a" myth as something
separate from its verbal embodiments, even though such a separation
cannot really exist.

   This brings us to a question we have not yet asked. Granted that
the narratives in the Bible are myths in the sense we have given the
word, whether they are histories or fictions, are they histories or
fictions? There are certainly verbal areas, such as the daily newspaper,
where it is important for us to know whether the stories we encounter
are true or only made up; and the kind of importance given traditionally to the Bible seems to indicate that it too is one of these areas.
Besides, the question is not an anachronism: the Old Testament, even
though its oldest parts are older than Herodotus, is still recent
enough for its writers to have been capable of giving us actual history
if they had chosen to do so. And no one denies that the Bible is
passionately interested in historical issues. Still, the Bible's answer to
the question is a curiously quizzical one: so quizzical that there must
be something wrong with the either-or way of formulating it.

   We begin, as remarked, with stories of a creation and a flood,
which seem to be myths not merely in the secondary sense of sacred
stories, but also in the colloquial and negative sense of being accounts
of events that can hardly have happened in just that way. They
resemble other creation and deluge myths over the world, and are not
the oldest forms we have of such myths. We pass on to what looks like
legend and folktale, stories of Jephthah's uttering a rash vow and
Elisha's making an iron axe-head float, which again belong to familiar
patterns of story. Familiar, too, is the type of story called etiological,
which leads up to the explanation of a place name. Samson kills a
thousand Philistines with the jawbone of an ass, and consequently
"called that place Ramath-lehi" ("the hill of the jawbone," Judges
15:17). From the analogy of such things elsewhere, the name suggested the story, not the other way around.

   The stories of Abraham and of the Exodus belong in an area best
called historical reminiscence. That is, they doubtless contain a
kernel of actual history, but what historical basis there may be for the
narrative we have is another matter. It seems to be not yet possible,
for instance, for Egyptologists to fit the exodus of Israel to anything
else they know about Egyptian history. It seems clear that the

Egyptians knew nothing of an exodus, just as the Emperor Augustus knew nothing of the birth of Christ. When we move into what looks like actual history, to which we can attach some dates and supporting evidence, we find that it is didactic and manipulated history. The kings of northern Israel and Judah are given simple black and white characterizations: white if they promoted the cult of Jehovah, black if they did not.

Ahab, for instance, is portrayed in the main as a kind of sinister clown, whose effete and corrupt dynasty was wiped out by Jehu in a whirlwind of righteous fury. One episode, however (I Kings 29:1-34), from a different source, presents Ahab as an able and popular ruler, so convincingly as to make us wonder if the Biblical writer is not deliberately choosing less reliable sources for the most part. The Assyrian monuments show some unwilling respect for the house of Omri, to which Ahab belonged, and portray the furiously driving Jehu as an abjectly submissive vassal. What is portrayed and stated may be paranoid, but that very fact makes it useful corrective evidence. Clearly, the Bible is a violently partisan book: as with any other form of propaganda, what is true is what the writer thinks ought to be true; and the sense of urgency in the writing comes out much more freely for not being hampered by the clutter of what may actually have occurred.

The general principle involved here is that if anything historically true is in the Bible, it is there not because it is historically true but for different reasons. The reasons have presumably something to do with spiritual profundity or significance. And historical truth has no correlation with spiritual profundity, unless the relation is inverse. The Book of Job, never seriously regarded as anything but an imaginative drama, is obviously profounder spiritually than the lists of choir singers and the like in the Book of Chronicles, lists that may well be or contain genuine historical records. What is more important is that whenever we move from the obviously legendary to the possibly historical, we never cross a clear boundary line. That is, the sense of historical fact as such is simply not delimited in the Bible, anywhere.

We get an indication of the Bible's bias of interest, perhaps, in the Book of Judges. This book, a collection of stories about heroes who were originally tribal leaders, has been edited to present the appearance of a history of a united Israel going through a series of crises, all of much the same shape. Israel, in whom the spirit of apostasy appears to be remarkably consistent, deserts its God, gets enslaved, cries to its God for deliverance, and a "judge" is sent to deliver it. Here there is a series of different contents, along with a repeating mythical or narrative form which contains them. The heavy emphasis on the structure, where because of the moral interest we are in effect being told the same kind of story over and over again, indicates that the individual stories are being made to fit that pattern. They are as distantly related to historical events as an abstract painting is to realistic representation, and related in a similar way. The priority is given to the mythical structure or outline of the story, not to the historical content.

And just as the historical books of the Old Testament are not history, so the Gospels are not biography. The Gospel writers care nothing about the kind of evidence that would interest a biographer—remarks of disinterested travelers and the like; they care only about comparing the events in their accounts of Jesus with what the Old Testament, as they read it, said would happen to the Messiah. The actual sequence of events does not seem crucially significant to them, and while Pontius Pilate and Herod are historical characters, other historical pointers, like the reference to Quirinius in Luke 2:2, are more embarrassing than helpful.

To repeat an example I have given elsewhere: Renan, a century ago, began a rationalized "historical" life of Jesus with the confident statement that Jesus was born in Nazareth in Galilee, the story that he was born in Bethlehem in Judea having been added later to reconcile his birth with the prophecy in Micah 5:2. But, arguing on those grounds, there is no reason for associating Jesus with Galilee except to reconcile his appearance with the prophecy in Isaiah 9:2, or for connecting him with Nazareth except that some unknown prophecy said, apparently, that the Messiah would be a "Nazirite" like Samson (Matthew 2:23). A connection with *netzer*, branch, has also been suggested, but the principle is the same: Renan's credible fact dissolves into two more Messianic prophecies as soon as we look up a few more references. Even the question of whether there was such a village as Nazareth at the time specified has been disputed.

We are sometimes urged to "demythologize" the Gospels in order to make them more relevant to modern canons of credibility. "Modern" in such contexts usually means about a hundred years out of date, but still an impulse to try to remove whatever seems obviously incredible is natural enough. It would be interesting to see, if we could, what the original "historical" Jesus was like, before his teachings got involved in the mythical and legendary distortions of his followers. But if we try to do this with any thoroughness, there will be, quite simply, nothing left of the Gospels at all. The Gospel writers, or editors, have been too clever for us, and whenever we think we have found something unique and "real," in historical terms, we also find that they have blocked up that exit too with some echo from or parallel with the Old Testament or contemporary Jewish ritual that suggests some other reason for its being there. And yet they do not seem to be clever men, in that sense: their aim is clearly to try to tell us something, not to prevent us from knowing something else. There is early secular evidence for the rise of Christianity, but there is practically no real evidence for the life of Jesus outside the New Testament, all the evidence for a major historical figure being hermetically sealed within it. But it seems clear also that the writers of the New Testament preferred it that way.

Nothing said here will be new to Biblical scholars, who are well aware that the Bible will only confuse and exasperate a historian who tries to treat it as a history. One wonders why in that case their obsession with the Bible's historicity does not relax, so that other and more promising hypotheses could be examined. Trying to extract a credible historical residue from a mass of "mythical accretions" is a futile procedure, if the end in view is Biblical criticism rather than history. It has been obvious for at least a century that "mythical accretions" are what the Bible is: it is the bits of credible history that are expendable, however many of them there may be. In Homeric criticism, scholars may have acquired a considerable and increasing respect for Homer's sense of fact, in both history and geography; but no increasing respect for such matters will make Achilles' fight with the river-god or the hurling of Hephaistos out of heaven historical. That is, Homer's sense of history does not mean that he is writing history. Similarly with the Bible. If the historical element in the Bible were a conscientious, inaccurate, imperfect history like the Anglo-Saxon Chronicle, we could understand how important it would be to make a fuller reconstruction of that history. But when it shows such an exuberant repudiation of everything we are accustomed to think of as historical evidence, perhaps we should be looking for different categories and criteria altogether.

An analogy from secular literature may give us a clue to our further procedure. The Icelandic Greenland and Eirik sagas are literary productions: they are intended to be such, and conform to the conventions of literature. But because they allude to Norse explorations and settlements on the coast of America, the extent to which they may be incidentally historical is naturally of great interest to many people. Hence they have also been studied as documents in a historical problem. In that context, what is or may be historical is true, and what belongs to myth and literature is false or imaginary.

These sagas tell us that the Norsemen were attacked by natives with catapults or ballistae. Scholars say that the Algonquins, at least, are known to have used ballistae in warfare; so here is something that may be historically true. We read of "unipeds," or people who had only one foot. No scholar will buy the unipeds: they came out of a book, and are therefore literary and false. We are told that two Scottish members of the expedition, a man and a woman, disappeared into the bush and returned, one with a sheaf of grain and the other with a bunch of grapes. Perhaps not inherently incredible, but there is an echo of Numbers 13:23 and, more important, a most suspicious symmetry. Symmetry, in any narrative, always means that historical content is being subordinated to mythical demands of design and form, as in the Book of Judges. Then again, of the three explored lands mentioned, "Helluland" sounds like Baffin Island and "Markland" like the coast of Labrador or Newfoundland; but "Vinland," though identified with any number of places from Nova Scotia to Florida, still sounds more like Hy Brasil or the Garden of the Hesperides than anything mundane enough to be marked on a map. However, the kernel of it may be an actual place: such categories in such narratives refuse to be definitely characterized as true or false.

In these sagas we have only the two elements of history and literature, and so are not disturbed by hysterics screaming that we must accept everything including the unipeds, in fact especially the unipeds, or face the wrath of a God who deliberately created the unipeds as a "test of faith" to make things as difficult as possible for intellectually honest people to believe anything he says. But a principle is involved which also applies to the Bible: we cannot get an inch further without new archaeological evidence, and such evidence would carry the authority that we have ceased to assign to the sagas themselves. Similarly, for the historian of the Biblical period, the primary historical authority is not the Bible but what (the written sources having been exhausted long ago) archaeology can still dig up in the way of acceptable evidence.

The degree to which the Bible does record actual events can perhaps never be exactly ascertained. We read in Joshua 10:12-14:

Then spake Joshua to the Lord in the day when the Lord delivered up the Amorites before the children of Israel, and he said in the sight of Israel, Sun, stand thou still upon Gibeon; and thou, Moon, in the valley of Ajalon.

And the sun stood still, and the moon stayed, until the people had avenged themselves upon their enemies. Is not this written in the book of Jasher? So the sun stood still, in the midst of heaven, and hasted not to go down about a whole day.

And there was no day like that before it or after it, that the Lord hearkened unto the voice of a man: for the Lord fought for Israel.

Our first reaction to this would be to say that the fine bold metaphor of the poet of the Book of Jasher has been vulgarized by an overcredulous and unimaginative prose commentator into a pointless miracle. Yet Immanuel Velikovsky, a writer with still a considerable vogue, has written books to show that this event, along with an equally improbable story about Hezekiah in II Kings 20, did take place in much the way described, the cause being, he tells us, the settling of the new planet Venus into its orbit.

Velikovsky illustrates in particular a perennial urge to explain myths that finds a curious satisfaction in aligning ancient stories with contemporary interests. In the seventeenth century, fossils and similar geological phenomena were being used to demonstrate the veracity of the Genesis account of the Flood. In an age of science fiction Ezekiel's vision of a chariot of "wheels within wheels" seems more relevant if what he saw was a spaceship from another planet; and an age of drug cults and popular occultism feels attracted by the notion that Jesus and his disciples were devotees of the agaric mushroom, or that Moses produced such miracles as bringing water out of a rock through his training in Egyptian magic, which would naturally have included dowsing. I am not dismissing such explanations: one should doubtless keep an open mind about them, though an open mind, to be sure, should be open at both ends, like the foodpipe, and have a capacity for excretion as well as intake. What I am saying is that all explanations are an *ersatz* form of evidence, and evidence implies a criterion of truth external to the Bible which the Bible itself does not recognize.

Thus someone recently asked me, after seeing a television program about the discovery of a large boat-shaped structure on Mount Ararat with animal cages in it, if I did not think that this alleged discovery "sounded the death knell of liberal theology." The first thing that occurred to me was that the Bible itself could not care less whether anyone ever finds an ark on Mount Ararat or not: such "proofs" belong to a mentality quite different from any that could conceivably have produced the Book of Genesis. Similarly, if a historical record of Jesus' trial before Pilate were to turn up that corresponded in any detail to the Gospel account, many people would hail that as a definitive vindication of the truth of the Gospel story, without noticing that they had shifted their criterion of truth from the Gospels to something else.

I labor this point, partly because it is connected with one of the central issues of the present book, the nature of "literal" meaning, and partly because of its relation to the historical perspective on the development of language given in the preceding chapter. Tradition, or some of it, says that the historical element in the Bible must be regarded as "true" in a simplified form of the sense I have associated with third-phase, or descriptive, writing. When such matters were controlled by an intellectual elite, or priesthood, it would be natural for such an elite to feel that the real truth in such matters was hard enough for the subtlest and profoundest of intellects to attain, if possible at all, and that therefore for the masses the appropriate criterion of belief would be their own "demotic" one. Later on, the attitude develops that if we find something incredible in the Biblical story, so much the better: that enables us to offer up our intellects as a willing sacrifice; and if we believe it, or believe that we believe it, we acquire a special virtue by doing so. With the general acceptance of demotic and descriptive criteria in language, such literalism becomes a feature of anti-intellectual Christian populism. This attitude says, for example, that the story of Jonah must describe a real sojourn inside a real whale, otherwise we are making God, as the ultimate source of the story, into a liar.

It might be said that a God who would deliberately fake so unlikely a series of events in order to vindicate the "literal truth" of his story would be a much more dangerous liar, and such a God could never have become incarnate in Jesus, because he would be too stupid to understand what a parable was. However, to set up standards of the "credible" is often equally hazardous, because no one knows what is possible, or more accurately what is impossible. Many writers assume or assert that the miracles of healing in the Gospels are incredible, and that the stories of casting out devils relate to very primitive notions of mental disease and must be rejected too, it being unreasonable to ask modern people, living in the century of Hitler and Idi Amin, to believe in evil spirits. But there are now other accounts of miraculous healings in various parts of the world, and perhaps the recent vogue for "exorcism" indicates a growing feeling that a "devil" might be as therapeutically useful a conception as, say, a superego. Of course, the more "credible" such things become, the less significant they are as testimonies to the uniqueness of Jesus' powers.

What all this amounts to is not that "literalism" of the kind described here is simply a matter of running scared: many people who would reject or ridicule such an approach to the Bible would apply much the same criteria in areas where it was equally inappropriate. What it amounts to, I think, is that credibility, as a factor in the response to the particulars of the Biblical narrative, is very largely a pseudo-issue. When the apostle Thomas demanded visible and tangible evidence for the Resurrection, he was told that he would have understood the Resurrection more clearly if he hadn't bothered with it. I doubt that the implication of this story is that an uncritical attitude is spiritually closer to truth than a critical one. I think the implication is rather that the more trustworthy the evidence, the more misleading it is.

The intimate and inevitable relation between mythology and poetry, then, seems to be operating here to some degree as well. Perhaps the myths of the Bible should be read poetically, just as we read Homer and the Gilgamesh epic poetically. Certainly the poetic parts of the Bible are genuinely poetic in a way that the historical parts are not historical. And if we ask why the Biblical myths are closer to being poetic than to being history, Aristotle's principle, which I have referred to so constantly in my criticism, will supply an answer, up to a point. History makes particular statements, and is therefore subject to external criteria of truth and falsehood; poetry makes no particular statements and is not so subject. Poetry expresses the universal in the event, the aspect of the event that makes it an example of the kind of thing that is always happening. In our language, the universal in the history is what is conveyed by the *mythos*, the shape of the historical narrative. A myth is designed not to describe a specific situation but to contain it in a way that does not restrict its significance to that one situation. Its truth is inside its structure, not outside.

Our stock example of a history, Gibbon's *Decline and Fall of the Roman Empire*, shows us that the same development can take place even with a work originally intended to be a history. History as such has continually to be rewritten: as time goes on, and historians learn more about the later Roman Empire, Gibbon's work "dates" as the definitive account of it. Two things happen in this process that are instructive for us here. In the first place, Gibbon's work survives by its "style," which means that it insensibly moves over from the historical category into the poetic, and becomes a classic of English literature, or at any rate of English cultural history. In proportion as it does so, its material becomes universalized: it becomes an eloquent and witty meditation on human decline and fall, as exemplified by what happened in Caesarian Rome. The shift in attention is simultaneously from the particular to the universal and from what Gibbon says to his way of saying it. We read him for his "style" in the sense that the stylizing or conventionalizing aspect of his writing gradually becomes more important than the representational aspect, just as a Cimabue painting of the Crucifixion comes to be, in the course of time, more important as a picture than as an icon of the death of Christ.

And yet, while reading Biblical myth poetically is a more liberal exercise than reading it as factual history, trying to reduce the Bible entirely to the hypothetical basis of poetry clearly will not do. There is no difficulty with Homer or the Gilgamesh epic, because they are poetic throughout, but large areas of the Bible are clearly not poetic. To put it another way, the Bible taken as a poem is so spectacularly bad a poem that to accept it all as poetry would raise more questions than it solves. Besides, we should have no criteria for distinguishing, say, Jesus from the prodigal son of his own parable, both being equally characters in fictions, and nobody would take such an approach to the Bible very seriously, whatever his degree of commitment to it. There are and remain two aspects of myth: one is its story-structure, which attaches it to literature, the other is its social function as concerned knowledge, what it is important for a society to know. We now have to consider this second aspect of myth, remembering that just as the poetic aspect had already developed toward literature by Biblical times, so the functional aspect had developed toward historical and political thought.

It is sometimes said that the reason for the Bible's oblique approach to history is that what we call history is *Weltgeschichte*, whereas the Bible is interested in *Heilsgeschichte*, in the history of God's actions in the world and man's relation to them. To give an illustration of what is meant here: Dante's *Commedia* presents a Paradiso above our own world, an Inferno below it, and two other worlds on the surface of this earth. On one side of the earth is thirteenth-century Italy, busily producing *Weltgeschichte*; on the other is the mountain of purgatory, where souls are grouped solely in relation to the eternal world above them, and where the only historical "event" is the passing of a soul into that world. In the Bible the two areas of history occupy the same space and time, but they are still two different perspectives on human life. *Weltgeschichte* uses the criteria of ordinary history, and attempts to answer the question, What should I have seen if I had been there? *Heilsgeschichte*, as we have it for instance in the Gospels, may say to us rather, "This may not be what you would have seen if you had been there, but what you would have seen would have missed the whole point of what was really going on." This distinction is no doubt sound enough, but leaves us with the question: What is the relation of *Heilsgeschichte* to myth, as I have been outlining it, or to poetic history, as we have it in Aeschylus' *The Persians* or Shakespeare's *Macbeth*?

We have spoken of the repeating quality in literature, its allusiveness and its almost obsessive respect for tradition. One of the first things I noticed about literature was the stability of its structural units: the fact that certain themes, situations, and character types, in comedy let us say, have persisted with very little change from Aristophanes to our own time. I have used the term "archetype" to describe these building blocks, as I thought in its traditional sense, not realizing how completely Jung's more idiosyncratic use of the same word had monopolized the field. This quality of repetition is essential to myth in all its contexts. A society, even one equipped with writing, cannot keep its central myths of concern constantly in mind unless they are continually being re-presented. The normal way of doing this is to associate them with ritual, setting apart regular intervals of sacred time when certain symbolic things are done, including the rehearsing of myth. Mircea Eliade tells us that for many societies all events in time are regarded as repetitions of mythical archetypal events that took place before time began, or what Australian indigenes call the eternal dream time.

Myth is thus inseparable from *dromena*, things to be done or specified actions. The ritual actions that accompany the rehearsing of myth point in the direction of the original context of the myth. The stories of creation and exodus in the Pentateuch form part of a context of law—the prescribing of certain forms of action—just as the parables of Jesus often have as their moral "Go and do thou likewise" (Luke 10:37). Obedience to law makes one's life a predictable series of repeating conditions: peace, prosperity, freedom. Disobedience to law also makes life a predictable series of repeating disasters: conquest, slavery, misery, as in the Book of Judges. In actual history or *Weltgeschichte* nothing repeats exactly: hence *Heilsgeschichte* and *Weltgeschichte* can never coincide. Accurate history brings out differentiating and unique elements in every situation, and so blurs and falsifies the point that *Heilsgeschichte* is trying to make. But what value is there in a point that can be made only by the falsifying of history?

In the preceding chapter we spoke of the oratorical style of the Bible as a uniting of the poetic and the concerned. Myth has two parallel aspects: as a story, it is poetic and is re-created in literature; as a story with a specific social function, it is a program of action for a specific society. In both aspects it relates not to the actual but to the possible. What a man essentially is is revealed in two ways: by the record of what he has done, and by what he is trying to make of himself at any given moment. Adopting provisionally the legal metaphor that runs all through the Bible, and sees man as under a trial and subject to judgment, we may say that the former is the case for the prosecution, the voice of the accuser. The accuser is the primary role of Satan in the Bible, and so Byron is very accurate when he refers to history, the record of what man has done, as "the devil's scripture." This aspect of history does not diminish its importance: quite the contrary. It is the function of literature, however, not to run away from the actual, but to see the dimension of the possible in the actual. And a program of action, while it cannot ignore history, may often set itself in opposition to history. This is most obvious with myths of deliverance, which speak of something that history gives us little encouragement to believe in.

Thus the Exodus is a myth of the deliverance of Israel from Egypt which clearly bears only the most oblique relation to the historical events of whatever period it may assume. The historical Egypt's record for cruelty and ruthlessness was no worse than that of any other Near Eastern nation, including Israel itself, and in the later Biblical period many Jews were living quite contentedly in Alexandria. It is the symbolic Egypt only that is the "furnace of iron" (I Kings 8:51), the hell-prison destroyed by a miracle. The evidence from history seems to suggest that Israel continued to be at least nominally subject to Egyptian power through most of the period covered by the stories of the judges. But the symbolic Egypt is not in history: it extends over past, present, and future. Several thousand years after the period of the Exodus we have the well-known spiritual:

Go down, Moses,
Way down in Egypt land,
Tell old Pharaoh
Let my people go.

The Israelites were not black, and nineteenth-century American blacks had no quarrel with ancient Egypt. The point is that when any group of people feels as strongly about anything as slaves feel about slavery, history as such is dust and ashes: only myth, with its suggestion of an action that can contain the destinies of those who are contemplating it, can provide any hope or support at all. Such myth does not overrule *Weltgeschichte*: by avoiding actual history and its criteria, it sets the historian free to do his own job in his own way. A more traditional language would say that myth *redeems* history: assigns it to its real place in the human panorama.

It is easiest to see this in myths of deliverance, but then the central myth of the Bible, from whatever point of view one reads it, is also a myth of deliverance. There are other myths, like the great tragedies in Greek drama, that are directed to increasing and illuminating our awareness of the human condition. But they too take us well beyond the habitual reflex that contrasts what is really there or actually happened with self-indulgent illusions about them: that regards the dream as only helpless wish, and waking life the invincible censor that represses it again. A serious human life, no matter what "religion" is invoked, can hardly begin until we see an element of illusion in what is really there, and something real in fantasies about what might be there instead. At that point the imaginative and the concerned begin to unite.

In the Bible, *Weltgeschichte* and *Heilsgeschichte* cannot be simply opposed to one another: if they were, *Heilsgeschichte* would become purely poetic again. We come much closer to this kind of separation in Classical and non-Biblical Near Eastern cultures, because they follow the cycle of *langage* that we have outlined more closely. Their religions are polytheistic, hence more purely metaphorical; and they show a much greater flexibility in assigning authority to their myths. Some say that Dionysus was born at Thebes; others that he was born in India or Africa or Thrace. In Classical mythology it does not matter much: obviously he got born, or his temple would not be here now. The Bible's attitude toward such things is more rigorous, and the reason for this takes us into the final stage of our discussion of myth.

All human societies are insulated to some degree by a culture that surrounds them and separates them from nature. There are no noble savages, in the sense of purely natural men for whom this integument of culture has disappeared. What we live in, says Wallace Stevens, is a description without place. This "description," on its verbal side, is a mythology or body of sacrosanct stories, rituals, traditions: a social

skin that marks the boundary between ourselves and the natural
environment. In its early stages it is difficult to separate or distinguish the various aspects of mythology, but as society becomes more
complex, different areas of culture—literature, religion, philosophy,
history, science, art—become increasingly distinct from one another.
The primary function of mythology is to face inward toward the
concerns of the society that possesses it—which is why science, which
faces outward toward the operations of nature itself, is a late cultural
development.

We have spoken of the tendency of myths to expand into a
mythology, and mythology has an encyclopedic quality about it: it
tends to cover all the essential concerns of its society. When we move
into the metonymic phase of *langage*, tension arises between the
growing separate elements of culture and the unifying mythology of
its social concern. At this stage it is quickly discovered that a unified
mythology is a powerful instrument of social authority and coercion,
and it is accordingly used as such. About two generations ago there
was a fashion for crying up the Middle Ages as a golden era in which
all aspects of human life were united in a common body of beliefs and
values. The intellectual unity of that time, however, was largely a
rationalizing of its centralized authority. Marxism makes a similar
appeal today as a unifying instrument of authority which includes an
all-encompassing metaphysic, though of course it is not called that.

But it is hard to see how the centrifugal drift toward cultural
pluralism could be stopped, even if we were agreed that it should be.
Sooner or later, astronomy had to accept a heliocentric view of the
solar system even though social anxieties demanded a geocentric one;
sooner or later British history had to give up King Arthur even
though the British imagination clung to him. That is, historians and
scientists found that they had not only a social function, but a
discipline of their own that demanded loyalty to its principles. It may
be more difficult for some to see that the writer or artist also may owe
a loyalty to his own discipline, and may have to defend that discipline
against the concerns of society, but the same principles hold there. In
the opposition to Galileo and Bruno it seems clear that it was social
concern that was wrong; but in this age of atom bombs and energy
crises it is equally clear that social concern has its case too. We have
still the problem of establishing the social function and responsibility
of the different aspects of culture while respecting their autonomy
and authority. It is a big problem, but we have no choice about
dealing with it.

The basis of the problem, once more, is the simultaneous sense of both the social relevance and the inner integrity of all the elements of human culture. Without the integrity, we go around the cycle again, back to a subordination of everything creative and scholarly to the expediencies and superstitions of authority. Without the sense of relevance, we fly apart into a chaos of mutually unintelligible elites, of which those nearest the center of society would soon take control, with the same result as in the opposite movement. So atavistic a social regression, in the present stage of technological development, might well wipe the human race off the planet. Hence we are back to the dilemma of Deuteronomy 30:19: "I have set before you life and death; therefore choose life." In that context the dilemma is presented from a perspective that only God is assumed to be able to attain: a concern for the continuation of human life in time that goes far beyond the purely imaginative, together with a view of the human situation that goes equally far beyond the purely historical. We have now to consider separately the imaginative and the metahistorical elements in this *Heilsgeschichte* vision.

CHAPTER THREE

METAPHOR I

Once we have realized that the Bible is not primarily literary in intention, it may seem curious that it should be so full of figures of speech, in their conventional or rhetorical forms. It becomes less curious when we realize how much of the Bible is contemporary with a metaphorical phase of language, where many aspects of verbal meaning cannot be conveyed except through metaphorical and poetic means. Not only are large blocks of the Old Testament written in verse, but the prose, with its frequent verse interludes, shows a strong affinity with the associative and figured speech of verse. Puns and popular etymologies appear everywhere in the Hebrew text: they are naturally untranslatable, but translations have to take account of them, at least in the marginalia. Foreign words are assimilated to the Hebrew, sometimes violently. Babel, which means gate of God, is associated with a Hebrew word meaning confusion; the story of the finding of Moses derives his name, which looks Egyptian, from a Hebrew word meaning "drawn out"; and so on.

The New Testament continues with the same patterns. In Matthew 16:18 we find the celebrated "Thou art Peter, and upon this rock (*petra*) I will build my church," a Greek pun which by a curious accident, if that is what it is, works also in the Aramaic that Jesus was more likely to have been speaking. Another Aramaic pun is probably involved when John the Baptist says (Matthew 3:9) that God is able of these "stones" (*'ebhanim*) to raise up "children" (*banim*) to Abraham. This also coincides with a Greek pun, though one that takes us outside the Bible: in the Hesiodic myth of the deluge the survivors of the flood, Deucalion and Pyrrha, were told to throw stones (*laas*) behind them: they did so and people (*laos*) sprang up. As we sometimes use the phrase "gospel truth" to mean the quintessence of demotic language, or veridical fact, it is interesting that of all figures of speech, the hyperbole, or intentional exaggeration, is the one that departs most explicitly from the representation of fact, and that the very last "gospel truth" uttered, the closing verse of the Gospel of John, should be a dazzling hyperbole:

And there are also many other things which Jesus did, the which, if they should be written every one, I suppose that even the world itself could not contain the books that should be written.

There are also some curiously violent hyperboles in the discourses of Jesus, as when we read of camels being swallowed or going through the eye of a needle, or of people having "beams" in their eyes.

We notice too that the Bible is full of explicit metaphors, of the this-is-that, or *A*-is-*B* type. Such metaphors are profoundly illogical, if not anti-logical: they assert that two things are the same thing while remaining two different things, which is absurd. Yet we read in Genesis 49: "Issachar is a strong ass"; "Naphtali is a hind let loose"; "Joseph is a fruitful bough." Ah yes, we say, but these are "just" metaphors, or ornaments of language: we may even hail them with relief as belonging to a "merely poetic" passage that we do not need to take too seriously. We could also stretch this poetic use of metaphor to cover, for example, Jesus' reference to Herod Agrippa as "that fox" (Luke 13:32). But then we notice that Jesus makes a number of metaphorical statements about himself: "I am the door"; "I am the vine, ye are the branches"; "I am the bread of life"; "I am the way, the truth, and the life." How "seriously" are we to take these? He seems to have meant them rather seriously. It is true that these "I" metaphors, as we shall see, are in a different class from the metaphors in Genesis 49, but they are still metaphors. We clearly have to consider the possibility that metaphor is, not an incidental ornament of Biblical language, but one of its controlling modes of thought.

We get into a more rarefied area of literary criticism with Jesus' aphorism "The kingdom of God is within you" (*entos hymon*, Luke 17:21). The New English Bible, which seems particularly unhappy with this remark for some reason, translates it "For in fact the kingdom of God is among you," and offers as alternates: "For in fact the kingdom of God is within you," "For in fact the kingdom of God is within your grasp," and "For suddenly the kingdom of God will be among you." Several critical principles may be dimly discerned in this. First, the translator's own attitude is important for the translation. Those who feel that psychological metaphors express the profoundest truths will prefer "within"; those who want a more social gospel—and these translators clearly have a social conscience—will prefer "among." Second, Jesus may very well have meant, or even said, what is recorded in the Gospel of Thomas: "The kingdom is inside you and it is outside you," although the Gospel of Thomas was not discovered until 1945. What Jesus meant may not be so easy to say, but everyone is united on what he did not mean. He did not mean that the kingdom of God is "within" in the sense that our heart and lungs are inside us, or in the sense, say, that a swallowed safety pin is within a baby. All serious discussion of the passage begins by rejecting the demotic or descriptive meaning, and then discusses what kind of metaphor is signified by the word *entos*.

The sense in Christianity of a faith beyond reason, which must continue to affirm even after reason gives up, is closely connected with the linguistic fact that many of the central doctrines of traditional Christianity can be grammatically expressed only in the form of metaphor. Thus: Christ *is* God and man; in the Trinity three persons *are* one; in the Real Presence the body and blood *are* the bread and the wine. When these doctrines are rationalized by conceptions of a spiritual substance and the like, the metaphor is translated into metonymic language and "explained." But there is a strong smell of intellectual mortality about such explanations, and sooner or later they fade away and the original metaphor reappears, as intransigent as ever. At that point we are back to a world in which St. Patrick illustrates the doctrine of the Trinity by a shamrock, a use of concrete paradox that enlightens the mind by paralyzing the discursive reason, like the koan of Zen Buddhism. The doctrines may be "more" than metaphors: the point is that they can be stated only in a metaphorical this-is-that form.

In descriptive language, metaphors are something of an obstacle because of their ambiguity. Accurate and precise definition, so far as words can convey it, is a descriptive ideal, and the descriptive axiom, "to mean any number of things is really to mean nothing," works fairly well in that context. The situation is somewhat different in metonymic writing, where the versatility of a single word, such as form, idea, substance, being, or time, may afford a key to a whole system of thought. And it is totally different in poetry, where the axiom does not work at all. It seems clear that the Bible belongs to an area of language in which metaphor is functional, and where we have to surrender precision for flexibility.

Similarly, we are told in the New Testament itself that the mysteries of faith have to be "spiritually discerned" (I Corinthians 2:14). This is in a passage where Paul is contrasting the letter, which, he says, "killeth," with the spirit that "giveth life." He is not saying that there is no literal basis for Biblical meaning, but that that literal basis cannot be "natural": its authority is not from the external world outside the Bible. The word "spiritually" (*pneumatikos*) means a good many things in the New Testament, but one thing that it must always centrally mean is "metaphorically." Thus in Revelation 11:8:

And their dead bodies shall lie in the street of the great city, which spiritually is called Sodom and Egypt, where also our Lord was crucified.

That is, the earthly Jerusalem, which had probably been sacked by the Emperor Titus shortly before the Book of Revelation was written, is metaphorically the same demonic city as the Sodom sunk under the Dead Sea and the Egypt whose army was sunk in the Red Sea.

So far we have been speaking of explicit metaphors, such as "Joseph is a fruitful bough," which contain a predication in the word "is." Ezra Pound, however, emphasizes the fact that we can have metaphor without the word "is," that in fact the predication may often be only an unnecessary concession to a prose mind. Once we take out "is," we move from explicit to implicit metaphor, which is produced by the juxtaposition of images only. Pound developed his idea from Fenellosa's study of the Chinese character, where a group of radicals are combined to produce a single verbal picture—a significant link with Vico's term "hieroglyphic." Pound's best-known example of metaphor by juxtaposition is his two-line poem on the Paris Metro:

> The apparition of these faces in the crowd,
> Petals on a wet, black bough.

Here any such predication as "is," "is like," "reminds me of," "suggests to me," or whatever, would, besides ruining the little poem, greatly weaken the metaphorical power of simply putting together the two images. Similarly, we read in Proverbs 11:22, omitting the connective tissue supplied by the AV and other translations:

A jewel of gold in a swine's snout,
A fair woman without discretion.

Once we raise the matter of implicit metaphor, however, or metaphor by juxtaposition, we have moved into a whole new dimension of figured speech. At this point we have to return to a critical principle discussed in *Anatomy of Criticism* as well as in many other books concerned with different aspects of verbal theory. A word, let us say, has its dictionary or conventional meaning, which exists independently of what we are reading; and it also has its particular meaning in the context of what we are reading. Our attention as we read is thus going simultaneously in two directions, outward to the conventional or remembered meaning, inward to the specific contextual meaning. In some verbal structures there comes a point at which we realize that the dictionary meanings are forming a second pattern parallel to the words. This is a sign that what we are reading is descriptive in intention: the verbal structure reproduces in its terms the body of phenomena it is describing, and a comparison between the two is implied throughout. At other times there seems to be no such secondary structure of meaning outside the words, and this in turn is a sign that what we are reading is "literary," which means provisionally a verbal structure existing for its own sake. To illustrate:

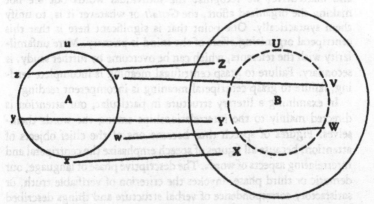

Here *A* is the verbal structure we are reading and *B* is the world outside it, where all the things that the words mean are to be found. The letters *uvwxyz* are the individual words in the verbal structure *A*, and the letters *UVWXYZ* are the things that they individually mean. The circle *A* represents the interrelating of words in what we are reading, and the dotted circle in B represents the corresponding structure in the non-verbal world, which exists only when the verbal structure is descriptive. If A were literary, $UVWXYZ$ would not have a symmetrical pattern corresponding to $uvwxyz$, but would be a purely random pattern with each element going back into A to find its contextual meaning. If we begin reading Carl Sandburg's poem on the fog:

> The fog comes
> On little cat feet

it is clear that we are not going to find anything structured outside the poem about fogs or cats' feet: the suggestion of something silent and furry comes back into the metaphorical structure of the poem itself. In A above, the movement through u, v, w, x, y, and z is the narrative or *mythos* already discussed, and $uvwxyz$ represents the whole of A, whereas $UVWXYZ$ is only the most infinitesimally small part of B.

There are two forms of half-reading that indicate how two processes are always involved. If we are reading a technical treatise on a subject we know little about, we can see that the sentences make grammatical sense, but we do not have enough external referents to complete the operation. Similarly with reading something in a language we imperfectly know. If, on the other hand, our reading is lazy and inattentive, we recognize the individual words but are not making the organized effort, the *Gestalt* or whatever it is, to unify them syntactically. One point that is significant here is that this centripetal organizing effort of the mind is primary. Mere unfamiliarity with the referents, which can be overcome by further study, is secondary. Failure to grasp centrifugal meaning is incomplete reading; failure to grasp centripetal meaning is incompetent reading.

In examining a literary structure in particular, our attention is directed mainly to the interrelationships among the words themselves. Figures of speech thus become one of the chief objects of attention, because all figures of speech emphasize the centripetal and interrelating aspects of words. The descriptive phase of language, our demotic or third phase, invokes the criterion of verifiable truth, or satisfactory correspondence of verbal structure and things described by it. Expressing such truth normally calls for a minimal use of figures of speech, which in such a context, as remarked earlier, seem to be "merely verbal." The predominance of metaphor and other forms of rhetorical figuration in the Bible make it impossible to read the Bible in this way.

The principle of implicit metaphor means among other things that when a "true" meaning is decided on for a word, it will usually be a choice among a number of metaphorical possibilities, and those other possibilities will still be there. This is particularly obvious when the word is a connective, like the *entos* of Jesus' aphorism. Suppose, for example, we were to decide that the "true" meaning of the word "in" was being contained by a container, as with "peas in a pod." In all other cases the word "in" would be metaphorical, including the "in" that stands at the beginning of this sentence. It will soon become clear that nobody can use language like that: all language is permeated by metaphor simply because words are juxtaposed.

We may note in passing that all speech contains a great deal of unconscious, additional, or implied meaning that comes from the nearness of words to one another, where many relations exist that need not or cannot be explicitly stated. In Wittgenstein's *Philosophical Investigations* one of the problems of conveying meaning through ordinary language is illustrated as follows: *A* says to *B*, "Teach these children a game"; *B* teaches them to gamble with dice, and *A* says, "I didn't mean that sort of game." What *A* "meant," evidently, was what he expressed by putting "children" and "game" so closely together: games appropriate to, or otherwise associable with, children. This principle of implicit meaning conveyed by the juxtaposing of words is the general principle of what in literary criticism used to be called *explication de texte*, and is also part of what is called hermeneutics. If there were not so many additional meanings within the contiguity of words, most such explication would be mere free association or daydreaming. Here is another critical principle that is ultimately of Biblical origin, as hermeneutics began originally in the exegesis of the Bible. In such exegesis, even in any intelligent sermon that sticks to its text, a large amount of attention is devoted to bringing out the "hidden" meanings involved in pure juxtaposition.

We are now back to the question raised in the previous chapter, What does the Bible literally mean? and have to reconsider some points made there in another context. In a sense all possible answers are the same: the Bible, like other books, means literally just what it says. But there are at least two ways of applying this answer. Some verbal structures, we said, are set up as counterparts of external events, like histories, while others, like stories, exist for their own sake and have no such counterpart. The first group consists of, roughly speaking, descriptive or non-literary structures; the second group, of literary or poetic structures. As the Bible seems not to be literature even though it has all the characteristics of literature, its literal meaning has traditionally been regarded as the simply descriptive meaning. The Bible means literally just what it says; and in the traditional way of applying this principle, that means that what it says, in the historical area, for example, is a definitive transcript of actual events.

This view, whatever the obvious difficulties, some of them already dealt with, derives a great deal of strength from the traditional association of the word "truth" with descriptive verbal structures. In the poetic structure as such there is no direct criterion of truth, as Aristotle explained: the writer of poetry or fiction says only "Let this be," and adopts postulates that may be as far away from ordinary experience as those of *Alice in Wonderland*. We do not argue about the postulates: we accept them and ask only what is done with them. So in the world of ordinary clichés the distinction between the poetic and the descriptive, in which only the latter seems interested in truth, has come to be thought of as a moral one, like the choice of Hercules. A cultural prejudice, which influences us even when we are not aware of it, gives to all the words connected with centripetal or literary structure, such as "myth," "fable," or "fiction," the secondary coloring of "not really true" that we have noted. In one of his books on kabbalism, Gershom Scholem says that at times kabbalism seems to lose its sense of direction, and that when it does so it "degenerates into mere literature." I think I understand the context of the remark well enough; but considering how closely the techniques of kabbalism approximate those of literary criticism, the implied rating for literature, however unconscious, still seems a trifle ungracious.

The principle involved here applies to all books, but applies with considerable force to the Bible because the Bible is so deeply rooted in the characteristics of words and of language. The centripetal aspect of a verbal structure is its primary aspect, because the only thing that words can do with any real precision or accuracy is hang together. Accuracy of description in language is not possible beyond a certain point: the most faithfully descriptive account of anything will always turn away from what it describes into its own self-contained grammatical fictions of subject and predicate and object. The events the Bible describes are what some scholars call "language events," brought to us only through words; and it is the words themselves that have the authority, not the events they describe. The Bible means literally just what it says, but it can mean it only without primary reference to a correspondence of what it says to something outside what it says. When Jesus says (John 10:9), "I am the door," the statement means literally just what it says, but there are no doors outside the verse in John to be pointed to. And when the Book of Jonah says that the Lord prepared a great fish to swallow Jonah, there are no great fish outside the Book of Jonah that come into the story. We could almost say that even the existence of God is an inference from the existence of the Bible: in the *beginning* was the Word.

An externalized literalism, which subordinates words to "real" things, is the kind of "natural man's" comprehension that Paul rejected, in the passage from I Corinthians (2:14) already referred to. We may notice, as the point will be important later, that when idolatry is condemned in the Bible, it is often regarded as a "literal" projection into the external world of an image that might be quite acceptable as a poetic metaphor. Thus Jeremiah (2:27) ridicules those who say "To a stock, Thou art my father; and to a stone, Thou hast brought me forth." But Isaiah (51:1) urges his hearers to "look unto the rock whence ye are hewn, and to the hole of the pit whence ye are digged." The epistemological basis, so to speak, of idolatry is precisely that of Faust when he mistranslated "das Wort" as "die That."

Metaphorical meaning as I use the term, like myth, has for me a primary and a derived sense, the primary one being so broad that it is really a tautology. All verbal structures have a centripetal and a centrifugal aspect, and we can call the centripetal aspect their literary aspect. In this sense all verbal structures whatever have a literary aspect, even though normally we do not speak of literature unless a pattern of continuous descriptive reference is absent. The primary and literal meaning of the Bible, then, is its centripetal or poetic meaning. It is only when we are reading as we do when we read poetry that we can take the word "literal" seriously, accepting every word given us without question. This primary meaning, which arises simply from the interconnection of the words, is the metaphorical meaning. There are various secondary meanings, derived from the centrifugal perspective, that may take the form of concepts, predications, propositions, or a sequence of historical or biographical events, and that are always subordinate to the metaphorical meaning. I imagine that keeping this centralizing sense of context in mind is one of the things that Paul means by the analogy of faith (Romans 12:6; the AV renders *analogia* as "proportion"), though I am applying the principle to criticism rather than faith.

With other books we can go on to say: either there is a continuous reference of external meaning, which establishes a context for whatever descriptive truth it may have, or there is no such reference, and we are dealing with a work of literature, where the criterion of truth, if relevant at all, emerges entirely from the inner verbal consistency. In dealing with literature we frequently speak of its self-contained unity as "imaginative," and distinguish as "imaginary" its relation to actual events. The Bible, however, as we saw, evades this antithesis: it is neither literary nor non-literary, or, more positively, it is as literary as it can well be without actually being literature. In the Bible the literal meaning is the poetic meaning, first by tautology, in the context in which all literal meaning is centripetal and poetic; secondly, in a quite specific sense of confronting us with explicitly metaphorical and other forms of distinctively poetic utterance.

And yet we cannot do with the Bible what we can do with Homer or Dante, and stop with the explicitly poetic utterance as the containing category. A kind of *pons asinorum* dilemma appears at this point. Those who realize that my identification of poetic and literal meaning needs more context may feel that in searching for that context they must go back to square one and some connection with descriptive accuracy, however modified, and however often frustrated by the Biblical text itself. Others feel that as soon as we admit that there are factors other than the poetic, belief or commitment takes over. Neither attitude, in my opinion, gets us much farther. With the Bible we are involved in a more complex theory of meaning and truth than we are with other books, and my revision of the word "literal" is a first step only, however essential a first step, in clearing the ground for the next stage in the argument.

The centripetal context for the Bible extends over the whole of the book usually called "Holy Bible," and might well extend far beyond that, except that we have to stop somewhere. Wherever we stop, the unity of the Bible as a whole is an assumption underlying the understanding of any part of it. This unity is not primarily, we repeat, a metonymic consistency of doctrine addressed to our faith: it is a unity of narrative and imagery and what we have called implicit metaphor. We shall give the main outlines of this unified structure in later chapters.

In the preceding chapter we considered words in sequence, where they form narratives and provide the basis for a literary theory of myth. Reading words in sequence, however, is the first of two critical operations. Once a verbal structure is read, and reread often enough to be possessed, it "freezes." It turns into a unity in which all parts exist at once, which we can then examine like a picture, without regard to the specific movement of the narrative. We may compare it to the study of a music score, where we can turn to any part without regard to sequential performance. The term "structure," which we have used so often, is a metaphor from architecture, and may be misleading when we are speaking of narrative, which is not a simultaneous structure but a movement in time. The term "structure" comes into its proper context in the second stage, which is where all discussion of "spatial form" and kindred critical topics take their origin.

The stage of reading sequentially is, strictly speaking, a precritical experience. It is premature to start critical study until all the evidence is in, i.e., until all the words have been read. After the experience has been completed, we can move from experience to knowledge. A great mass of additional detail that we missed in the sequential reading then becomes relevant, because all the images are metaphorically linked with all the other images, not merely with those that follow each other in the narrative. Hence the intricacy of any serious critical study of a complicated text such as a Shakespeare play: a full explication of the network of words employed would be many times longer than the play itself.

I have described the process as a sequential reading followed by the study of the entire text as a simultaneous unit. But clearly this is oversimplified: we should lose our perspective on a Shakespeare play very quickly unless we continually went back to sequential reading, as well as seeing the play on the stage as often as possible. The experience of reading or listening has to be continuously re-created as well. In the study of the Bible it is even more obvious that the two operations have to go on concurrently, because the Bible does not, like Homer, present an unbroken surface of narrative, but is so digressive that it forces us into other perspectives along the way.

At the risk of prolixity, we may summarize the present stage of argument. If we read the Bible sequentially, the Bible becomes a myth, first by tautology, in the sense in which all myths are *mythoi* or narratives, and second in a more specific sense of being a narrative with the specially significant material that we find in all mythologies: stories of creation, of legendary history, lists of laws and rituals with narratives explaining their origin, and so on. If we "freeze" the Bible into a simultaneous unit, it becomes a single, gigantic, complex metaphor, first by tautology, in the sense in which all verbal structures are metaphorical by juxtaposition, and second, in a more specific sense of containing a structure of significantly repeated images. Traditionally, the Bible's narrative has been regarded as "literally" historical and its meaning as "literally" doctrinal or didactic: the present book takes myth and metaphor to be the true literal bases.

Our discussion of myth and history involved us in Aristotle's distinction between the poetic universal narrative and the particular historical one, and we saw that the narrative of the Bible is much closer to being universal and poetic. I have often expressed my regret, as have many other people, that Aristotle did not go on to discuss the other half of this question: the relation between poetic or universal meaning and particular meaning. The latter would consist of predications, which, like the assertions of the historian, would be subject to criteria of truth and falsehood. Hence it would include, for example, metaphysical thinking, which also consists of predications judged by readers as true or false. What would universal or poetic meaning be like? This question would perhaps have formed part of the argument of the unwritten, or unrecorded, second book of the *Poetics*, and it would be interesting to know how Aristotle would have dealt with a question that would have forced him to consider more carefully the nature of mythological thinking, which he dismisses with such contempt in the *Metaphysics* (in a slightly different context, it is true). Partly as a result of there being no Aristotelian directive, the question of primary and secondary meaning has been, in my opinion, turned around.

Philosophers often provide concrete "illustrations" for their thinking: sometimes the illustration takes the form of a diagram, as with the "divided line" of the *Republic*, but is more commonly an image or a story. When we come to such a work as Carlyle's *Sartor Resartus*, we say that it is a literary work using a body-and-clothes image to illustrate the Romantic German philosophy of the Fichtean school. "Body" illustrates the world in itself that we never see, which Fichte derived from Kant's noumenal world of things in themselves, and "clothes" stands for the phenomenal world that simultaneously reveals and conceals the noumenal world. Such a concrete illustration, for all its simplistic crudity, is useful in helping to make difficult abstract thought more accessible to naïve minds—or so at any rate goes the customary cliché, which is a residue from Plato's crusade for dialectic against metaphor.

Suppose we turned this explanation inside out. Suppose we were to say that Carlyle's body-and-clothes metaphor is the poetic and therefore the primary or universal meaning of Fichte's construct, the germ out of which it grew, and that Carlyle has come closer to the genesis of Romantic philosophy than that philosophy itself could ever have come by using predicative language. Suppose we thought of Plato's myths, not as illustrating his dialogues but as the primary meaning of which the dialectic discussions form a commentary. This would lead us to the principle that metaphorical meaning has the same relation to discursive meaning that myth has to history: it is a universal or poetic meaning, and can sustain a number of varying and yet consistent renderings of its discursive meaning, just as a myth can sustain a number of historical *exempla*. Thus:

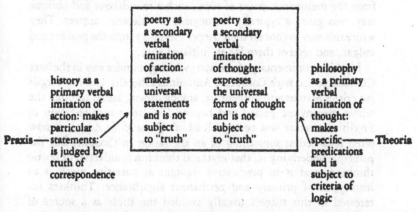

	poetry as a secondary verbal imitation of action: makes universal statements and is not subject to "truth"	poetry as a secondary verbal imitation of thought: expresses the universal forms of thought and is not subject to "truth"	
history as a primary verbal imitation of action: makes particular statements: is judged by truth of correspondence			philosophy as a primary verbal imitation of thought: makes specific predications and is subject to criteria of logic

Praxis ———————————————————————————————— Theoria

A two-dimensional diagram, however, may conceal the principle just given: that all verbal structures whatever, whether historical, poetic, or discursive, have a moving and a static aspect. The Bible, we said, has a historical myth that by-passes conventional historical criteria: it is neither a specific history nor a purely poetic vision, but presents the history of Israel, past and future, in a way that leaves conventional history free to do its own work. Similarly, it has, or rather is, a structure of universalized or poetic meaning that can sustain a number of discursive theological interpretations. When the Catholic Church achieved temporal power, it was able to confine acceptable discursive renderings of the Bible's meaning to a very narrow orbit, but after the Reformation it became obvious that secondary or discursive meanings of the Bible could take on many different but internally consistent forms, by no means all of them theological.

The same principle was applied to Classical mythology, where critics had a great deal more freedom, and where the principle itself therefore emerged much more clearly. All through the metonymic period we have a tradition of commentary on myth informed by the general principle that a story-myth can carry a great number of "interpretations" or "meanings." Every example illustrates any number of precepts, just as any precept can be the moral of a fable. Major Classical poets, notably Homer and Virgil, came to be regarded as inexhaustible treasure-troves of metonymic ideas. Even Francis Bacon wrote a treatise on the "Wisdom of the Ancients," in which most of the standard Classical myths turned out to be prototypes of the principles of Baconian philosophy. The question why poets and similar makers of myths expressed themselves in what was, from the metonymic point of view, such a roundabout and oblique way, was given a typically metonymic or "hieratic" answer. They wrote this way to conceal their deeper meanings from the profane and vulgar, and reserve them for an initiated elite.

Mythical commentary of this sort, which got under way in the later Classical period with Cornutus, Antoninus Liberalis, and the Virgilian critics Servius and Fulgentius, among others, lasted through the whole metonymic period and beyond. Its latest manifestation in English literature was perhaps Ruskin's *Queen of the Air*. It is now often regarded as something of an aberration in thought, but the principle underlying it, that mythical thinking is universal or poetic thinking, and is to predicative thought as narrative myth is to history, is of primary and permanent significance. Thinkers interested in this subject usually avoided the Bible as a source of mythology, to avoid clashing with dogmatic authority, though they drew many parallels between Biblical and Classical myth. In the descriptive period these moral and didactic interpretations of myth were replaced by quasi-anthropological ones, in which, for example, the life of Jesus could be interpreted as anything from a sun myth to a mushroom cult. The same principle, that a myth can sustain an indefinite variety of such interpretations, clearly holds here as well. The likelihood that one of these is the "true" one is weakened by the equal plausibility of several dozen others.

With the descriptive phase, modern science and its mathematical language entered the picture. I have previously explained why I think that the so-called conflict of science and mythology, in which scientific explanations supersede mythological ones, affects only the accidents of mythology and not real mythology, this latter being re-created by the poets. Poets continue to think mythically and metaphorically, and cannot absorb scientific language beyond a very limited point. If one approaches the Bible without irrelevant anxieties, one soon finds that its attitude toward natural knowledge is precisely parallel to its attitude toward history. That is, natural knowledge is regarded as something that man can be left to get for himself. The Bible has no direct reference to science, which would be an anachronism in any case, but it does not block its development either, except for readers who provide their own blocks. We are told in the Book of Enoch that the sun and moon are much the same size but that the sun's light is seven times greater: a statement that would have been a considerable nuisance if the Book of Enoch had become canonical. There seems to be a kind of inherent tactfulness, if we may put it so, in the canonical books that prevents them from making statements of this kind.

Certain cosmological assumptions seem to be present which are no longer with us, such as the assumption in Genesis and elsewhere of a sea of water above the heavens and a freshwater sea below the earth. But these are assumptions that remain metaphorical, on the same plane as the words "sunrise" and "sunset," not enforcing a belief any more than the words "sunrise" and "sunset" enforce or even imply a belief in a geocentric solar system. Job's "he hangeth the earth upon nothing" (26:7) is a bold metaphor, but one that does not get in the way of the future growth of astronomy. The conception of wisdom in the Bible is never associated with any kind of esoteric knowledge. "In secret I have said nothing," was Jesus' remark to Caiaphas (John 18:20): he was speaking primarily of subversive political activity, but the remark may serve as an epitaph for most "secret gospels" of the *Pistis Sophia* type. It is curious but significant that "gnostic" and "agnostic" are both dirty words in the Christian tradition: wisdom is not identified either with knowledge or with the denial of knowledge. It is an existential wisdom with its center in human concern, not in the exploration of nature or other worlds (cf. Job 28:14: "The deep saith, It is not in me"). But in looking at the Bible as a myth we found that the Biblical myth was a form of *Heilsgeschichte* and had its own kind of history. In looking at it as metaphor, or a metaphor complex, we come up against the word "revelation," a word that does imply knowledge of a sort, even though it may not be knowledge of history or nature.

The polytheistic gods, we suggested, are metaphors begotten of man's close association with nature and his sense that nature has a life and energy identifiable with his own. Local deities—the nymphs, fauns, and satyrs of a later mythology—are part of the sense of *natura naturans*, the "paganism" that is the instinctive belief of the *paganus* or peasant who is closest to such a nature and farthest from the centers of social development. Here the gods are mysterious beings whose presence is sensed or who may appear unpredictably in epiphanies. Their background is a nature that is primarily a force of growth or energy (the original sense of the Greek word *physis*). There is nothing here that is confined to paganism, however: the poets continue to insist on the sense of identity with what Dylan Thomas calls "the force that through the green fuse drives the flower" as something we ignore at our peril. Wordsworth speaks of the "huge and mighty forms" that seep from nature into the human soul, and Baudelaire conveys the sense of tantalizing mystery that comes from the same direction:

> La Nature est un temple où de vivants piliers
> Laissent parfois sortir de confuses paroles;
> L'homme y passe à travers des forêts de symboles
> Qui l'observent avec des regards familiers.

But there are also many beautiful and eloquent passages in the Bible, like the one beginning "Consider the lilies" in the Sermon on the Mount (Matthew 6:28), that indicate a profound sensitivity to the power and beauty of *natura naturans*. What the Bible condemns is only what it calls idolatry: the feeling of the numinous, of divine presence, may be experienced in or through nature, but should not be ascribed to nature. That puts man in the grip of an external power, which, as he has projected it from himself, means that he is enslaving himself to it. Nature is a fellow creature of man, and there are no gods in it: the gods that have been found in it are all devils, and for his knowledge of God man has to turn to the human and verbal world first. The opposition, then, is to the myths formed from the perception of *natura naturans*, when they become cults of a deity constructed out of it.

No principle is without many exceptions in mythology, but one very frequent mythical formulation of this attitude to nature is an earth-mother, from whom everything is born and to whom everything returns at death. Such an earth-mother is the most easily understood image of *natura naturans*, and she acquires its moral ambivalence. As the womb of all forms of life, she has a cherishing and nourishing aspect; as the tomb of all forms of life, she has a menacing and sinister aspect; as the manifestation of an unending cycle of life and death, she has an inscrutable and elusive aspect. Hence she is often a *diva triformis*, a goddess of a threefold form of some kind, usually birth, death, and renewal in time; or heaven, earth, and hell in space.

We catch many glimpses of this earth-goddess in the Bible, along with her subordinate, usually male, companion who represents the cycle of life and death itself, as she represents the continuing process underlying it. This companion may be her son, her lover, or a "dying god," a victim either of herself or of some aspect of the "dead" time of year, whether winter or the late summer drought. Venus and Eros (Cupid), Venus and Mars, Venus and Adonis, are the familiar forms of this threefold relationship in Classical mythology. The first and third have their Christian counterparts in the Madonna-Child and *Pietà* pictures; for many reasons, some of them obvious, maternal and bridal figures have to be separated in Christian mythology. In the dying-god cults of surrounding nations, often referred to in the Bible, the death of the male god is mourned by a chorus of women representing the earth-mother, whose productivity is latent during the "dead" times of the year, but who, though a mother, is also, according to Robert Graves, a virgin mother, renewing her virginity every spring and waiting for a new lover, obliterating the memory of the past. Artemis in Greek mythology was both a virgin and a protector of mothers in childbirth; an even clearer manifestation of the identity of the two aspects is the many-breasted "Diana of the Ephesians" who appears in Acts 19.

This mythology is dominated by the conception of cyclical movement, more particularly the cycle of the seasons of the year and of the animal and vegetable life geared to it. The cycle presided over by the earth-mother of *natura naturans* is, in Plato's phrase, the cycle of the different, the life that emerges being always different from the life that gave birth to it. Hence the emphasis on renewal and the obliterating of the past. Eventually, as society becomes more complex, mythology expands toward the conception of *natura naturata*, nature as a structure or system; and the symbolism of cyclical movement shifts to the sky. This is because the sky illustrates rather the cycle of the same, it being clearly the same sun that comes up the next morning, the same moon that returns from the dark. Such a cycle suggests planning and intelligence rather than mysterious power, and as this sense begins to dominate mythology the supreme god comes to be thought of increasingly as a sky-father. He is a father because he is a deity who does not bear or nurse his children, and hence a god who *makes* the world rather than one who brings life into existence by giving it birth.

One would think that the sky-father would probably be later in cultural development than the earth-mother, a mother being more appropriate for a farming economy and a father for the tool-using, patriarchal, city-dwelling life that is usually thought to succeed it. There is no certainty in such matters, and in any case no god is ever new, only a new emphasis may be given to a conception potentially present from the beginning. We are told that a belief in a transcendent sky-god is a very ancient and primitive belief, but when a social system is undeveloped, this deity remains correspondingly unfunctional: he is commonly a *dieu fainéant* who leaves the effective control of the world to subordinates. Hesiod, in any case, established for Greek mythology the conception of an earth-mother far older than Zeus the sky-father, a late usurper and third in a line of sky-gods, succeeding Cronos and Ouranos. By Stoic times the sky-father who begets has prevailed over the earth-mother who brings to birth, and the great hymns to Zeus by the Stoic poets Cleanthes and Aratus of Soli speak of mankind as being Zeus's offspring—a phrase of Aratus to this effect is quoted approvingly by Paul in Acts 17:28.

This is part of a social development in which subordinate gods move from local deities of woods and rivers and fields into an analogy of a human aristocracy like the Olympian gods of Greece. The Olympians treat humanity as aristocrats do their inferiors, with a kind of rough justice, especially vigilant to put down anything that threatens their privileges. Their habitation on the top of a mountain is symbolically "over" mankind. In a still further stage they move up from the earth altogether into the stars, and by late Classical times most of the effective gods had become star-gods. The earth-mother also tends to take on the characteristics of a sky-goddess: we can see something of this development even in the Bible. In the period of the judges a fertility goddess was worshiped in Israel, usually called Asherah, because she was a tree-goddess, and *asherah* or wooden poles were her emblem (Judges 6:25 and elsewhere). By Jeremiah's time (Jeremiah 44:15ff.) she was a Queen of Heaven. When Jeremiah reproached the women of Jerusalem for returning to her cult, they told him calmly that they had had no luck since they deserted her, and they had nothing to lose by renewing their fidelity—a line of argument not greatly different from Jeremiah's own. Similarly, Isis in Egypt moved her center of gravity from the lower to the upper cycle, although there had always been sky-goddesses in Egypt. In Christianity the Virgin Mary took on some of the attributes of a Queen of Heaven, with her blue robe and her star (*stella maris*) emblem, which had also been attached to Isis. Some developments in Judaism assigned something parallel to a female Schekinah or divine presence. Neither was ever regarded as in any sense a supreme God, who remained thought of as symbolically male in all Biblical religions.

In this development from *natura naturans* to *natura naturata* there is a curious analogy to the shift in the critical process we have traced from participating in a narrative movement in time to studying a structure that is spread out before us in space. If we "freeze" a myth, we said, we get a single metaphor-complex; if we "freeze" an entire mythology, we get a cosmology. Paganism, thus frozen, seems to be dominated by the vision of cyclical recurrence. Nature suggests no beginning or end in itself, because we see it within the mental categories of time and space, and beginnings and ends in time and space are not really thinkable, easy as it may be to talk about them. We do perceive, however, a repeating pattern in nature, and we can expand this to visions of the most colossal cycles, like the days and nights of Brahma in Hinduism and the successive cycles ended by fire (*ekpyrosis*) in Stoicism. The universe may have started off with a big bang billions of years ago, but the question of what happened before that goes on nagging.

The Biblical myth, in contrast, stresses a total beginning and end of time and space. The Creation was an absolute beginning, and to ask what God was doing before the Creation is a question in bad taste—at least, Augustine quotes someone, doubtless himself, as saying in answer to it that God was probably preparing a hell for those who ask such questions. But to be told that we should not ask a question merely increases its urgency, in any healthy mind. The nearest we can get to an answer, perhaps, is to say that we experience time in such a way that we cannot imagine a beginning to it, and the reason for postulating an absolute beginning in the Bible is to make it clear that time does not represent an ultimate reality. Similarly, the Old Testament prophesies an end, not precisely to time, but to history as we have known it, a "day of Yahweh" ("Jehovah" in the usual anglicization, "the Lord" in AV), which is thought of as a day of appalling disaster for the heathen and the Israelite unfaithful. A magnificent prophecy of this Day of the Lord in Zephaniah 1:14-16 is the ultimate source for the medieval "Dies Irae" hymn incorporated into the Requiem Mass. In the New Testament this "Day of the Lord" is thought of as more specifically a *kairos*, a time that has an end. The AV rendering of Revelation 10:6, "that there should be time no longer," is not quite accurate, but the general principle holds for that prophecy.

This conception of two levels, a level of time and space and a level of "eternity" above it, turns on the meaning of "resurrection" in the New Testament as a vertical ascent from a world of death to a world of life. Resurrection is thus not renewal or rebirth or revival or restoration: all these words mean a new cycle of time, and are in the last analysis the opposite of resurrection. There is no doctrine of resurrection in the Old Testament (except perhaps in Daniel 12:2), but all the images of restoration, such as Ezekiel's vision of the valley of dry bones in which the bones take on flesh (37), were identified with resurrection by Christian readers. Similarly, Jesus' teaching recurs often to the fact that human life, whether cyclical in shape or not, is a confused and inseparable mixture of joy and suffering, good and evil, life and death, and that the eternal realities of this life are its two poles, worlds of life and death which are outside time. The Bible, we said, is traditionally called a revelation, and the "spiritual" kingdom of God of Jesus' teaching is primarily, from the Christian point of view, what it has to reveal.

This kingdom of God is an idealized world, metaphorically identical, as we shall see in more detail later, with the "spiritual" garden of Eden and the Promised Land, including the future Promised Land of the restored Israel and the New Testament apocalypse. Its imagery is drawn from two main sources. One source is the top half, so to speak, of the natural cycle: the area of youth and spring and all the vigor and energy of life. Traditionally, the earthly paradise is a *ver perpetuum*: a world where, as Milton says, spring and autumn danced hand in hand, where there are flowers and fruits but no winter, where the human inhabitants are in the prime of life, with no aging or senility.

The other source is that of creative or productive human work. A good deal of human activity is wasted or perverted energy, making war, feeding a parasitic class, building monuments to paranoid conquerors, and the like. The genuine work which is founded on the human need for food and shelter moves in the direction of transforming nature into a world with a human shape, meaning, and function. The animal world is transformed into a pastoral environment of flocks and herds; the vegetable world, into a cultivated land of harvests and vintages and gardens; the mineral world, into cities and buildings and highways. There is a creative element in such work, because the mere need for food and shelter, in itself, would not have got far beyond gathering roots and hiding in caves. The world of work is also an expression of desire as well as of need: what man really wants is what the positive and productive work he does shows that he wants.

In literature there are two great organizing patterns. One is the natural cycle itself; the other, a final separation between an idealized and happy world and a horrifying or miserable one. Comedy moves in the general direction of the former, and traditionally closes in some such formula as "They lived happily ever after." Tragedy moves in the opposite direction, and toward the complementary formula "Count no man happy until he is dead." The moral effect of literature is normally bound up with its assumption that we prefer to identify ourselves with the happy world and detach ourselves from the wretched one. The record of history, in itself, does not indicate this: it indicates that man is quite as enthusiastic about living in hell as in heaven. To see misery as tragic, as a destroyed and perverted form of greatness and splendor, is a primary achievement of Greek literature. The Bible's vision of misery is ironic rather than tragic, but the same dialectical separation of the two worlds is quite as strongly marked.

In ordinary experience our ultimate categories are those of time and space, and these categories are in themselves unending, as we have just seen. Hence, as long as we associate the eternal with endless time, and the infinite with endless space, we have done nothing to get beyond our ordinary categories of thought and perception. We sometimes try to arrive at the conception of "eternity" by simply subtracting the essence of time, which is movement and change, from time. This is what gives us all the metaphors about God or ultimate reality as unchanging Being, in contrast to the world of Becoming that we inhabit. In this construct the eternal is described as a state of continuous peace, rest, and repose. One can understand the appeal of such metaphors after seventy years or so of human behavior, but after all they are metaphors drawn from death, and seem hardly definitive for a conception of something genuinely beyond life.

When "eternal" is taken to mean "endless time," then, we are still simply talking about time, from which the conception of endlessness cannot be detached. This has had its sinister as well as its misleading aspect in historical Christianity. The phrase "You can't take it with you" is proverbial for "life after death," but in this very phrase the word "after" implies that our ordinary experience of time is in fact taken with us. For Jesus, heaven and hell, the extremes of bliss and of pain, were the two permanent realities of existence. The AV renders his term *aionios* as "everlasting," an eloquent testimony to the limitations of language. Hell thus became for later Christianity a hopelessly mixed metaphor meaning (*a*) the human life created by human evil; (*b*) the world of eternal death which is the abyss or deep of nothingness; (c) a world of externally applied torture going on endlessly in time. This last aspect proved to be a very powerful political lever: as a friend of mine once remarked, good news will not sell in a mass market until it is perverted into bad news.

The author of the early Apocalypse of Peter, after contemplating the torments of the damned as something, in La Rochefoucauld's phrase, not wholly disagreeable, is given a broad hint that these torments may not after all be endless, but that he must on no account say so, or he will encourage people to sin. By such devices the nightmare of a hell in unending time after death entered the foreground of Christian teaching. The only thing to be said for this foul doctrine is that it made sin creative: that is, humanity owes infinitely more to the sinners who went on sinning in spite of it than it does to the preachers who tried to restrain sin by threatening it.

In man's transformation of nature into a humanized pastoral, cultivated, civilized world there is, of course, a good deal of exploitation, waste, and wanton destruction. Perhaps our religious traditions have encouraged us to regard nature as a limitless field of exploitation; certainly the growing sense of alienation from nature that accompanied the rise of modern science did. From Copernicus onward, man seemed increasingly to have only an accidental relation to the spatial world of the stars, where conscious life has not so far been found, and to the temporal world of evolution, in which man is a late and perhaps an intrusive development. As the sheer size of scientific time and space expanded so hugely, the traditional view of creation began to look paranoid, a complacent and unwarranted illusion on man's part that everything had been created for him.

Before modern times, there had been a sense of correspondence or affinity between man and nature, of which the most imaginative expression was perhaps the doctrine of the microcosm, the assumption that man contains an epitome of the whole of reality, being half spirit and half physical substance. This conception of correspondence was closely associated with magic, because it provided a basis for divination, for examining natural phenomena in terms of a supposed connection with the patterns of human destiny. The most important form of such divination is astrology, and astrology is based on a conception of coincidence, which is, as Jung says, a synchronic and acausal conception. Even astrologers now could hardly accept astrology on the old causal basis of "influence," assuming that some physical substance emanates from constellations billions of miles away. The assumption is rather that the world is set up in such a way that there is a pattern of coincidence between configurations of stars and human lives that can be systematically studied.

I do not find any consistent astrological symbolism in the Bible, but there are many allusions to divination in it, many of them practiced in Israel, such as the mysterious "Urim and Thummim" on the high priest's costume in Exodus 28:30 and elsewhere. This is a highly technical subject beyond our scope. There are also such patterns of correspondence as the emphasis on sevens and twelves in the Book of Revelation. Perhaps they are so prominent there because by the time this book was written, seven was the number of days in the week and of the planets, and twelve the number of months in the year and of the signs of the Zodiac. Hence these numbers would suggest, more than others, a world where time and space have become the same thing. But correspondence does not seem to be the central thing that the Bible is saying about the relation between man and nature.

We get instead a strong feeling that there are assumed to be two levels in that relation. The lower level is outlined in God's contract with Noah, after the deluge had receded:

And the fear of you and the dread of you shall be upon every beast of the earth, and upon every fowl of the air, upon all that moveth upon the earth, and upon all the fishes of the sea; into your hand are they delivered.

Every moving thing that liveth shall be meat for you; even as the green herb have I given you all things. (Genesis 9:2-3)

We notice, first, that no restrictions are placed on what man is to eat, in striking contrast to the elaborate dietary laws later imposed on Israel alone. It was to this general contract with Noah that Christianity decided to return, after rejecting the Jewish law as no longer binding on Christians (Acts 10:15). Second, man's attitude to nature is assumed to be one of domineering exploitation, a reign of terror over all "inferior" creatures, and illustrating Schopenhauer's remark that the animals live in a hell of which mankind are the devils.

The upper level of man's relation with nature is the one assigned to Adam and Eve in the garden of Eden, where man lived only on the fruits of trees and in which all animals were domestic pets to be given names (Genesis 2:16, 20). This world has disappeared, and with the "fall" of Adam and Eve man descended into the indifferent and alien nature that we see around us now, where he was forced to work. But there is an element in work, we saw, that is an image of the world man has lost and has still to regain. He will never really gain it until he knows thoroughly what hell is, and realizes that the pleasure gained by dominating and exploiting, whether of his fellow man or of nature itself, is a part of that hell-world. Once we separate ourselves completely from that world, the natural order takes on a very different appearance:

The wolf also shall dwell with the lamb, and the leopard shall lie down with the kid; and the calf and the young lion and the fatling together; and a little child shall lead them. . . .
They shall not hurt nor destroy in all my holy mountain: for the earth shall be full of the knowledge of the Lord as the waters cover the sea. (Isaiah 11:6, 9)

The question we have tried to lead up to in this chapter is: What does the Bible look like when we try to see it statically, as a single and simultaneous metaphor cluster? We are perhaps not too surprised to discover that there is a factor in it that will not fit a static vision. Ordinarily, if we "freeze" an entire mythology, it turns into a cosmology, and of course there were Christian and Jewish cosmologies as well as non-Biblical ones. But what the Bible gives us is not so much a cosmology as a vision of upward metamorphosis, of the alienated relation of man to nature transformed into a spontaneous and effortless life—not effortless in the sense of being lazy or passive, but in the sense of being energy without alienation:

And in that day will I make a covenant for them with the beasts of the field, and with the fowls of heaven, and with the creeping things of the ground: and I will break the bow and the sword and the battle out of the earth, and will make them to lie down safely. (Hosea 2:18)

The ultimate secrets of nature will not be revealed until man has stopped the self-destructive activity that prevents him from seeing what kind of world he is really in. The real world is beyond time, but can be reached only by a process that goes on in time. As Eliot says, only through time time is conquered. We shall try to deal with this factor of creative time in the next chapter, but here we may simply set out the general conclusion that our examination of Biblical metaphor leads us to, though it will take a good deal more documentation to make it fully intelligible.

The Christian Bible is a written book that points to a speaking presence in history, the presence identified as the Christ in the New Testament. The phrase "word of God" applies both to the Bible and to that presence. As long as we accept the referential meaning of the Bible as the primary one, and read the words only for their revelation of something beyond themselves, applying the same phrase to such different things is only a dubious syllepsis. But we saw that the Bible deliberately subordinates its referential or centrifugal meaning to its primary, syntactical, centripetal meaning. It is our only real contact with the so-called "Jesus of history," and from this point of view it makes good sense to call the Bible and the person of Christ by the same name. It makes even better sense to identify them metaphorically. This is a conception of identity that goes far beyond "juxtaposition," because there are no longer two things, but one thing in two aspects. The remainder of this book is devoted largely to what is implicit in that identification.

CHAPTER FOUR

TYPOLOGY I

Let us turn back to a remark made above, that there is no real evidence for the life of Jesus outside the New Testament, and that even there the Evangelists did not bother to collect the kind of material that we should call historical or biographical evidence. Primitive Christians wanting evidence were told to read the "Scriptures," meaning the Old Testament. The "Scriptures" did not then exist in so fixed a form, and one or two allusions in the New Testament that seem to be to the Old Testament cannot now be traced, but the general procedure is unaffected by this. The New Testament insists a great deal on what it calls faith and truth, but its guarantees for such things seem very strange, even when we have understood something of the principle involved. How do we know that the Gospel story is true? Because it confirms the prophecies of the Old Testament. But how do we know that the Old Testament prophecies are true? Because they are confirmed by the Gospel story. Evidence, so called, is bounced back and forth between the testaments like a tennis ball; and no other evidence is given us. The two testaments form a double mirror, each reflecting the other but neither the world outside.

The New Testament writers, then, regard the Old Testament as a source of anticipations of the events in the life of Christ. These are often explicitly alluded to, and the source given. Thus, in the Crucifixion, the piercing of Jesus' hands and feet, the mockery of the passers-by, and the fact that his legs were not broken on the cross, are related to passages in Psalm 22. Jesus' great cry on the cross, "My God, why hast thou forsaken me?" is a quotation of the first verse of this psalm. Sometimes the relationship is implicit only. The thirty pieces of silver and the potter's field of the Judas story are found in Zechariah 11:12-13; a resurrection on the third day is mentioned in Hosea 6:2; the suffering servant of Isaiah 53 is close behind the account of the Passion; and the "Emmanuel" prophecy earlier in Isaiah (7:14) is related to the Incarnation. Even in more doctrinal passages Christian conceptions are presented not as new doctrines but as realizations of Old Testament conceptions. Thus Paul's central axiom, "The just shall live by faith" (Romans 1:17) is a quotation from Habbakuk 2:4.

There is a very large number of these references to the Old Testament in the New: they extend over every book—not impossibly every passage—in the New Testament; and some New Testament books, notably Revelation and the Epistle to the Hebrews, are a dense mass of such allusions, often with direct or oblique quotations. The details of this relationship will constitute a good deal of the next chapters, as well as the next volume, of this work. The New Testament, in short, claims to be, among other things, the key to the Old Testament, the explanation of what the Old Testament really means. Jesus' disciples could not understand even the Resurrection until Jesus had explained its relation to Old Testament prophecy (Luke 24:44).

The general principle of interpretation is traditionally given as "In the Old Testament the New Testament is concealed; in the New Testament the Old Testament is revealed." Everything that happens in the Old Testament is a "type" or adumbration of something that happens in the New Testament, and the whole subject is therefore called typology, though it is typology in a special sense. Paul speaks in Romans 5:14 of Adam as a *typos* of Christ; the Vulgate renders *typos* here as "forma," but the AV's "figure" reflects the fact that "figura" had come to be the standard Latin equivalent of *typos*. What happens in the New Testament constitutes an "antitype," a realized form, of something foreshadowed in the Old Testament. In I Peter 3:21 Christian baptism is called the *antitypos* of the saving of mankind from the flood of Noah, and here again the AV has "figure."

This typological way of reading the Bible is indicated too often and explicitly in the New Testament itself for us to be in any doubt that this is the "right" way of reading it—"right" in the only sense that criticism can recognize, as the way that conforms to the intentionality of the book itself and to the conventions it assumes and requires. The typological organization of the Bible does present the difficulty, to a secular literary critic, of being unique: no other book in the world, to my knowledge, has a structure even remotely like that of the Christian Bible. To find analogues we have to go to larger structures than the individual book. There are aspects of Plato's work, for example, that remind us of a gigantic effort to compose a one-man Bible. The Old Testament Torah is thought to be derived from traditional documents by editors working under the influence of the teachings of the earliest prophets. Similarly, Socrates in the *Republic* constructs an ideal state out of his prophetic dialectic, and one of his hearers remarks on the similarity between this state and ancient legends of Atlantis. Hence we proceed to the creation and deluge myths in the *Timaeus* and *Critias*, after which Plato gets involved with the *Laws*, just as the Torah gets involved with its six hundred-odd regulations. In most of the dialogues, again, Socrates is the central figure, and his eventual martyrdom, corresponding to the Passion in the Gospels, is the ultimate focus of much of the argument. Even so, Plato is not typological in the way that the Bible is.

In our day, Marxism might be said to have something like a typological scripture in its canonical texts, where the nineteenth-century prophecies of Marx and Engels are fulfilled in Lenin's tactical organization of the Bolshevist revolution. We shall see in a moment why such a movement as Marxism might be expected to have an affinity for typology. Naturally, being the indicated and obvious way of reading the Bible, and scholars being what they are, typology is a neglected subject, even in theology, and it is neglected elsewhere because it is assumed to be bound up with a doctrinaire adherence to Christianity. I am concerned here with typology as a mode of thought and as a figure of speech. I say "and," because a mode of thought does not exist until it has developed its own particular way of arranging words. Typology is a form of rhetoric, and can be studied critically like any other form of rhetoric.

The three phases of language that we discussed in the first chapter, the metaphorical, the metonymic, and the descriptive (there seems to be no better adjective for simile), are all based on two units assumed to exist simultaneously. Typology is a figure of speech that moves in time: the type exists in the past and the antitype in the present, or the type exists in the present and the antitype in the future. What typology really is as a mode of thought, what it both assumes and leads to, is a theory of history, or more accurately of historical process: an assumption that there is some meaning and point to history, and that sooner or later some event or events will occur which will indicate what that meaning or point is, and so become an antitype of what has happened previously. Our modern confidence in historical process, our belief that despite apparent confusion, even chaos, in human events, nevertheless those events are going somewhere and indicating something, is probably a legacy of Biblical typology: at least I can think of no other source for its tradition.

There is another form of rhetoric, or way of arranging words, which also moves in time, and that is causality. Causality has played a major role in both second- and third-phase writing: Hume's discussion of it marks its assimilation to the third phase, where its basis comes to be an inductive collection of instances. Over a century later, Whitehead inquired, in *Science and the Modern World*, why philosophers were still as committed to causality as though Hume had never pointed out the limitations of the idea. The literary critic's answer, at least, would be that they are writing in continuous prose, and continuous prose is a way of arranging words so bound up with causality that we can hardly have one without the other. Almost any simple prose statement ("The man opened the door") will show the link between the subject-predicate-object arrangement of prose and what we think of as a movement from cause to effect.

In the process of thought that precedes causal writing, the temporal order of typology is normally reversed. The causal thinker is confronted with a mass of phenomena that he can understand only by thinking of them as effects, after which he searches for their prior causes. These causes are the antitypes of their effects, that is, revelations of the real meaning of the existence of the effects. The backward movement reminds us of, and is not impossibly connected with, Plato's view of knowledge as *anamnesis* or recollection, the recognizing of the new as something identifiable with the old. An exposition founded on causality, however, is likely for the sake of greater clarity to reverse this movement again, and proceed forward from cause to effect. Hence causality and typology are rhetorically similar in form, and typology might in fact be thought of as an analogy of causality, a development of Aristotle's formal and final causes. A retrospective procedure is often followed in typology also. Even the most traditional Christianity does not need to claim that Isaiah or the Psalmist knew, on any level of consciousness, that they were prophesying the coming of Jesus. The types are frequently established, or at least interpreted as such, only after the antitypes have appeared.

Causality, however, is based on reason, observation, and knowledge, and therefore relates fundamentally to the past, on the principle that the past is all that we genuinely or systematically know. Typology relates to the future, and is consequently related primarily to faith, hope, and vision. When we want what the funeral service calls the comfort of a reasonable religion, we may deliberately attach a typological belief to some causal process, and say that the latter provides evidence for the former. We shall come to examples of this in a moment. Such an assimilation, however, is really justified only when the future phenomena are genuinely predictable, i.e., when they are mechanical or behave mechanically, as with the astronomical prediction of an eclipse or statistical predictions of general trends.

Kierkegaard's very brief but extraordinarily suggestive book *Repetition* is the only study I know of the psychological contrast between a past-directed causality and a future-directed typology. The mere attempt to repeat a past experience will lead only to disillusionment, but there is another kind of repetition which is the Christian antithesis (or complement) of Platonic recollection, and which finds its focus in the Biblical promise: "Behold, I make all things new" (Revelation 21:5). Kierkegaard's "repetition" is certainly derived from, and to my mind is identifiable with, the forward-moving typological thinking of the Bible. Perhaps his book is so brief because he lived too early to grasp the full significance of his own argument, as typological rhetoric was then only beginning to take on many of its new and remarkable modern developments.

Another distinction between causality and typology is of great importance. Causal thinking tends not to move out of the same dimension of time: especially in third-phase causality, the causes have to be in the same temporal plane as their effects, or they are not genuine causes. Ascribing a disease to the will of God or to the malice of a witch is not causal thinking. Typology points to future events that are often thought of as transcending time, so that they contain a vertical lift as well as a horizontal move forward. The metaphorical kernel of this is the experience of waking up from a dream, as when Joyce's Stephen Dedalus speaks of history as a nightmare from which he is trying to awake. When we wake up from sleep, one world is simply abolished and replaced by another. This suggests a clue to the origin of typology: it is essentially a revolutionary form of thought and rhetoric. We have revolutionary thought whenever the feeling "life is a dream" becomes geared to an impulse to awaken from it.

The most important single historical fact about the Old Testament is that the people who produced it were never lucky at the game of empire. Temporal power was in heathen hands; consequently history became reshaped into a future-directed history, in which the overthrow of the heathen empires and the eventual recognition of Israel's unique historical importance are the main events, though events that are still to come. Typology in the Bible is by no means confined to the Christian version of the Bible: from the point of view of Judaism at least, the Old Testament is much more genuinely typological without the New Testament than with it. There are, in the first place, events in the Old Testament that are types of later events recorded also within the Old Testament. Thus Aaron's making of a "golden calf" at the time of the Exodus (Exodus 32:4) is a type of the later schismatic cult set up in the kingdom of Northern Israel (I Kings 12:28), which also featured golden calves. For Judaism the chief antitypes of Old Testament prophecy are, as in Christianity, the coming of the Messiah and the restoration of Israel, though of course the two contexts differ.

Judaism has also the great advantage, for a typological outlook, of keeping its crucial antitypes in the future. In Christianity the transcending of history by the Resurrection did not bring about an end of time in ordinary experience, and so a belief in a future "second coming" grew up *pari passu* with the belief that the crucial victory over death had already been achieved. The expectation of what appears to be an imminent end of the world runs through all the New Testament itself, and though Christianity as a social institution survived it, it still has a strong appeal for what I have called the populist elements in Christianity. There are considerations here that we shall return to later.

To use two familiar terms in a new context: the typological structure and shape of the Bible make its mythology diachronic, in contrast to the synchronic mythology characteristic of most of the religions outside it. This is the basis for the commonplace that Biblical religions have a distinctive sense of history, to which we may add personality, as it is only within a historical context that personality can emerge. Jesus and Adonis are both "dying gods," in the sense of being objects of cults with similar imagery and ritual attached to them; but Jesus is a person and Adonis is not, however many sacrificial victims may have represented him. Some of the stories about Hercules or Theseus or Perseus may have been originally attached to human figures, as were, much earlier, the stories about Gilgamesh. But they tend to lose the sense of historical personality when they become assimilated to a synchronic mythology.

Causality develops with second-phase, or metonymic, writing: its first-phase, or metaphorical, counterpart is the tendency on the part of many societies to see their myths as archetypal events in a distant past (Mircea Eliade's *in illo tempore*), of which events in ordinary life, more particularly ritual events, are repetitions. What we are calling typology is a specialized form of the repeatability of myth, discussed earlier: it carries on the primitive perspective but reverses its significance. In some primitive societies, when boys go through the initiation rites that turn them into men, they are taught the essential myths and laws of their society as part of that initiation. This kind of traditional teaching is an embryo of what Judaism means by Torah—the sacred instruction in the first five books of the Old Testament which includes the law and which is often translated "law," although the Torah includes a great deal that is not law. Judaism still finds the Bible's center of gravity in the Torah: the Talmud, which in some respects is the Jewish counterpart of the New Testament, takes mainly the form of a commentary on the Torah. For Christianity the Old Testament was primarily a book of prophecy, foretelling the future event of the Incarnation and thereby pointing to the transcendence of the law.

A warning that the law, even if transcended, was not to be regarded as destroyed or annihilated by the gospel appears in Matthew 5:18, where it was perhaps inserted to guard against the Gnostic tendency to think of Christianity as totally discontinuous with Judaism, even to think of the Old Testament God as an evil being. The Old Testament ceremonial and dietary laws were, however, considered no longer binding on Christians, and that meant that they had to be thought of as allegories of the spiritual truths of the gospel. Paul himself uses the word "allegory" (Galatians 4:24) in speaking of the story of Abraham's two wives; and the extent to which the allegorizing of the ceremonial law can go in Christianity may be illustrated by a passage in *The Pilgrim's Progress*:

Faithful. This brings to my mind that of Moses, by which he describeth the beast that is clean. He is such a one that parteth the hoof and cheweth the cud; not that parteth the hoof only, or that cheweth the cud only. The hare cheweth the cud, but yet is unclean, because he parteth not the hoof. And this truly resembleth Talkative; he cheweth the cud, he seeketh knowledge, he cheweth upon the word; but he divideth not the hoof, he parteth not with the way of sinners; but as the hare, he retaineth the foot of a dog or bear, and therefore he is unclean.

Christian. You have spoken, for aught I know, the true gospel sense of those texts.

Typology is not allegory: allegory is normally a story-myth that finds its "true" meaning in a conceptual or argumentative translation, and both testaments of the Bible, however oblique their approach to history, deal with real people and real events. But the above allegorizing of the law indicates something of the difficulty that the continuation of history posed for Christianity. As century after century passed without a second coming, the Church developed a progressive and forward-moving structure of doctrine, one that carries the typology of the Bible on in history and adapts it to what we have called second-phase, or metonymic, language. This structure of doctrine became increasingly the compulsory means of understanding the Bible; and so, as Cardinal Newman remarked in the nineteenth century, the function of the Bible, for the Church, came to be not to teach doctrine but to prove or illustrate it. What this means in practice, whatever may be true of theory, is that the doctrines of Christian theology form the antitypes of which the stories and maxims in the Bible, including those of the New Testament, are types.

The full thrust of New Testament typology goes in two directions: into the future and into the eternal world, the two things coinciding with the apocalypse or Last Judgment. The one thing that would naturally be resisted by a socially established Church by every means in its power would be the suggestion of a transcending of its authority within history. Such teachings as those of Joachim of Floris about a third historical age of the Spirit, which would succeed the Jewish age of the Father and the Christian ecclesiastical age of the Son, consequently were regarded as heretical. In the sixteenth century the conception of a transcending of the Church within history came into focus as the Protestant Reformation. By "Reformation" the Protestants meant, not simply the reforming of abuses within the Church, to which no one objected in principle, but the setting up of the Bible as a model of belief and action to which the Church would be required to conform. Thus the Church's role was to enter into a dialogue with the Word of God and not to replace it as the source of revelation. Milton, who, being a poet, understood that changes in metaphor were far more important than changes in doctrine, remarked that this involved thinking of the Church not as a "mother" but as a young bride about to be instructed in her duties. The analogy between this conception of reformation and the growth of a descriptive approach to language is clear enough. The ramifications of this issue do not concern us at present, but the Protestant Reformation was an intensifying of the original revolutionary impulse in Biblical religion, and a renewed emphasis on the typological importance of the Old Testament was one of the results. With the great capitalist revolutions of the eighteenth century, typological thinking entered the secular arena.

For believers in progress in the democracies, contemporary events are proceeding toward their own antitypes in the future, toward a state of human existence that will make what is now happening intelligible as a series of signposts pointing in that direction. For Marxist and other revolutionaries, a worldwide revolution is the central future event that will constitute the antitype of history as a whole. Both of these are essentially forms of religious belief, but, in the nineteenth century, the biological conception of evolution was often assumed to have provided a scientific and causal basis for them. Typology is a one-directional and irreversible conception of history, and evolution was assumed to endorse such a conception because evolution was looked at from our own point of view, as a one-way development with its climax in us, and as capable of further development only through us. Hence evolution became assimilated, by analogy, to the conceptions of history, progressive, Christian, Marxist, democratic, which looked forward to an end to history as we have known it. The old tension between typological and cyclical views of time recurs in Nietzsche, who developed a conception of a "Superman" surpassing the "all too human" level of existence that we know—another of the diachronic conceptions suggested by evolution. But because of his preference for the synchronic deity Dionysus, Nietzsche was compelled to incorporate his Superman into a cyclical framework of identical recurrence, a framework that I should think would effectively destroy the dynamic of the conception for most of his readers.

There is another aspect of typology to be considered. The Old Testament is concerned with the society of Israel; the New Testament with the individual Jesus. The society Israel, then, is the type of which the individual Jesus is the antitype. This relation of society to individual corresponds to certain elements of ordinary life: we belong to something before we are anything, and we have entered a specific social contract before birth. I was predestined to be, for example, a middle-class mid-twentieth-century male white English-speaking Canadian in the instant of conception. But as the individual develops within his society, all the essential aspects of thought and imagination and experience take place in him. Social freedom, however essential, is general and approximate; real freedom is something that only the individual can experience. The individual grows out of society like a plant out of its soil; but he does not break away from it. The progress of his education includes increasing awareness of his social conditioning and context, and hence a reabsorbing of his society into an individual form, though it may include an absorption of many other influences originating elsewhere.

We spoke of the simple metaphor, of the "Joseph is a fruitful bough" type, as an identifying of *A with B*, and said that such a metaphor is anti-logical. In logic *A* can only be *A*, never *B*, and to assert that *A* "is" *B* overlooks all the real differences between them. But there is another form of identification that we do not think of as metaphorical but as the basis of all ordered categorical thinking. There is identification *as* as well as identification *with*. We identify *A* as *A* when we make it an individual of the class to which it belongs: that brown and green object outside my window I identify *as* a tree. When we combine these two forms of identification, and identify an individual *with* its class, we get an extremely powerful and subtle form of metaphor, which I sometimes call the royal metaphor, because it underlies one of the most symbolically pervasive of institutions, that of kingship.

The function of the king is primarily to represent, for his subjects, the unity of their society in an individual form. Even yet Elizabeth II can draw crowds wherever she appears, not because there is anything remarkable about her appearance, but because she dramatizes the metaphor of society as a single "body." Other societies have other figures, but there seems to be a special symbolic eloquence, even a pathos, about the *de jure* monarch, whose position has been acquired by the pure accident of birth, and who has no executive power. At the same time most societies have done away with monarchical figures; "charismatic" leaders, dictators, and the like, are almost invariably sinister and regressive; the mystique of royalty that Shakespeare's plays take for granted means little to us now; and theologians talking about the "sovereignty" of God risk alienating their readers by trying to assimilate the religious life to the metaphors of a barbaric and outmoded form of social organization. It is natural that our news media should employ the royal metaphor so incessantly in telling us about what France or Japan or Mexico "is" doing, as though they were individual beings. But the same figure was used in my younger days, to my own great annoyance, to boost the prestige of dictators: "Hitler is building roads across Germany," "Mussolini is draining the marshes in Italy," and the like. Those who employed this figure were often democratic people who simply could not stop themselves from using the royal metaphor. It seems as though the "sovereign" may be either the most attractive of icons or the most dangerous of idols.

Herman Melville recorded in his journal, after a visit to the pyramids:

I shudder at idea of ancient Egyptians. It was in these pyramids that was conceived the idea of Jehovah. Terrible mixture of the cunning and awful.

The kernel of truth in this statement may be that the Israelites also found something in pyramid-building to shudder at, even though the pyramids are not directly mentioned in the Bible. It is quite possible that some of the characteristics of Hebrew religion derive partly from a reaction against Egyptian religion: some kind of cultural trauma seems to be concealed behind the Exodus story. Ancient Egypt went further than any other society on record in the direction of making what we have called the royal metaphor a social force. The Pharaoh was not only the shepherd of his people, high priest as well as king, but also an incarnate god, identified with Horus in his life and with Osiris after his death. All the symbolism of an immortal afterlife bound up with the mummifying of bodies and the like was originally attached only to him. The amount of labor and wealth expended in burying a Pharaoh and constructing his tomb would be incredible to us without direct evidence; but perhaps the ordinary Egyptian found an identity within the mystical body of Pharaoh of a type that our mental processes can no longer recapture.

The Semitic peoples of Western Asia did not go to such lengths in deifying their rulers, and Mesopotamian kings were thought of rather, in the imagery of the second Psalm, as "begotten" (adopted or chosen) sons of the national god. Israel itself embarked on monarchy with great misgivings and trepidation, and its historians are frank about the human shortcomings of all their kings, including David and Solomon. It is clear both from the accounts in Kings and from many of the Psalms that the king of Israel originally had many priestly functions as well, but on the whole a distinction between spiritual and temporal power is clearly marked in the Old Testament; and the episode of Uriah's wife, in which David's behavior was denounced by the prophet Nathan, indicates that the prophet too was assumed to have an independent authority. On the other hand, the *de jure* aspect of David's authority was rigidly adhered to: it was evidently wrong for northern Israel to break with the line of David, despite the folly of the southern king Rehoboam, who represented that line; and the assumption that the future king who would restore the power of Israel would be lineally descended from David remains constant throughout the rest of the Bible.

The central figure of the New Testament is called "Messiah," a word which means "anointed one" and of which the Greek equivalent is "Christ." In the Old Testament the word "Messiah" means only a legitimate ruler, whose right to rule has been symbolized by an anointing ceremony, real or assumed. The word is applied to the rejected king Saul and, once, to someone outside the Israelite community altogether, Cyrus of Persia (Isaiah 45:1). But by the time of Jesus, with the successful rebellion of the Maccabees fresh in the Jewish mind, there was a good deal of discussion about a figure called "the" Messiah, a figure of a type known as eschatological, concerned with not merely restoring Israel's power but with bringing about an end of what we have known as history. It is fairly common knowledge that the identification of "the" Messiah with Jesus of Nazareth is the issue that divides Christians from Jews.

We have previously remarked on the significance of the fact that Israel was never a powerful or prosperous empire. The Bible records only two periods of relative independence and prosperity for Israel, and the reason was the same in both cases: one world empire had declined and its successor had not yet risen. The period of David and Solomon came between the decline of Egypt and the rise of Assyria; the period following the Maccabean wars, between the decline of Syria and the rise of Rome. This fact throws another aspect of the royal metaphor into great prominence in the Bible. If the king represents the unity of his society, he represents it also in defeat and humiliation. Thus in the elegy over the destruction of Jerusalem by Nebuchadnezzar it is said of the unlucky Zedekiah, the last king of an independent Judah:

> The breath of our nostrils, the anointed of the Lord, was taken in their pits, of whom we said, Under his shadow we shall live among the heathen. (Lamentations 4:20)

The phrase "breath of our nostrils" indicates that the word "represent," used above, is an accommodation to our present framework of language: the king *is* his people, their existence as a "body." A similar and even more famous elegy, thought to have come from the period of the Babylonian captivity, describes a sacrificial victim known as the "suffering servant":

> He is despised and rejected of men; a man of sorrows, and acquainted with grief: and we hid as it were our faces from him; he was despised, and we esteemed him not. (Isaiah 53:3)

It is idle to inquire whether this originally referred to a specific individual or to Israel as a society. The great oracle is not moving in this kind of either-or world at all, but in the world of the royal metaphor, where society and individual interpenetrate with each other. Even in total isolation the individual victim is still the identity of those who reject him.

It was of course not only in Israel that the king was regarded as an embodiment of the misfortunes and disasters of his people as well as of their triumphs. If a severe drought hits a country, its ruler, whether David in Jerusalem (II Samuel 21) or Oedipus in Thebes, must consult an oracle of the appropriate god or gods to find out the reason, and take the blame if it is his fault. A king of Babylon, we are told, such as Nebuchadnezzar, would have to go through a ceremony of ritual humiliation at each new year, with his face slapped by the high priest, in order to renew his title to the kingdom. Nebuchadnezzar was a successful monarch as such things go, and therefore the omission of such a ceremony might provoke the envy of his tutelary god. The parallel with David is interesting. The greatest triumph of David's reign, from the Biblical point of view, was his bringing of the "ark of the covenant" into the newly captured Jerusalem; and David showed his sense of the importance of the occasion by dancing in front of it "with all his might." His wife Michal, Saul's daughter, watched him and sneered at him as having made an exhibitionistic fool of himself in front of the servants. David's reply was:

> And I will yet be more vile than thus, and will be base in mine own sight: and of the maidservants which thou hast spoken of, of them shall I be had in honour. (II Samuel 6:22)

It is not hard to understand why David became the traditional author of most of the Psalms. In a hymn sung by a group, such a phrase as "I will praise the Lord" expresses the unity of that group by the metaphor of the individual, who in this case is identified with the author of the hymn. The verbal figure involved is an extension of the royal metaphor, and is easily absorbed into it. The confessional psalms in particular, where the "I" is a sinner needing acceptance or a persecuted victim needing help, take on a peculiar eloquence and power when the "I" is thought of as also a king, whether a real king or a hypothetical one.

With this background, what Paul calls the scandal of the cross (Galatians 5:11; AV reads "offence") attached to Jesus becomes more comprehensible. It was agreed that the Messiah would be lineally descended from David, hence Matthew and Luke trace the ancestry of Jesus through David to Joseph, even though Joseph was not Jesus' father. But his lineage was unrecognized throughout his life: at his birth he was confronted with another "King of the Jews," Herod, and at his trial his accusers remarked "We have no king but Caesar" (John 19:15). What associations there are with royalty, including the crown of thorns and the inscription "King of the Jews" over the cross, are in a context of mockery and torture. In all this he is the individual form of the society of Israel, with its unique spiritual mission and its almost unbroken record of isolation and exile. Even more significant for our immediate context is that Jesus' claim that he was a real king, though of a spiritual kingdom "not of this world," while at the same time behaving like a servant and identifying himself with "the least" of others (Matthew 25:40), is intended among other things to resolve the master-slave dialectic on which the whole of human history turns. History symbolically ends at the point at which master and servant become the same person, and represent the same thing.

In our discussion of types and antitypes we remarked that in the metonymic period the structure of Christian doctrine eventually became the antitype of the Bible. In the descriptive period archaeology opened the door between the Biblical and the pre-Biblical worlds. For well over a century the Bible has been seen to have many traces of pre-Biblical thought and ritual, and it is clear that cults older than the Bible are involved, or were originally involved, in such episodes as Jephthah's sacrifice of his daughter or Jacob's setting up of a sacred stone at Bethel. Accompanying archaeology was a vast expansion of comparative data from religions, folktales, customs, and rituals from every part of human time and space, all suggesting affinities to something Biblical. Hence there was a growth of comparative studies that tended to look at the Bible centrifugally, collecting analogues of its themes on the assumption that there is nothing in the Bible that cannot be found in some parallel form outside it. Such an approach, in Frazer and others, introduces the student to the whole panorama of imagery and narrative that human mythology has produced, and thereby implies that we may finally come to some understanding of a universal language of symbolism.

The only trouble with this is that while the parallels are suggestive and even tantalizing, an endless diffusion of analogies does not seem to be getting anywhere, much less nearer an understanding of universal symbolism. To adapt a phrase of Wallace Stevens, there is a continuous dazzle that never yields to clarity. We might get more sense of direction if we looked at the situation from something closer to the Bible's own point of view. From its own point of view, surely, the Bible is providing the antitypes of which Canaanite and other pre-Biblical cults are types. It claims, by implication, to indicate what the symbolism of such cults "really means" by relating them to the worship of the true God. If we accept such a claim as a heuristic principle, the critical axiom above goes into reverse. If there is so little in the Bible for which some analogy cannot be found somewhere else, there is correspondingly little to be found anywhere else that cannot be found in some form in the Bible. If we take the Bible as a key to mythology, instead of taking mythology in general as a key to the Bible, we should at least have a definite starting point, wherever we end.

Most of these pre- and extra-Biblical types are presented in the Bible as parodies or demonic perversions: we shall come to more detail in this kind of imagery later. But by no means all of them are: the dragon-killing creation myth, for example, found in so many Near Eastern mythologies, appears in the Bible too, not as a matter of belief or ritual but of poetic imagery. Again, the Christian conception of "Israel" as the Church of the Gentiles makes it possible for, say, Classical mythology to become a type of Christian mythology. Parallels between Classical and Christian myth were a commonplace of Renaissance critical scholarship, and helped immensely to enrich Christian culture as well as to provide a cultural citizenship for the Classics within Christendom.

We need one more critical principle to bring all this into focus. In discussing the relation of myth and history, we said that a work originally intended to be a history, such as Gibbon's *Decline and Fall*, may in the course of time, if well enough written, shift its center of gravity from history to myth and literature after it begins to date as a history. What we did not then say was that it also acquires a new kind of historical identity. Gibbon's book eventually becomes an *eighteenth-century* book, a monument of one of the most fascinating periods of English culture. Could we apply such a principle to the

Bible? Not to the whole Bible, perhaps, as it covers so long a period, but the focus of the Christian Bible, the first century A.D., the age of Jesus and Paul, might assume a distinctive kind of historical significance. This was the age of the founding of the Roman Empire under Augustus, and the historical situation contemporary with the New Testament may have a symbolic significance of its own. The question in the background is, Was there a reason within history itself for Christianity to begin at that particular time? The dramatic confrontation between Christ and Caesar was felt more vividly in the period of the Renaissance and Reformation than it is now, though the two kinds of interest expressed by these two words naturally differed a good deal. Here our main concern is with the Renaissance view of the Augustan Age as providing a kind of Gentile type for the emergence of Christianity.

In the preceding chapter we noted that the mythology of paganism seems to show a development parallel with that of the social organization that makes it cultic. It begins with local epiphanic gods and moves on to departmental gods with established functions, in proportion as societies grow from tribal to national entities. At this point we should take one more step. With the rise of empires, whose rulers begin to think of themselves as rulers of the "world," we get a kind of monotheism. This is, however, an imperial monotheism, quite different from the revolutionary monotheism of the Bible. Imperial monotheism is usually an umbrella structure, and is normally tolerant of local cults, which it tends increasingly to regard as manifestations of a single god. This single god, who as a rule is a sky-god, is in a peculiar sense the patron of the world ruler; and the world ruler, from Ikhnaton in ancient Egypt to the Caesars of Rome and even later, has had a curiously persistent symbolic association with the sun.

The Bible does not regard the world ruler as necessarily an evil or sinister person. It is only that he rules the kind of world in which one of his successors will sooner or later become so. The Pharaoh who knew Joseph and welcomed Israel into Egypt was finally succeeded by a Pharaoh who tried to exterminate the Hebrews by genocide. Cyrus of Persia, and to some extent Darius, are referred to with the deepest respect, but their successor Xerxes, the Ahasuerus of the Book of Esther, is very nearly persuaded into an anti-Jewish pogrom. Alexander the Great gets very little attention in the Bible, though Josephus has him welcomed into Jerusalem by the high priest with many mutual expressions of esteem. But eventually his empire produced Antiochus Epiphanes, who began the ferocious persecution of Jews that provoked the Maccabean rebellion. Under the Roman Empire Paul maintains that "the powers that be are ordained of God" (Romans 13:1), but before long we have Nero and other persecuting emperors.

The reason for this degeneration of the world ruler is one that takes us back to the two forms of social contract that we saw arising out of the pagan and Biblical cultures. The Classical social contract is the one that we see in the trial scene at the end of Aeschylus' *Oresteia*. It is a vision of justice and equity in which man, nature, and gods are all included. The gods ratify it, and if they were not there we should have nothing but the purely automatic reactions of nature represented by the Furies, the agents of the natural force of *nemesis*, to keep a balance in human affairs. In the Biblical contract, as we saw, nature is not an immediate participant: the contract is between God and his people, and if the people are as loyal to it as God is, the nature around them will be transformed into a quite different world.

As social conditions change to those of empire, however, it becomes more and more obvious that the ruler is the one essential force that holds the contract together. Hence he begins to take on divine qualities, as the adopted son or, as in Egypt, the incarnation of his god. It is at this point that Jesus' principle, that one should render to Caesar what is Caesar's and to God what is God's (Mark 12:17), runs into trouble. Sooner or later there will be a Caesar who will demand what is due only to God, that is, divine worship.

The act of Antiochus Epiphanes that outraged the Jews even more than his cruelties was his desecrating of the temple by rededicating it to Zeus and erecting an altar and perhaps a statue there (I Maccabees 1:54). This sacrilege is called, in the AV's somewhat cumbersome rendering, "the abomination that maketh desolate" (Daniel 11:31). It is referred to again in the Gospels (Matthew 24:15) in connection with the calamities of further persecutions, not impossibly with reference to a supposed desire expressed by the Emperor Caligula to put his own statue in the same place.

In any case a cult of the divine Caesar was established at Rome, and an act of observing it, however perfunctory, was obligatory. Society is never tolerant about anything it attaches real importance to, and this act was important as the symbol of the Roman way of life. But it was, of course, precisely the act that Jews and Christians could not observe. Hence, although Christianity was not set up on a revolutionary basis, and on the contrary stressed its loyalty to the secular power, it was compelled to behave exactly like a revolutionary organization. There have been many explanations for Christianity's triumph over all other religions of its time, but the most visible explanation was the brilliance of its revolutionary tactics. It set up a counterpart of imperial authority in the Church which could go underground in times of persecution, until the time came for it to emerge and take over, or at least merge with, temporal power. Marcus Aurelius spoke of the *parataxis*, the military discipline, of the Christians as their strongest asset.

Already in the New Testament a conception has emerged of an "Antichrist," the enemy of everything Christ stands for, and who seems to have some connection with the persecuting emperors. Paul, despite his emphatic counsel of submission to the Roman power, gives us a description of

. . . The son of perdition, Who opposeth and exalteth himself above all that is called God, or that is worshipped; so that he as God sitteth in the temple of God, shewing himself that he is God. (II Thessalonians 2:3-4)

The imagery here is clearly derived from Daniel's "abomination." In the Book of Revelation (13:18), a "beast," a figure of the Antichrist type, is referred to by a cipher, the number 666, which is generally thought to spell out the name of Nero, even though the author of Revelation may have lived under a later emperor.

The Book of Revelation was later assumed to be a prophecy of the future troubles of the Church, which left commentators on it free to identify its sinister images of Antichrist and Great Whore with whatever they were most afraid of in their day. The Great Whore, of whom more later, is identified in the text with the Babylon that carried the Jews into captivity, and evidently also with the Rome of the persecuting Caesars who represented the same kind of thing in the author's own day. Dante identified these images with Philip of France and the Avignon Papacy. Some Protestant polemic of the sixteenth century regarded the Roman Church as an extension of the Roman Empire, identifying that Church with the Whore, and the Pope with Antichrist. Blake identified them, more traditionally, with a recrudescence of state power that he saw taking shape in his day; this he called "Deism" and saw as leading to the annihilation warfare that he identified as a degenerate form of "Druidism." We should call it "totalitarianism": the effort to conceive the state as a single body incarnate in its leader, the "Ein Reich, Ein Volk, Ein Führer" of Hitler's Germany. It might even be said, from some points of view, that the only mark of genuine distinction in that otherwise rather shabby tyrant was the seriousness with which he took his Antichrist role, as a figure to whom everyone in Germany was to render thanks for his daily bread.

The time of Christ was also the period of the great consolidation of Classical literature under Virgil and Ovid. Here, as we should expect, the controlling imagery is that of cyclical movement, which had expanded to take in such larger rhythms as the precession of the equinoxes. Hence there were many theories about a new cycle of history, just as there are theories about an "age of Aquarius" now. One famous expression of these theories is Virgil's Fourth Eclogue, a congratulatory poem on the birth of a child, thought to be influenced by the apocryphal, or rather pseudepigraphical, "Sibylline Books." This poem speaks of a new golden age when nature will resume its paradisal shape and "the serpent shall die." Christianity promptly seized on this poem as an unconscious prophecy of the Christian Messiah, but at the same time it ignored or rejected all cyclical theories of history. Augustine's attack on this kind of cyclical specu- lation in *The City of God* is much later, but reflects a consistent Christian view.

In Dante's *Commedia* Virgil serves as guide for the whole area that is controlled by the natural cycle—the hell at the center of the earth and the mountain of purgatory on its other side. At that point Virgil has to leave Dante, who from there on is guided by Beatrice instead, because Virgil is never to see the beatific vision. His vision on earth got as far as renewal, but never broke through to resurrection. In our day we have the reverse movement in D. H. Lawrence's story *The Man Who Died*, which assimilates Jesus to the revolving cycle of nature. In this story Jesus, reviving in the tomb, becomes the lover of a priestess of Isis who has been told to "wait for the reborn man," and at the end of the story he leaves her with a promise to return. Other assimila- tions of the Christian story to the cycle of rebirth are in Robert Graves's *King Jesus* and in Yeats's *Vision*. In the latter the planetary conjunctions symbolized by the phrase "A Full Moon in March" embrace both the assassination of Caesar and the crucifixion of Christ.

The *Aeneid* is also dominated by the cycle of revolving years, and its main theme is the establishment of a new Troy and a new cycle of history. The crucial point of its vision is in Aeneas' journey, in the sixth book, to the lower world, where he sees the great wheel of history turning to bring Rome to world power. Some conception of reincar- nation, which is of course entirely consistent with such a vision, seems to be included. It is clear that in the Stoical world view, as expounded by Posidonius and others, which was a strong influence on Virgil, the pagan contract is beginning to narrow down. The gods are nature spirits in origin, but as the sense of natural law, as manifested in the cycle, develops, the arbitrary characteristics of such gods, derived as they are from unpredictable elements in nature, fade into the background. In the action of the *Aeneid* Juno's willful aggressiveness is not only childish but futile, and even Venus is hardly more than decorative. The real power is an inscrutable will that manifests itself only in the divine supervision of Aeneas' struggles to establish a beachhead in Italy and bring about a new phase of history. Virgil is still a long way from saying that only one god is necessary—the divine will that holds together social and natural law—and that Caesar is the central manifestation of this will. But the tendency is there, the *Aeneid* being essentially a poem in which the house of Caesar occupies much the same place as the line of David in the Bible.

Around the same period, Ovid's *Metamorphoses* provides what was accepted for centuries as a kind of pagan counterpart of the Bible, beginning with stories of creation and flood and proceeding to stories of metamorphosis. In these stories, beings who were originally conscious are turned into various objects of nature and fall silent, sometimes as a reward, sometimes as a punishment, but always as something no longer capable of speech or response, except for the plaintive songs of those turned into birds. Metamorphosis is thus an image of what in the Bible is called the fall of man, which traditionally has involved his alienation from nature. There are no metamorphoses in the Bible except that of Lot's wife (Genesis 19:26), who became a pillar of salt because, like Orpheus, she made the fatal mistake of looking back when escaping from a demonic world (see Luke 17:32). The Bible, as we saw, thinks rather in terms of a future metamorphosis of nature in an upward direction, when it will gain the power of articulateness instead of losing it:

> For ye shall go out with joy, and be led forth with peace: the mountains and the hills shall break forth before you into singing, and all the trees of the field shall clap their hands. (Isaiah 55:12)

In Ovid the vision of nature is carried through to a melancholy survey of the kind of mutability that the cycle brings with it, until the whole process of nature finally runs down in a kind of entropy. At the end of the poem, however, comes the deifying of the two great Caesars, the Caesar figure being here, as in Virgil, the one whose presence seems to hold the entire vision together much as the Messiah does the Biblical vision.

The coming of Jesus into the world, then, seems to have taken place historically at one of those dialectical confrontations in which history suddenly expands to myth and indicates a dimension beyond the historical. The poet W. H. Auden has attempted, in his *For the Time Being* and elsewhere, to show how the completeness of the pagan achievement, along with its obvious limitations, formed an appropriate background for the Incarnation. Everything was there: resignation, acceptance of law and order and of its accredited images of authority, an understanding too of the principle of change and mutability, a feeling that all was for the best if one could really absorb the great and overruling law of causality:

Felix qui potuit rerum cognoscere causas.

Everything was there except the revolutionary challenge to make a complete break with all of it. The break involved a good deal of cruelty and fanaticism on both sides, but the bloody historical record, as usual, only muddles the real issue.

And, of course, the challenge itself, for many early Christians, rested on the illusion that the end of time would take place almost at any moment. But, as time went on without so dramatic an event, Christianity found that it could no more do without a synchronic ritual calendar of observances than any other religion. We cannot in fact trace Christianity back to a time when the Jewish ceremonial law had not been replaced by a Christian one—that is, to a time when this synchronic ritual calendar did not exist. Even as Paul was saying "Circumcision is nothing" (I Corinthians 7:19), the Church was saying something more like "Baptism is practically everything," and could claim the authority of Paul for doing so. The cyclical calendar of observances formed an "analogy," as Joseph Butler later called it, a sacramental imitation of life in the eternal world, in which the ritual observance was the type and eternal life the antitype. The Resurrection, strictly speaking a leap out of time altogether, could be celebrated only by an annual spring festival full of images of renewal and rebirth, including eventually eggs and rabbits. Whatever Paul meant by his sardonic remark to the Galatians (4:10): "Ye observe days, and months, and times, and years," he also gave his support to such "observance" in the Christian Church.

I have said that this synchronic ritual calendar was present in

Christianity from the beginning; hence I am not suggesting any betrayal of the original Christian impulse. What I am saying is that the central royal metaphor—that we are all members of one body—was expressed in terms of unity and integration, as the unity of a social body into which the individual is absorbed. The Church claimed to be the continuing Body of Christ in history, and as early as the letters of Ignatius we are completely in the atmosphere of the Church Militant, with its emphasis on military analogies and its disciplined organization, where no authority is to be followed except what comes through the bishop. In the Catholic Church the Body of Christ was visibly present in the host of the Mass; some of the Protestant churches formulated the sense of presence differently and put more emphasis on other elements, such as the proclamation of the Word of God in the sermon, but made no change in the central metaphor. Naturally a good deal of similar imagery continued in the secular world: Elizabeth I absorbed much of the cult of the Virgin in Protestant England, and Louis XIV of France was once again, like the deified Caesars, a sun-king. This was because sacred and secular authority had the same metaphorical construct: State and Church were equally larger social bodies to which individuals are related as individual cells are to our own bodies. This formulation of authority was largely unquestioned down to our own time: if we look at religious conversions in the nineteenth century, for example, we see how regularly the search for true religion and the search for a true church, or larger social body with which to identify oneself, are assumed to be the same quest.

In our day, we said, the "Antichrist" social complex is encapsulated for us in the word "totalitarian," where again the individual is a member of a larger body, and exists primarily as a function of that body. There are no divine Caesars any more, though there is usually a dictatorial figure to whom inspired or preternatural powers are attributed. Such movements owe their strength largely to habit and tradition: they are an intensification of a feeling that has always been with us. Loyalty, though a very central and essential element of experience, has no "rational" basis, and is not an "emotion" either. It is the result of basing one's life, or the essential part of it, on the realizing of a metaphor, specifically some form of the royal metaphor.

Most of us outside totalitarian regimes feel that these are anything but the highest form of social organization, and prefer a different set of values which we associate not so much with our religious traditions as with the secular conception of "democracy." For us democracy, as a source of loyalty, does not mean only the machinery of elections or a greater tolerance of religion and art or a greater relaxation of leisure, privacy, or freedom of movement, but to what all these things point to: the sense of an individuality that grows out of society but is infinitely more than a social function. It is easy to formulate this sense in egocentric terms, as a right to do what we like and so forth, but it is even easier to demonstrate that the notion of a socially detached individual is an illusion. What is significant here is that religious bodies do not effectively express any alternative of loyalty to the totalitarian state, because they use the same metaphors of merging and individual subservience.

And yet there are quite different ways of formulating the royal metaphor that are equally consistent with the way it is stated in the New Testament and elsewhere, and yet totally inconsistent with totalitarian ways of stating and thinking it. Paul, for example, says that he is dead as what we should call an ego, and that only Christ lives within him (Galatians 2:20, and similarly elsewhere). This is the same metaphor, but the metaphor is turned inside out. Instead of an individual finding his fulfillment within a social body, however sacrosanct, the metaphor is reversed from a metaphor of integration into a wholly decentralized one, in which the total body is complete within each individual. The individual acquires the internal authority of the unity of the Logos, and it is this unity that makes him an individual. Paul's phrase "not I" means that he is not talking about any form of private judgment or any egocentric formulation of the metaphor. Private judgment is for dreams, where, as Heraclitus says, every man is his own Logos. Naturally what is expressed here is an ideal and not a permanent achievement, even for Paul; but then no permanent achievement is ever enough.

In our day Simone Weil has found the traditional doctrine of the Church as the Body of Christ a major obstacle—not impossibly *the* major obstacle—to her entering it. She points out that it does not differ enough from other metaphors of integration, such as the class solidarity metaphor of Marxism, and says:

Our true dignity is not to be parts of a body. . . . It consists in this, that in the state of perfection which is the vocation of each one of us, we no longer live in ourselves, but Christ lives in us; so that through our perfection Christ . . . becomes in a sense each one of us, as he is completely in each host. The hosts are not a *part* of his body.

I quote this because, whether she is right or wrong, and whatever the theological implications, the issue she raises is a central one in metaphorical vision, or the application of metaphors to human experience. We are born, we said, within a pre-existing social contract out of which we develop what individuality we have, and the interests of that society take priority over the interests of the individual. Many religions, on the other hand, in their origin, attempt to be re-created societies built on the influence of a single individual: Jesus, Buddha, Lao Tzu, Mohammed, or at most a small group. Such teachers signify, by their appearance, that there are individuals to whom a society should be related, rather than the other way around. Within a generation or two, however, this new society has become one more social contract, and the individuals of the new generations are once again subordinated to it.

Paul's conception of Jesus as the genuine individuality of the individual, which is what I think Simone Weil is following here, indicates a reformulating of the central Christian metaphor in a way that unites without subordinating, that achieves identity *with* and identity *as* on equal terms. The Eucharistic image, which she also refers to, suggests that the crucial event of Good Friday—the death of Christ on the cross—is one with the death of everything else in the past. The swallowed Christ, eaten, divided, and drunk, in the phrase of Eliot's "Gerontion," is one with the potential individual buried in the tomb of the ego during the Sabbath of time and history, where it is the only thing that rests. When this individual awakens and we pass to resurrection and Easter, the community with which he is identical is no longer a whole of which he is a part, but another aspect of himself, or, in the traditional metonymic language, another person of his substance.

Whatever the social importance of achieving a symbolic counterpart within Christianity to the political ideal of democracy, I am speaking here about the connection of this decentralizing approach to Christian metaphors with the imagery and narrative of the Bible. In the second part of this book we shall try to look further into that connection.

PART TWO

THE
ORDER
OF
TYPES

CHAPTER FIVE

TYPOLOGY II
Phases of Revelation

The Biblical religions are strongly moral and voluntaristic, and throw their main emphasis on salvation, whether individual or social. The two forms are interconnected, of course, and social organization and individual duty keep alternating with each other. They also preserve the tension of creature and creator to the limits of their revelation, and they are theistic, in that they deny that any category of being higher than the personality of God can exist. To many people today, some of these characteristics seem rather primitive in contrast to what is provided by certain forms of Hindu and Buddhist belief. Here we are expected to pass beyond the external and objective barrier of the divine personal creator, who is usually thought of in these Oriental religions as largely a projection of the ego, and seek instead what is generally called enlightenment. This enlightenment is attained by destroying the notion of the individual subject, for whom all the rest of the world is objective, a mirror that reflects back to the subject all its desires and aggressions. If attained, enlightenment brings about the same kind of obedience to the moral code (*dharma*) that "salvation" does in the West, but without the legalism that Christianity is regarded as having abolished only in theory. In the Western world, it is urged, such a conception as salvation by the will implies at once a prolonged argument over whether it is man's will or God's will or some proportion of both that gets involved in the saving: in the

Eastern quest for enlightenment all such either-or questions are simply left behind.

Such Oriental perspectives have made a good deal of headway in the West, where they are removed from their own social context. In that context however, we noted, Marxism, which we have characterized as a Western gospel descended from the social aspect of the Biblical religions, has been a major influence. Still, it would perhaps be profitable to inquire what elements in the Biblical tradition correspond to the more metaphorical and less conceptual appeal of the Oriental conception of enlightenment. This is part of our central question, What in the Bible particularly attracts poets and other creative artists of the Western world? If this interest on my part is kept in view, some of the emphases in what follows may be easier to understand.

The content of the Bible is traditionally described as "revelation," and there seems to be a sequence or dialectical progression in this revelation, as the Christian Bible proceeds from the beginning to the end of its story. I see a sequence of seven main phases: creation, revolution or exodus (Israel in Egypt), law, wisdom, prophecy, gospel, and apocalypse. Five of these phases have their center of gravity in the Old Testament and two in the New. Each phase is not an improvement on its predecessor but a wider perspective on it. That is, this sequence of phases is another aspect of Biblical typology, each phase being a type of the one following it and an antitype of the one preceding it.

First Phase: Creation

We have noted the main characteristics of the creation myth in the Bible: it is an artificial creation myth in which the world was originally made by a sky-father, in contrast to sexual creation myths in which it is brought into being by (frequently) an earth-mother. In Genesis, however, the forms of life are *spoken* into existence, so that while they are made or created, they are not made out of something else. Christian doctrine speaks of a creation *ex nihilo*, and denies that the waste and empty chaos we meet at the beginning could have been coeternal with God. So we should not oversimplify the antithesis between making and bringing to birth. Another antithesis is more important. Sexual creation myths tend to become cyclical, because the conception of birth leads us only to an earlier birth in the past and a renewal of birth in the future. The Genesis myth starts with what

Aristotle would call the *telos*, the developed form toward which all living things grow, and the cycle of birth and death follows after.

Three questions arise in studying the creation myth in the Bible. First, why is the deity to whom exclusive devotion is to be paid so intolerably patriarchal? We know only of a world in which every human and animal form is born from a female body; but the Bible insists, not only on the association of God with the male sex, but that at the beginning the roles of male and female were reversed in human life, the first woman having been made out of the body of the first man. Second, why is creation contained within the image of the week, and alleged to have occupied six days? Third, what is meant by saying that death came into the world with the fall of man? All these questions have immediate answers. God is male because that rationalizes the ethos of a patriarchal male-dominated society; creation took six days because that rationalizes the law of the sabbath; death came with the fall because that rationalizes the very primitive feeling that death, the most natural and inevitable of all events, is still somehow unnatural, and that if we die someone or something else must be responsible. All these answers are true as far as they go, so we shall ignore their truth in order to try to get a little farther.

In the older, or Jahwist, account of the Creation, which begins in Genesis 2:4, not all the imagery of sexual creation is eliminated. That account begins with the watering of a garden, and Adam emerges from the dust of the ground, the *adamah* or mother earth. The association between gardens and female bodies runs all through literature, and is found elsewhere in the Bible, notably in the Song of Songs. If we look at the imagery of *Paradise Lost*, we can see how subtly and delicately Milton has associated the body of the garden of Eden with the body of Eve; Adam is associated rather with the lower sky. The maleness of God seems to be connected with the Bible's resistance to the notion of a containing cycle of fate or inevitability as the highest category that our minds can conceive. All such cycles are suggested by nature, and are contained within nature—which is why it is so easy to think of nature as Mother Nature. But as long as we remain within her cycle we are unborn embryos.

The chief point made about the creation of Eve is that henceforth man is to leave his parents and become united with his wife (2:24). The parent is the primary image of the extension of what we are beyond ourselves in time, but that image has to give way to the image of the sexual union of bridegroom and bride. This is a modulation of a principle to be dealt with farther on, that the anxiety of continuity in

time has to be superseded sooner or later by a break with it. Of the
two parents, the mother is the one we have to break from in order to
get born at all. The embryonic life in Mother Nature, enclosed in the
mechanical cycle of repetition, is also mechanical, with no freedom to
escape. The embryo is mentioned in Psalm 139:16, where the Hebrew word is *golem*, and in later Jewish legend the *golem* became, very
appropriately, a mechanical monster like the one in Mary Shelley's
Frankenstein.

From this point of view we can see how important it is that the first
word of the Bible is "beginning." Nature itself suggests no beginning: it exists in an indefinite dimension of time and space. Human
life is a continuum that we join at birth and drop off at death. But,
because *we* begin and end, we insist that beginnings and endings
must be much more deeply built into the reality of things than the
universe around us suggests, and we shape our myths accordingly.
We have previously noted how tenaciously Christianity clung to the
notion of a finite beginning and end in time and space, as part of the
emphasis it gave to the eternal and infinite beyond it. It gained little
by that emphasis, we saw, because, at least in the general social
imagination, the usual views of the eternal and infinite did not get
beyond the perspective of endless time and space.

We get a little closer to this question when we realize that the
central metaphor underlying "beginning" is not really birth at all. It
is rather the moment of waking from sleep, when one world disappears and another comes into being. This is still contained within a
cycle: we know that at the end of the day we shall return to the world
of sleep, but in the meantime there is a sense of self-transcendence, of
a consciousness getting "up" from an unreal into a real, or at least
more real, world. This sense of awakening into a greater degree of
reality is expressed by Heraclitus, in an aphorism referred to earlier,
as a passing from a world where everyone has his own "logos" into a
world where there is a common "logos." Genesis presents the Creation as a sudden coming into being of a world through articulate
speech (another aspect of logos), conscious perception, light and
stability. Something like this metaphor of awakening may be the real
reason for the emphasis on "days," and such recurring phrases as
"And the evening and the morning were the first day," even before
the day as we know it was established with the creating of the sun.
The fact that this phrase starts with the evening, too, follows the
rhythm of awakening.

In the earth-mother, or sexual, type of creation myth, death is not a problem. Death is built into a myth that concerns only living things, all of which die; and in fact death is the only element that makes either the process itself or the myth about it intelligible. But an intelligent God, it is felt, can have made only a model world, a world he could see to be "good" (1:10, etc.), and consequently it could not have had any death or sin or misery originally in it. Such a myth therefore must have an alienation myth of a "fall" to account for the contrast between the perfect world God must have made with the world we live in now.

The story of the fall of man in Genesis seems originally to have been one of the sardonic folktales of the Near East that explain how man once had immortality nearly within his grasp, but was cheated out of it by frightened or malicious deities. We have earlier versions from Sumerian times on that are less rationalized than the one in Genesis. But the Genesis account, in its turn, has very little of the desperate anxiety to prove that the Fall was all man's fault and not the least little bit God's fault that we find, for example, in *Paradise Lost*. The Genesis account permits itself a verse (3:22) in which God seems to be telling other gods that man is now "one of us," in a position to threaten their power unless they do something about it at once, with a break in the syntax that suggests genuine terror. On the other hand, it is not easy to hear either in the Genesis story what Paul and the author of II Esdras heard in it, the terrible clang of an iron gate shut forever on human hopes. To make the "fall" story an intelligible account of man's present alienation from nature, a very complex fall within nature itself has to be postulated. Milton devotes the tenth book of *Paradise Lost* to showing how every inconvenience man suffers in nature, from frostbite to thorns on the rose bushes, resulted from a fall of nature that completed the human fall. But this is pure reconstruction: there is not a word about any such fall in Genesis, the cursing of the ground in 3:17 being removed in 8:21.

What man acquires in the Fall is evidently sexual experience as we know it, and something called the knowledge of good and evil, obviously connected with sex but not otherwise explained. Man becomes ashamed of his body and performs his sexual acts in secret: certain features of that body, such as the fact that in most climates he needs clothing and consequently is the world's only naked animal, indicate a uniquely alienated relation to his environment. The reason for the creation of woman, we are told (2:24), is that in the sexual relation man should be not alone and yet "one flesh" with his wife. In sex as we know it there is no complete union of bodies, and therefore sex, even with synchronized orgasms, has a residual frustration built into it. The knowledge that accompanied the discovery of sex in its present form seems to have been a genuine wisdom that put man, at least potentially, on the level of the true gods or angels (see II Samuel 14:17). But it was clearly a knowledge founded on self-consciousness, as is sexual knowledge itself, in which man becomes a subject confronting an objective environment. Consciousness of this sort, the philosophers tell us, is founded on a consciousness of death, so that mortality is a part of it. The "subtle" serpent, with its ability to renew its vitality by shedding its skin, is the symbol of the cyclical world of objective nature that man entered with his "fall." In the Genesis account the world of the Fall is symbolized only by the serpent: the assumption that the serpent was a disguise for Satan comes much later. Man's chief and most distinctive assets are his sense of sex as an imaginative experience and his consciousness: these two are closely connected, but have a common and fatal flaw.

It is with the "fall" that the legal metaphor begins that persists all through the Bible, of human life as subject to a trial and judgment, with prosecutors and defenders. In this metaphor Jesus is the counsel for the defense, and the primary accuser is Satan the *diabolos*, a word from which our word devil comes, and which originally included a sense of the person opposed to one in a lawsuit. In the emotional response to Christianity at any rate, the role of God as Father, however defined in dogma, keeps shifting from the benevolent to the diabolical, from a being genuinely concerned for man to an essentially malicious being compounded of wrath and condemnation. One consequence of having a creation myth, with a fall myth inseparable from it, has been the sense of being objective to God, or, more specifically, of being constantly watched and observed, by an all-seeing eye that is always potentially hostile.

Such emotional uncertainty, it could be said, is the result of a fallen state in which there are radical limitations to our vision. But when we move back from the story of the Fall to the Priestly account of creation in the first chapter, we meet some puzzling features there too. The world God made was so "good" that he spent his seventh day contemplating it—which means that his Creation, including man, was already objective to God, even if we assume that man acquired with his fall a new and more intense feeling of the "otherness" of both God and nature. The Creation, we are told, imposed light and order on a chaotic darkness, a deep symbolized by the sea of death. Yet the acts of creation include the separating of land from sea and the alternating of light and darkness with the creation of the sun and moon. So chaos and darkness can be thought of in two ways. They may be thought of as enemies of God outside his creation; but they are dialectically incorporated into creation, and are creatures of God as well. The second is the view taken in the Book of Job; the first is the more usual view of the prophets. But the prophets also suggest that God is above such distinctions as those that the knowledge of good and evil provides:

> I form the light, and create darkness; I make peace, and create evil: I the Lord do all these things. (Isaiah 45:7)

Perhaps, then, the sense of alienation traditionally attached to the fall may be latent in the original creation too, with its recurrent darkness and its stability menaced by the sea and other images of chaos (see Job 38:11). Furthermore, it is not said that man was immortal before his fall, only that there is a danger of his becoming so after it. We have seen that the traditional Christian view of the verse "And God said, Let there be light, and there was light" is that it is the Word of God that creates, and that therefore Christ, identified with the Word of God in John and elsewhere, was the original creator. But to speak is to enter the conventions of language, which are a part of human death-consciousness; so if we push the image far enough, we come to the possibility that as soon as God speaks, and transforms himself into a Word of God, he has already condemned himself to death.

The fact that modern English has preserved the two words "sunlight" and "daylight" may suggest that at one time daylight was not causally associated with the sun at all. Similarly, the primordial light of Genesis 1:3 is not the light of the sun or moon. The emphasis on the sacredness of the week, the period of the lunar phase, is one of several indications of an original lunar cult among the Hebrews, as would be natural for desert dwellers for whom the sun is a killer and the moon a friendly guide in darkness. Jesus is described as a light shining in darkness (John 1:5), which suggests the moon or a bright star like the one heralding his birth. And yet the "Day of the Lord" imagery often recurs to a catastrophe in which "the sun shall be turned into darkness, and the moon into blood" (Joel 2:31, quoted in Acts 2:20). After that, the new light that would enlighten the redeemed survivors would have to come from the fire of life which was neither sun nor moon but rather the original light of creation. In Psalm 72:7 it is said in the AV that God's people will have peace "as

long as the moon endureth," but the sense of the original is closer to
"until the moon is destroyed." It seems almost as though in the last
phase of revelation the first phase, the artificial creation, will become
a gigantic illusion to be swept away.

The Creation, in short, seems to belong to the complex we have
associated with the metaphor of integration. To create is to create a
designed unity, with the craftsman's care in which every detail
acquires a function, a distinctive relationship to a whole. Critics from
Elizabethan times at least have noted the analogy between God as
Creator and the poet, whose name means "maker." We should be
more inclined now to reverse the analogy, and say that the conception
of God as Creator is a projection from the fact that man makes things.
The analogy was originally intended to confer dignity on the poet,
but it ends by cutting God down to a bargain-basement demiurge. As
Wallace Stevens says, one confides in what has no concealed creator:
the sense of the beauty and majesty and splendor of nature is in the
long run cheapened by what used to be called the argument from
design. The argument from design did not survive the evolutionary
structures of thought in the nineteenth century, but the assumption
that the only alternative vision to a designing deity is something
mindless and random seems also a trifle glib. Clearly there is something essential about the place of creation in the total Biblical vision,
but our ways of comprehending it seem to be grossly inadequate.
When we turn to human creative power, we see that there is a quality
in it better called re-creation, a transforming of the chaos within our
ordinary experience of nature.

The ambiguity in the Biblical conception of creation is a very
deep-seated one, and in the New Testament period those who pressed
the issue hardest were the Gnostics. They maintained that the created
order was essentially alien to man and could therefore never have been
produced by a God who had any interest in man's redemption or
emancipation. There were pagan and Jewish Gnostics as well as
Christian ones, and it was not their Christian opponents but Plotinus
who attacked them most sharply on this point. Plotinus reproaches
them for adopting what seems to us an utterly obvious principle: that
all men are brothers, "including the base," as he says, but that men
are not brothers to the stars. The beauty and perfection of the
established order of nature was a central element of faith to him,
however that order may be obscured by human ignorance.

Christianity clearly had to steer some sort of middle course between the Gnostic contempt for nature and the pagan adoration of it. Paul speaks of Jesus' teaching as a new creation, one that puts the old creation in the position of a mother in childbirth (Romans 8:20-22), although the latter is still a manifestation, or secondary Word of God (Romans 1:20). Down to the eighteenth century, Christianity worked out this position on the basis of a conception of two levels of nature. The upper level was the "good" divine creation of Genesis; the lower level was the "fallen" order that Adam entered after his sin. Man is born now on the lower level, and his essential duty in life is to try to raise himself to the higher one. Morality, law, virtue, the sacraments of the Church, all help to raise him, as does everything genuinely educational. Whether the arts are genuinely educational in this sense was disputed, but the general principle remained: Milton, for example, defines education as the attempt to repair the fall of Adam by regaining the true knowledge of God.

The "good" creation, in this view, was the world man was intended to live in, and is therefore the order specifically of human nature. The world of animals and plants we now inhabit is a physical nature that human nature is in but not of: man is confronted with a moral dialectic at birth and must either rise above physical nature or sink below it into sin. The nature around us is permeated by death and corruption, but we can discern within it the original "good" creation. The symbol of this original nature, and all that is now really left of it, is the sky. The stars give out, according to legend, a music or harmony that expresses the sense of perfected structure. The two levels of nature thus make up for man a purgatorial order, a means whereby he attains his own "true nature."

This symbolic structure wore out in the eighteenth century for two main reasons. First, the images of the sky's perfection disappeared: the stars were not made out of immortal quintessence, and the planets did not revolve around the earth in perfect circles. The sky joined the rest of nature as an image of alienation, often in fact as the most extreme form of it. Second, there was no real evidence that the "natural" on the upper human level really was natural to man except the assertions of custom and established authority. The Lady in Milton's *Comus* regards her chastity as natural on her level of nature, but the arguments used are circular: she wishes to remain chaste, and that is that. For us, human creativity is still thought of as purgatorial, as a way of raising the level of human nature. But that it imitates or restores an original divine creation of nature is not a principle now defended with much confidence. The essential meaning of the creation story, for us, seems to be as a type of which the antitype is the new heaven and earth promised in Revelation 21:1.

Second Phase: Revolution

In the Book of Genesis God makes a series of contracts or testaments with Adam, with Noah, with Abraham, with Isaac (Genesis 26:3), and with Jacob (Genesis 35:11). The sixth, with Moses, begins the Book of Exodus and the real story of Israel, and the seventh comes with the law itself, delivered in the wilderness after the Exodus. In many respects it would have been much simpler if the Biblical story had begun with the colloquy with Moses from the burning bush. Such a beginning would have wiped out at once the dreary chess problem of "theodicy," of how to derive a bad world from a good God without making God responsible in any way for its badness, that we have just been stumbling over. In the burning-bush story a situation of exploitation and injustice is already in existence, and God tells Moses that he is about to give himself a name and enter history in a highly partisan role, taking sides with the oppressed Hebrews against the Egyptian establishment.

The burning-bush contract introduces a revolutionary quality into the Biblical tradition, and its characteristics persist through Christianity, through Islam, and survive with little essential change in Marxism. Of these characteristics, the most important are, first, a belief in a specific historical revelation as a starting point. Israel's story begins here and in this way; Christianity begins with Christ and not, say, with the Essenes; Islam begins with the Hegira of Mohammed, Communism with Marx and not, say, with Owen or Fourier. Second is the adoption of a specific canon of texts, clearly marked off from apocryphal or peripheral ones, along with a tendency to regard the heretic who differs on minor points of doctrine as a more dangerous enemy than the person who repudiates the whole position. Third is the dialectical habit of mind that divides the world into those with us and those against us.

The Israelites made their great contribution to history, as is the wont of human nature, through their least amiable characteristic. It was not their belief that their God was the true God but their belief that all other gods were false that proved decisive. I spoke earlier of the contrast between the revolutionary monotheism of the Bible and the imperial monotheisms in Egypt, Persia, Rome, and elsewhere.

For an educated and tolerant monotheist of the latter type, the conception "false god" would be almost unintelligible, certainly in bad taste. In Japan, when Buddhism was introduced, there was a good deal of tension with the indigenous Shinto religion, until a Buddhist theologian proposed that the *kami*, the miscellany of gods, nature spirits, and ancestral spirits in Shinto, could all be regarded as emanations of the Buddha, after which the two religions coexisted. No such compromise was ever possible for Judaism, Christianity, Islam, or (*mutatis mutandis*) Marxism.

Israel's Syrian neighbors, like most ancient peoples, assumed that when they went to war with Israel they would be fighting Israel's gods as well, whose existence and reality they did not question, and that they should, for example, try to get the Israelites into flat country because the gods of a hilly country would be expert hill-fighters (I Kings 20:23). The assumption proved disastrous for them because Jehovah took offense at the suggestion that he was not equally good in valleys. The great story of the contest of Elijah and the priests of Baal on Mount Carmel, on the other hand, is designed to show that Baal does not exist at all, not that Jehovah is the stronger god. True, an earlier story about a contest between Jehovah and the Philistine god Dagon (I Samuel 5) does not appear to deny the reality of Dagon. There is a good deal of flexibility in such matters, because logically the reality of a "false god" would have to be a devil, and elaborate demonologies belong to a later period.

The main historical preoccupation of both Judaism and Christianity was not with demonology but with the expectation of a *culbute générale* in the future, a kind of recognition scene when those with the right beliefs or attitudes would emerge on top with their now powerful enemies rendered impotent. The simplest version of this *culbute* is the one given in the Book of Esther, when a proposed anti-Jewish pogrom with Haman for its leader and Mordecai for its chief victim is reversed by a stratagem. Haman is hanged on the gallows he built for Mordecai, and the resulting massacre is of his party. But even this intransigent book reflects the general tendency of Judaism to come to terms with the secular power rather than colliding with it. The king of Persia is left in possession of his kingdom, as are Nebuchadnezzar and Darius in Daniel. Paul, we saw, also urged compliance with secular power. But the general feeling persists, in Christianity, in Islam, and now in Marxism, that nothing will ever go right until the entire world is united in the right beliefs.

There is one obvious feature of the Bible that is of great importance in considering its revolutionary aspect: its strong emphasis on metaphors of the ear as compared with those of the eye. Much is said about the word of God, and there is never any difficulty about God's speaking. But any suggestion that God has been seen is hedged about with expurgation and other forms of editorial anxiety: the explanation is generally that it was only an angel of God that was seen. The miraculously burning bush, as a visible object, is there only to catch Moses' attention: it is what is said from within it that is important. Similarly, Hagar's confused question in Genesis 16:13, rendered by the AV as "Have I also here looked after him that seeth me?" probably means "Have I really seen God and lived?" Similarly, Gideon and the parents of Samson assume that seeing the face of God means death (Judges 6:23 and 13:22). In Exodus 33:20ff., God, aware of a similar danger to Moses, considerately turns around and presents the prophet with his "back parts," carefully explained in later exegesis as the symbol of the material world. The importance of the invisibility of God's presence in the Holy of Holies has already been noted.

We come a little closer to an actual vision of God in the two great epiphanies of Isaiah 6 and Ezekiel 1. The AV ascribes to Isaiah the statement "I saw also the Lord sitting upon a throne, high and lifted up." There is an ancient legend, which could conceivably be more than a legend, that Isaiah was martyred by King Manasseh on the charge of having claimed to have had a direct vision of God. Ezekiel's vision of God's chariot, however, is diverted to the "wheels within wheels" (giving rise to a later tradition of a separate class of angels called "wheels") and to the four "living creatures" drawing it, identified as a man, a bull, a lion, and an eagle. In Christianity there would be less difficulty about such a vision, because what was seen would be the Son or Word of God, and it would be typologically easy for Christians to identify the four living creatures of Ezekiel (which reappear in Revelation 4:6ff.) with the writers of the four Gospels, that is, the carriers of the divine Word.

But even Christianity had its difficulties, as we see in the curious wording of John 1:18: "No man hath seen God at any time; the only begotten Son . . . hath declared him." The spoken words of Christ are recorded with great care, but his physical appearance, the fact that he was bound to resemble some people more closely than others, could never have been anything but an embarrassment. It is different with his second and final coming, when "every eye shall see him" (Revelation 1:7). The eye was satisfied before the beginning of history, in Eden where God made every tree "that is pleasant to the sight"

(Genesis 2:9), and the eye will be satisfied again in the last day, when all mysteries are revealed. But history itself is a period of listening in the dark for guidance through the ear.

The revolutionary context of this is clear enough. The word listened to and acted upon is the starting point of a course of action: the visible object brings one to a respectful halt in front of it. We have noted the persistent association of the world ruler with the sun, the starting point of the visible world; and the salute is said to have developed out of the ritual shading of one's eyes before the glory of a superior countenance. The metaphors "capital city" and "head of state" indicate how our social life is bound up with seeing heads, or more precisely faces. Greek culture focused on two powerful visual stimuli: the nude in sculpture, and the drama in literature. However important what is heard in a theater may be, the theater itself is primarily a visual experience, as the origin of the word "theater" (*theasthai*, to see) indicates. A polytheistic religion, again, must have statues or pictures to distinguish one god from another. The revolutionary tradition in Judaism, Christianity, and Islam has tended to a good deal of prudery about the naked body, to iconoclasm, and to a rejection of spectacular art, especially when representational.

The second commandment prohibits the making of "graven images" to represent either the true or any false god, and in Judaic and Islamic traditions particularly this has restricted, even eliminated, many aspects of representational art. In Christianity the intensifying of the original revolutionary impulse, such as we have in left-wing ("Puritan") Protestant movements, is regularly associated with iconoclasm. The use of icons in Christian churches was, of course, carefully protected by dogma against any confusion with idolatry, but that, also of course, did not prevent left-wing reformers from calling it idolatry, and going on periodic rampages of smashing stained glass and burning religious pictures. There were also some ferocious outbreaks of iconoclasm in Eastern Churches. Again, the Christian campaign against gladiatorial shows was prompted less by humanitarian motives than by a prejudice against spectacles. Tertullian, for example, urges the faithful to stay away from such spectacles and wait for the real spectacle, the sight of their enemies writhing in the torments of hell. The Puritan and Jansenist prejudice against "stage shows" is familiar, and needs only an allusion. The influence of the Greek tradition, or some aspects of it, has been of immense value to the Western world in counteracting the neuroses of its revolutionary religious tradition.

In all this it is easy to lose sight of the genuine feeling that underlies the hatred of idolatry. We have tried to show that the root of this hatred is a revolutionary impatience with a passive attitude toward nature and the gods assumed to be dominating it. This attitude of acceptance of external power, it is felt, assumes it to be far stronger than it is. Paul speaks (Galatians 4:9) of "the weak and beggarly elements, whereunto ye desire again to be in bondage." There is a great deal of visual imagery in the Bible, but that imagery has to be internalized, made the imaginative model of a transformed world. Of course the energy thereby withdrawn from nature is projected on God, but the attitude toward God is not intended to be passive. In the Old Testament God is naturally assumed to be capable of doing what Israel cannot do for itself, but his willingness to do it depends on their obedience to his law, and that is a strenuous and full-time activity. In the New Testament the activity described as faith is similarly assumed to be capable of generating miraculous results. Both are or include protests against any lotus-eating surrender to fate and the cycles of nature.

Third Phase: Law

Whatever the historical facts may have been, the Old Testament's narrative sequence, in which the giving of the law comes so soon after the Exodus, is logically and psychologically the right one. Mount Sinai follows the spoiling of the Egyptians as the night the day. A shared crisis gives a community a sense of involvement with its own laws, customs, and institutions, a sense of being a people set apart. Tocqueville noted, and Dickens in *Martin Chuzzlewit* satirized, this element in American life after the Revolution. The Revolution itself built a good deal on the New England Puritan feeling that their colony was an attempt to construct a new society in spite of the devil, so to speak, and was consequently exposed to his greater malice. A country founded on a revolution acquires a deductive way of thinking which is often encoded in constitutional law, and the American reverence for its Constitution, an inspired document to be amended and reinterpreted but never discarded, affords something of a parallel to the Old Testament sense of Israel as a people created by its law.

More extreme, more primitive, and to most of us far less desirable, is the sense of purity in a people linked together by common acts and beliefs. The conception of purity sets up an uncompromising superego model for human actions, which means that no society can live in a state of purity of any kind for very long. Hence the sense of purity soon modulates to the sense of a need for purging. The passages in Ezra and Nehemiah about Jews who are compelled to put away their foreign wives read very unpleasantly in this century of racism; yet the parallel with racism is not quite relevant. Any revolutionary society may have purges that are not necessarily on a racial basis. Closely associated with the purge is the idea of the saving remnant, a curiously pervasive theme in the Bible from the story of Gideon's army in Judges 7 to the exhortations to the seven churches of Asia Minor in Revelation. The feeling that a pure or homogeneous group, no matter how small, is the only socially effective one, and in times of crisis is the one to be kept for seed, so to speak, until a new age dawns, is an integral part of the revolutionary consciousness.

A society with a human hierarchy may be full of, or even founded on, injustice and exploitation. But the corruption that is bound to grow up in such a society at least affords loopholes that the wily, the indolent, and occasionally the genuinely honest, can take advantage of. The primitive Israelite society under Moses and Joshua is presented as living in the full glare of a theocratic dictatorship, where every rebellion is known to God and instantly annihilated. In the story of Achan in Joshua 7 we see how the acquisitiveness of one man, in keeping back for himself what is to be devoted to God, brought disaster to all Israel, and had to be atoned for by the destruction of Achan's entire family. The terrorism of an incorruptible society revived in the first generation of Christianity, and the corresponding story in the New Testament is that of Ananias and Sapphira in Acts 5.

The conception of law in the Bible is immensely complex, and we are concerned with it only as the third in our sequence of phases. We distinguish between two aspects of law: our obligations to society and the human observation of the repeating processes in nature. These two areas have little in common, and the grotesque pun on the word "law" which has connected or identified them entered our cultural heritage as the result of a conspiracy, so to speak, of Classical and Biblical tendencies. The conception of "natural law" was developed to establish a link between human law and the so-called laws of nature, but that belongs to the history of Western thought rather than to the study of the Bible. We have suggested that such a conception assumes two levels of nature, one intended by God for humanity alone, and the other the "fallen" or alienated nature that we see around us. Hence what is "natural" to man is not natural in the context of the world of animals and plants and stones, but includes the elements of culture and civilization. But as these are interpreted by the voice of established authority in human society, all arguments about what is really natural to man on the higher level are completely circular.

We spoke of the Greek sense of social contract, most obviously present at the end of the *Oresteia*, in which the gods, or at least the goddess of wisdom, are shown as endorsing a justice that extends over both moral and natural orders. At the heart of this justice is the sense of *nemesis*, the tendency in nature to recover its balance after an act of human aggression. This recovery of balance makes a tragic action in Greek drama not only morally but almost physically intelligible. Such *nemesis* may operate on the mechanical or *lex talionis* principle, as with the Furies, or in accordance with a higher form of equity; but in either case it demonstrates the return to balance that makes the scales the central emblem of justice. Such balance is very deeply rooted in nature: the Ionian philosopher Anaximander suggests that birth itself is a disturbance of balance, and that death is its inevitable *nemesis*.

The Bible has a very different view of nature, but it regards moral and natural orders as controlled by the same divine will, and hence it also identifies moral and natural law, in its own fashion. In a polytheistic religion there can be a clash of divine interests and wills, as there is a clash between Aphrodite and Artemis in *Hippolytus*, or a near-clash between Apollo and Athene in the *Oresteia*—to say nothing of the divine civil war provoked by the golden apple of the goddess Discord. Such clashes open the way to the conception of a fate overruling a variety of divine wills, and fate is really a metaphor for natural "law." Hence science develops more readily out of a polytheistic religion. In Homer there are sometimes suggestions that fate and the will of Zeus are the same thing, but there are other suggestions that the two are really different, and that fate is the stronger.

With an omnipotent personal God, however, we cannot really distinguish a miracle from a natural event, except by its rarity. Even after the rise of science, we suggested earlier, there is a persisting residual notion that in "natural law" too there is commanding and obedience, although it is clear that laws of nature are not "broken." If they appear to be, it is because there are other "laws" operating that we have not yet identified. Natural law in particular is traditionally regarded as the continuing of the divine creation in time, a view quite consistent with thinking of nature as having its own legal code which it automatically obeys. Hence in certain types of religious mind the right of God to suspend the "laws of nature" is vigorously defended, because law implies constraint and necessity, and overruling it affords a glimpse of a higher "providential" order manifesting the state before the fall, especially if the overruling is made in our favor. Natural law, however, like the divine creation of which it is an extension, is a conception we no longer know very clearly how to deal with, except to point out the difficulties of the metaphor involved and to say, with Sartre, that the problem of human freedom cannot be worked out wholly within the categories of man as we know him and nature as we see it.

Fourth Phase: Wisdom

The conception of wisdom in the Bible, as we see most clearly in some of the psalms, starts with the individualizing of law, with allowing the law, in its human and moral aspect, to permeate and inform all one's personal life. Law is general: wisdom begins in interpreting and commenting on law, and applying it to specific and variable situations. There are two wider principles in such wisdom. In the first place, the wise man is the one who follows in the accepted way, in what experience and tradition have shown to be the right way. The fool is the man with the new idea that always turns out to be an old fallacy. Such wisdom is dominated throughout by what may be called the anxiety of continuity. It goes with the authority of seniors, whose longer experience in the tried and tested modes of action makes them wiser than the young. The Book of Proverbs, traditionally assigned to Solomon, recommends the corporal punishment of one's sons, in a verse (19:18) that has probably been responsible for more physical pain than any other sentence ever written. In Ben Sirach's Ecclesiasticus, in the Apocrypha, this principle is expanded into a general enthusiasm for beating anyone within reach, including daughters and servants. What is behind this is not sadism but the attitude that has given so curiously penal a quality to the education of the young down to our own century. Education is the attaining of the right forms of behavior and the persistence in them, hence, like a horse, one has to be broken into them.

The second element in wisdom is inseparable from the first. The sense of continuity, or persistence in the right ways, relates primarily to the past: wisdom facing the future is prudence (Proverbs 8:12), a pragmatic following of the courses that maintain one's stability and balance from one day to the next. Perhaps the serpent is a symbol of wisdom because there is a good deal of wriggling and insinuating about choosing the wisest course of action. Prudent advice is communicated by the proverb, which is normally addressed to those without supreme advantages of birth or wealth, and provides advice on how to meet the various crises of social life. It is closely related to the fable, one of the few literary genres that are popular in the sense of possessing a genuine affinity with the lower ranks of society. The best-known purveyors of fables, Aesop and Phaedrus, were both slaves. The fable is not very prominent in the Old Testament, except that the Book of Job is an enormous expansion of one, but it comes into its own, as a vehicle of instruction, in the parables of Jesus. The proverb, on the other hand, is the kernel of wisdom literature, which consists largely of collections of proverbs. There seems to be something about the proverb that stirs the collector's instinct—which is natural if one accepts its usefulness as a key to success in life. Wisdom, as noted, is not knowledge: knowledge is of the particular and actual, and wisdom is rather a sense of the potential, of the way to deal with the kind of thing that may happen. It is this sense of the potential that the proverb is specifically designed to assist.

All the Near Eastern civilizations seem to have cultivated the proverb a good deal: the Egyptians, with their rigidly stratified society, were especially fond of it. Some ancient Egyptian proverbial material reappears in the Book of Proverbs, where it is already centuries old. Often the containing form is that of a father giving advice to his son, transmitting the ancestral and traditional wisdom of the culture in the manner of Polonius instructing Laertes in *Hamlet*, or, still later, Lord Chesterfield trying, in a series of letters, to make another Lord Chesterfield out of his lumpish offspring. Elsewhere it is a teacher instructing a pupil.

One typical piece of wisdom literature is the story of Ahikar, the sage and of course elderly counselor of the king of Nineveh (Assyria). Having no son, he adopts a nephew who turns out to be a scoundrel, plots against him, and manages to get him condemned to death. Ahikar escapes, through the usual romance formula in which a hired assassin develops a conscience, and goes to Egypt, where he also becomes a counselor. The king of Nineveh soon finds himself in difficulties, wishes audibly he had his adviser back, is told that Ahikar is still alive, sends for him and restores him to favor. Ahikar then takes a terrible revenge on his nephew by placidly reciting one proverb after another to him, an appreciable number of them concerned with the sin of ingratitude, until, the text demurely informs us, the nephew blows up and bursts. For a popular tale one can hardly miss with these ingredients: it has the superior wisdom and virtue of seniors, the dangers of trusting anyone under thirty, and any number of proverbs thrown in to improve the reader's mind. Ahikar has left his mark on at least the Apocrypha (Tobit is said to be Ahikar's uncle); on Greek literature, where he is identified with Aesop; and on the Koran (Sura 10), which as a rule has even less interest in secular literature than other sacred books.

The center of the conception of wisdom in the Bible is the Book of Ecclesiastes, whose author, or rather chief editor, is sometimes called Koheleth, the teacher or preacher. Koheleth transforms the conservatism of popular wisdom into a program of continuous mental energy. Those who have unconsciously identified a religious attitude either with illusion or with mental indolence are not safe guides to this book, although their tradition is a long one. Some editor with a "you'd better watch out" attitude seems to have tacked a few verses on to the end suggesting that God trusts only the anti-intellectual, but the main author's courage and honesty are not to be defused in this way. He is "disillusioned" only in the sense that he has realized that an illusion is a self-constructed prison. He is not a weary pessimist tired of life: he is a vigorous realist determined to smash his way through every locked door of repression in his mind. Being tired of life is in fact the only mental handicap for which he has no remedy to suggest. Like other wise men, he is a collector of proverbs, but he applies to all of them his touchstone and key word, translated in the AV as "vanity." This word (*hebel*) has a metaphorical kernel of fog, mist, or vapor, a metaphor that recurs in the New Testament (James 4:14). It thus acquires a derived sense of "emptiness," the root meaning of the Vulgate's *vanitas*. To put Koheleth's central intuition into the form of its essential paradox: all things are full of emptiness.

We should not apply a ready-made disapproving moral ambience to this word "vanity," much less associate it with conceit. It is a conception more like the *shunyata* or "void" of Buddhist thought: the world as everything within nothingness. As nothing is certain or permanent in the world, nothing either real or unreal, the secret of wisdom is detachment without withdrawal. All goals and aims may cheat us, but if we run away from them we shall find ourselves bumping into them. We may feel that a saint is a "better" man than a sinner, and that all our religious and moral standards would crumble into dust if we did not think so; but the saint himself is most unlikely to take such a view. Similarly, Koheleth went through a stage in which he saw that wisdom was "better" than folly, then a stage in which he saw that there was really no difference between them, as death lies in wait for both, and finally realized that both views were equally "vanity." As soon as we renounce the expectation of reward, in however refined a guise, for virtue or wisdom, we relax and our real energies begin to flow into the soul. Even the great elegy at the end over the failing bodily powers of old age ceases to become "pessimistic" when we see it as part of the detachment with which the wise man sees his life in the context of vanity.

We take what comes: there is no choice in the matter, hence no point in saying "we should take what comes." We soon realize by doing so that there is a cyclical rhythm in nature. But, like other wheels, this is a machine to be understood and used by man. If it is true that the sun, the seasons, the waters, and human life itself go in cycles, the inference is that "there is a time for all things," something different to be done at each stage of the cycle. The statement "There is nothing new under the sun" applies to wisdom but not to experience, to theory but not to practice. Only when we realize that nothing is new can we live with an intensity in which everything becomes new.

The creation began with air and light, the two symbols of "spirit." Air is the first thing we think of when we think of things that we can't see but know to exist, and in a sense we do not see light either: what we see is metaphorically fire, a source or reflection of light. We see by means of light and air: if we could see air we could see nothing else, and would be living in the dense fog that is one of the roots of the word "vanity." In the Bible the invisible world is not usually thought of as a separate and higher order of reality: it is thought of rather as the medium by which the world becomes visible (see Romans 1:20 and Hebrews 11:3). The invisible world, like the cyclical machinery of nature, is an opportunity for human energy, not a stifling darkness or a concealed revelation.

In Koheleth's inexhaustible treasury of common sense one of the shrewdest comments is that God has put *'olam* into man's mind (3:11). This word usually means something like "eternity," but in this context has rather the sense of mystery or obscurity. Eternity is a mental category that, in Keats's phrase, teases us out of thought: we do not know what it means, but as long as it is there we can never be satisfied with simplistic solutions. We are all born lost in a forest: if we assume either that the forest is there or that it is not there, we shall follow the rhythm of nature and walk endlessly in circles. The metaphor of fog or mist present in "vanity" suggests that life is something to find a way through, and that the way of wisdom is the way out.

The teaching of this book comes to a focus on a "work ethic" of "whatsoever thy hand findeth to do, do it with thy might" (9:10). The Preacher is not recommending activity for its own sake, but pointing to the release of energy that follows the giving up of our various excuses for losing our way in the fog: "Better is the sight of the eyes than the wandering of the desire" (6:9), as he says. But the phrase "work ethic" suggests the question of what is not work, and our normal habits of language tell us that one opposite of work, at least, is play. Work, as we usually think of it, is energy expended for a further end in view; play is energy expended for its own sake, as with children's play, or as a manifestation of the end or goal of work, as in "playing" chess or the piano. Play in this sense, then, is the fulfillment of work, the exhibition of what the work has been done for.

The Preacher is well aware of this connection, and emphasizes that we should "live joyfully" (9:9). But the point is even clearer in the Book of Proverbs, where Wisdom is personified as an attribute of God from the time of creation, expressing in particular the exuberance of creation, the spilling over of life and energy in nature that so deeply impresses the prophets and poets of the Bible. The AV speaks of this wisdom as "rejoicing in the habitable part of his earth" (8:31), but this is feeble compared to the tremendous Vulgate phrase *ludens in orbe terrarum, playing* over all the earth. Here we finally see the real form of wisdom in human life as the *philosophia* or *love* of wisdom that is creative and not simply erudite. We see too how the primitive form of wisdom, using past experience as a balancing pole for walking the tightrope of life, finally grows, through incessant discipline and practice, into the final freedom of movement where, in Yeats's phrase, we can no longer tell the dancer from the dance.

Fifth Phase: Prophecy

Wisdom, with its sense of continuity, repetition, precedent, and prudence, is the highest form of the ordinary functioning level of society. The revolution is far in the past; it is a part of tradition now, and without the fifth stage of prophecy the culture reflected in the Old Testament would have nothing unique about it. For prophecy is the individualizing of the revolutionary impulse, as wisdom is the individualizing of the law, and is geared to the future as wisdom is to the past.

Our earliest historical glimpse of the prophets of Western Asia is in the autobiographical account of the Egyptian envoy Wen-Amon, who encountered one at the court of Sidon in Phoenicia. They first appear in the Old Testament in ecstatic groups, working themselves into trance-like states with the aid of music, and then speaking with a different voice, no doubt assumed originally to have been the voice of the local god. Samuel says to Saul:

> Thou shalt meet a company of prophets coming down from the high place with a psaltery, and a tabret, and a pipe, and a harp, before them; and they shall prophesy:
> And the Spirit of the Lord will come upon thee, and thou shalt prophesy with them, and shall be turned into another man. (I Samuel 10:5-6)

The prophets, then, like the oracle priestesses in Greece, arose out of a primitive reverence for people with ecstatic powers. Not unnaturally there were those who discovered that there was a comfortable living to be made by the not very difficult effort of developing these powers, as long as one did not go far enough under to forget what the king wanted to hear. The great majority of prophets, the Old Testament itself makes clear, were well-broken-in functionaries either of the court or of the temple. So it is all the more interesting that the Old Testament should highlight so strongly a number of prophets who spoke out against royal policies and exposed themselves to persecution as a result. In the superbly told story of Micaiah (I Kings 22), in the dialogues with King Ahaz in the early part of Isaiah, in the account of Jeremiah's collisions with the last kings of Judah, the same point is constantly made: the prophet with the authentic message is the man with the unpopular message.

Many prophets, "cultic prophets" as they are called by scholars, were attached to the temple and spoke from within the orbit of priestly authority. But the distinction between prophetic and priestly authority is already established in the Pentateuch, where Moses is described as the greatest of Hebrew prophets (Deuteronomy 34:10), the priestly functions assigned to Aaron being quite separate. It is also Moses who wishes that all the Lord's people would become prophets (Numbers 11:29). Left to himself, Aaron goes wrong and makes an idolatrous golden calf; but though Moses makes human mistakes, the voice of prophecy in itself is conventionally regarded as infallible. Jesus, again, thinks of the prophetic tradition as one of martyrs to the testimony of God (Matthew 5:12), and clearly regards it as superior in authority to that of the "chief priests and the scribes."

Such prophets, though "called" by God and invariably claiming to speak with the voice or authority of God, are no longer simply ecstatics. They are advisers to princes even when their advice is furiously rejected, and they are rather people with what seems to be an open channel of communication between the conscious and the unconscious, if this way of putting it is not too anachronistic. As such, they represent an authority in society that most societies find the greatest difficulty in absorbing. The story of Cassandra is an example from a non-Biblical culture. Most prophets have to be accredited by either secular or spiritual authority as already established, because by what other criteria can a society distinguish a superior authority from an inferior one? Any self-deluded crank can call himself a prophet, and even the psychotics who assert that God has told them to murder somebody may appear sane enough at other times.

Both testaments reflect this difficulty: even in Saul's time there is a sharp distinction between the accredited prophets, whom Saul himself joined briefly, and such ecstatics as the Witch of Endor, who communicated with the spirits of the dead, conventionally assumed to have knowledge of the future. This contrast recurs also in Greek culture in a different form. There are gods above who appear in the *Iliad* and elsewhere in the disguise of a familiar person, in broad daylight, and giving advice on an immediate and specific situation. There are also sinister gods below who live with the spirits of the dead, and have to be invoked by midnight sacrifices of black animals and the like: these can reveal a more distant future, as when Odysseus consults the shade of Tiresias for information about his own death. The popular notion of a prophet is that of a man who can foretell the future, but the Biblical prophets as a rule take fairly short views, except when prophesying the future restoration of Israel.

The New Testament, like the Old, warns frequently against false prophets, but its criteria for distinguishing the genuine ones are not very precise. Paul, dealing with the ecstatic manifestations in the church of Corinth, says that "the spirits of the prophets are subject to the prophets" (I Corinthians 14:32), which apparently means that authentic prophets can control their ecstatic powers and are not taken over by them. The contrast between those inspired by the Holy Spirit and those who are possessed by devils recurs in I John 4, where it is proposed that spirits unwilling to testify to the Christian faith are to be known as evil, it being assumed that there are subjects on which even a lying spirit is afraid to lie. An uneasy transition is marked here between the early Christian detaching of prophetic authority from Jewish priestly authority and its later absorption into Christian priestly authority.

In the post-Biblical period both Christianity and Rabbinical Judaism seem to have accepted the principle that the age of prophecy had ceased, and to have accepted it with a good deal of relief. Medieval Europe had a High King and a High Priest, an Emperor and a Pope, but the distinctively prophetic third force was not recognized. The exceptions prove the rule. The career of Savonarola is again one of martyrdom, and the same is true of Joan of Arc, who illustrates the inability of a hierarchical society to distinguish a Deborah from a Witch of Endor. The liberty of prophesying was supposed to be one of the issues of the Reformation, but it can hardly be said that Protestantism succeeded in developing a prophetic authority distinct from a priestly one: its prophets never strayed very far from pulpits. It is Milton in the *Areopagitica* who, perhaps without fully realizing it, gives us a clue to some of the sources of the prophetic element in modern society. They may come through the printing press, more particularly from writers who arouse social resentment and resistance because they speak with an authority that society is reluctant to recognize. Such authority, in this context, is certainly not infallible, but it may be genuine insight nonetheless. Tolerance for creative minds as potentially prophetic, even without ready-made standards and certainly without any belief in their infallibility, seems to be a mark of the most mature societies. In the modern world, therefore, what corresponds to prophetic authority is the growth of what we called earlier a cultural pluralism, where, for example, a scientist or historian or artist may find that his subject has its own inner authority, that he makes discoveries within it that may conflict with social concern, and that he owes a loyalty to that authority even in the face of social opposition.

Prophecy in the Bible is a comprehensive view of the human situation, surveying it from creation to final deliverance, and it is a view which marks the extent of what in other contexts we could call the creative imagination. It incorporates the perspective of wisdom but enlarges it. The wise man thinks of the human situation as a kind of horizontal line, formed by precedent and tradition and extended by prudence: the prophet sees man in a state of alienation caused by his own distractions, at the bottom of a U-shaped curve. We shall come to this U-shaped curve later as the unit of narrative in the Bible. It postulates an original state of relative happiness, and looks forward to an eventual restoration of this state, to, at least, a "saving remnant." The wise man's present moment is the moment in which past and future are balanced, the uncertainties of the future being minimized by the observance of the law that comes down from the past. The prophet's present moment is an alienated prodigal son, a moment that has broken away from its own identity in the past but may return to that identity in the future. We can see from this that the Book of Job, though it is classed with wisdom literature and includes a eulogy of wisdom, cannot be understood by the canons of wisdom alone, but needs the help of the prophetic perspective.

Sixth Phase: Gospel

The gospel (restricting our comment on it to the perspective of this chapter) is a further intensifying of the prophetic vision. That vision, we suggested, had two levels: the level of the present moment and a level above it. The latter is both that of the original identity symbolized by the garden of Eden (along with, as we shall see, the Promised Land and the Temple), and the ultimate identity symbolized by the return to these things after the "Day of the Lord" and the restoring of Israel. Jesus' teaching centers on the conception of a present spiritual kingdom that includes all these upper-level images, and on earth he is thought of as living simultaneously in it and among us.

To express this there have to be secondary metaphors of "descending" from the higher level, or "heaven," and of "ascending" back into it again. Prophecies of the restoration of Israel such as Isaiah's prophecy of Emmanuel in Isaiah 7, and Ezekiel's vision of the valley of dry bones in Ezekiel 37, were interpreted by Christians as types of the Incarnation or the Resurrection. Paul's brilliant phrase for the Incarnation is "He emptied himself" (Philippians 2:7; the AV's rendering is not a translation but an inept gloss). That is, he "descended" or was born into the world of vanity or total emptiness. The return to the spiritual world is "resurrection," a conception which, though it is a return from death, can hardly be confined to the revival of a dead body in a tomb. Jesus sometimes speaks of his central doctrine of a spiritual kingdom as a mystery, a secret imparted to his disciples (though they often got it wrong too), with those outside the initiated group being put off with parables (Mark 4:11). It seems clear, however, that the real distinction between initiated and uninitiated is between those who think of achieving the spiritual kingdom as a way of life and those who understand it merely as a doctrine.

The way of life is described as beginning in *metanoia*, a word translated "repentance" by the AV, which suggests a moralized inhibition of the "stop doing everything you want to do" variety. What the word primarily means, however, is change of outlook or spiritual metamorphosis, an enlarged vision of the dimensions of human life. Such a vision, among other things, detaches one from one's primary community and attaches him to another. When John the Baptist says "Bring forth fruits worthy of *metanoia*" (Matthew 3:8), he is addressing Jews, and goes on to say that their primary social identity (descent from Abraham) is of no spiritual importance. What one repents of is sin, a word that means nothing outside a religious and individualized context. That is, sin is not illegal or antisocial behavior. The "deadly" or mortal sins that destroy the soul were classified in the Middle Ages as pride, wrath, sloth, envy, avarice, gluttony, and lechery; and of these, heavily moralized as they are, not one necessarily results in criminal or antisocial acts. Sin is rather a matter of trying to block the activity of God, and it always results in some curtailing of human freedom, whether of oneself or of one's neighbor.

The dialectic of *metanoia* and sin splits the world into the kingdom of genuine identity, presented as Jesus' "home," and a hell, a conception found in the Old Testament only in the form of death or the grave. Hell is that, but it is also the world of anguish and torment that man goes on making for himself all through history. Jesus describes it in imagery of an undying worm and an unquenched fire, taken from the last verse of Isaiah, which speaks of the dead bodies of those overthrown in the final *culbute*. As a form of vision, *metanoia* reverses our usual conceptions of time and space. The central points of time and space are now and here, neither of which exists in ordinary experience. In ordinary experience "now" continually vanishes between the no longer and the not yet; we may think of "here" as a hazy mental circumference around ourselves, but whatever we locate in ordinary space, inside it or outside it, is "there" in a separated alien world. In the "kingdom" the eternal and infinite are not time and space made endless (they *are* endless already) but are the now and the here made real, an actual present and an actual presence. Time vanishes in Jesus' "Before Abraham was, I am" (John 8:58); space vanishes when we are told, in an aphorism previously referred to, that the kingdom is *entos hymon* (Luke 17:21), which may mean among you or in you, but in either case means here, not there.

In its relation to the previous phrases, the gospel of *metanoia* makes man a "new creature" (II Corinthians 5:17), in which the original and now fallen order of nature becomes a mother bringing to birth a re-creation made through a union of God and man (Romans 8:21). It is the reappearance in human life of the higher or transfigured nature, the innocent world before the fall. The revolutionary thrust of the Exodus is also preserved, and Jesus often speaks of "faith" as though it gave the individual as much effective power as the Exodus gave the whole society of Israel. Such faith clearly includes a power of action informed by a vision transcending time and space. In the Old Testament law and wisdom follow the deliverance from Egypt. The totalitarian conception of law, in which the breaker of an obligation to God is to be wiped out with his family (Joshua 7:24), had already given way to the principle that the individual alone was responsible for what he did (Ezekiel 18:20). One of the pseudepigrapha, II Baruch, speaks of the law among us and the wisdom within us (48:24). But the gospel is a different kind of individualizing of the law, founded on the category of prophecy. We remarked earlier that Christianity thinks of the Old Testament as primarily a book of prophecy rather than of law; and the principle involved here needs careful stating.

We spoke earlier of the latent terrorism in the rule of law, which has been seen many times in history since the Old Testament, and is often a post-revolutionary feeling. A great experience has been shared: the society feels drawn together into a single body, and social and individual standards become, for a necessarily brief period, assimilated. Plato's *Republic* outlines an ideal society on the analogy of the wise man's mind, where the reason is a dictatorial philosopher-king, the will a ruthless thought-police hunting down every subversive impulse, and the natural impulses of appetite, though allowed to function, are rigidly controlled. At the end of the ninth book Socrates suggests that such a society could perhaps never exist, but that wise men may and do exist, and the wise man would live by the laws of such a republic, whatever his actual social context. As an allegory of the wise man's mind, the *Republic* is a powerful vision; as an ideal social order, it would be a fantastic tyranny.

Similarly, the Sermon on the Mount is in part a commentary on the Ten Commandments in which the negative commands not to kill or commit adultery or steal are positively stated as an enthusiasm for human life, a habitual respect for the dignity of a woman, a delight in sharing goods with those who need them. Such a gospel, Paul says, sets one free of the law—and of course we do not get free of the law by breaking the law, only more fouled up with it than ever. But the standards of the highly integrated individual are far more rigorous than those that apply to society in general, hence the gospel made into a new social law would again be the most frightful tyranny. Thus, according to Milton, Jesus condemns divorce because "marriage" for him means spiritual marriage, the model of which is Adam and Eve in Eden, for each of whom there was, very exactly, no one else. Such a marriage would not be "consummated," which means finished, at the first sexual union, but only by the death of one of the partners. But to assume that every sexual liaison or marriage contract in ordinary society is a spiritual marriage of this type would pervert the gospel into a new law.

Whether Milton is right or wrong, he is assuming a prophetic rather than a legal basis for the gospel. Let us go back to Plato for another illustration. The one thing which has caught everyone's imagination in Plato is the figure of Socrates, the archetypal teacher and prophet, "corrupting" the youth of Athens by showing them that when they express social stereotypes about love or courage or justice or pleasure they have not the faintest idea what they are talking about. We see this Socrates, in the *Apology* and the *Phaedo*, facing martyrdom without making any concession to the ignorance and stupidity of his accusers. But Plato himself was a revolutionary thinker, and in the *Laws* he draws up a blueprint for his own post-revolutionary society. In that society all teachers are to be most strictly supervised and instructed what to teach: everything depends on their complete subservience to the overall social vision. Socrates does not appear in the *Laws*, and no such person as Socrates could exist in such a society. We should be careful to understand what Plato is doing here. He is really assuming that those who condemned Socrates were right in principle, and wrong only—if wrong at all by that time—in their application of it.

Similarly, Christianity is founded on a prophet who was put to death as a blasphemer and a social menace, hence any persecuting Christian is assuming that Pilate and Caiaphas were right in principle, and should merely have selected a different victim. The significance of the life of Jesus is often thought of as a legal significance, consisting in a life of perfect morality, or total conformity to a code of right action. But if we think of his significance as prophetic rather than legal, his real significance is that of being the one figure in history whom no organized human society could possibly put up with. The society that rejected him represented all societies: those responsible for his death were not the Romans or the Jews or whoever happened to be around at the time, but the whole of mankind down to ourselves and doubtless far beyond. "It is expedient that one man die for the people," said Caiaphas (John 18:14), and there has never been a human society that has not agreed with him.

What primarily distinguishes Christianity (and Judaism) from most Oriental religions, it seems to me, is this revolutionary and prophetic element of confrontation with society. This element gives meaning and shape to history by presenting it with a dialectical challenge. From this point of view, the root of evil in human life cannot be adequately described as ignorance, or the cure for it correctly described as enlightenment. The record of human cruelty and folly is too hideous for anything but the sense of a corrupted will to come near to a diagnosis. Hence Jesus was not simply the compassionate Jesus as Buddha was the compassionate Buddha. His work, though it includes the teaching of ways of enlightenment, does not stop there, but goes through a martyrdom and a descent into death. Two implications here are of especial importance for our present purpose. One, a specifically historical situation is latent in any "enlightenment": man has to fight his way out of history and not simply awaken from it. Two, the ability to absorb a complete individual is, so far, beyond the capacity of any society, including those that call themselves Christian.

Anti-Semitism is a long-standing corruption of Christianity, and one of the more rationalized pretexts for it is the notion that the legalism condemned in the New Testament is to be identified with Judaism. But this is a very dubious interpretation of even the most polemical parts of the New Testament, and is not found at all in the teaching of Jesus. Jesus always attacks a quite specific elite or pseudo-elite of chief priests, scribes, lawyers, Pharisees, Sadducees, and other "blind guides" (Matthew 23:24), but not the precepts of the religion he was brought up in himself. What Jesus condemned in Pharisaism is as common in Christianity as in any other religion. The attack on legalism is in a quite different context: it means accepting the standards of society, and society will always sooner or later line up with Pilate against the prophet.

In the Book of Leviticus the ritual for the Day of Atonement, which we shall come to again, consisted in separating a symbolic figure of a goat ("scapegoat," as the AV calls it), which represented their accumulated sin, from the community of Israel. The antitype of this, in the Christian view, is the separation of Christ from the human community, an atonement that reunites God with man. It was unfortunate for the English language that the originally comic pronunciation of "one" as "wun" should have caught on, as it obscures the connection of "one" with other words derived from it, such as "alone" and "only." More relevant for us at the moment is its obscuring of the fact that the radical meaning of "atonement" is "unifying." The AV speaks of atonement mainly in the sense of making reparation for sin, and in an Old Testament context. The "unifying" implications of atonement take us much further than this. They suggest that a channel of communication between the divine and the human is now open, and hence the whole metaphorical picture of the relation of man and God has to be reversed. Man does not stand in front of an invisible but objective power making conciliatory gestures of ritual and moral obligation to him: such gestures express nothing except his own helplessness.

Let us take an example from outside the Biblical area. The Roman Saturnalia festival, in which masters waited on their slaves in memory of the golden age of Saturn, was a dumb, helpless gesture which said symbolically that the slave structure of Roman society was all wrong, but that nothing could or would be done about it. For Paul and the author of Hebrews the old sacrificial rituals, like the Saturnalia, were "vanity": empty actions in an empty world, even though the good will they expressed had a symbolic or typical value. In the changed metaphor man has an infinite energy behind him that is now available to him: a God who is invisible because he does the seeing. The metaphor of a God behind, a power that can do anything through man, seems implicit in Jesus' strong emphasis on God as a "Father," the hidden source of his own energy. Once again, changes in metaphor are fundamental changes, and here we may glimpse the possibility of getting past the pseudo-issues growing out of the metaphor of a divine presence in front of us, who may be believed or disbelieved "in" because he may or may not be "there." Theist and atheist are at one in regarding personality as the highest category known to experience. Whether it is possible for human personality to be connected with and open to a divine one that is its own infinite extension may still be a question, but the more solid the metaphorical basis for either side, the more possibility there is of mutual understanding.

So far we have spoken in individual terms, but the gospel also brings in a new conception of "Israel" as the citizens of the kingdom of God. The notion that any group of such citizens, such as women or slaves, is inherently second-class is nonsense (Galatians 3:28). Such a society is not the ordinary society out of which we grow from birth, but a re-created society growing out of an individual. Its type is the society descended from an eponymous ancestor, as the society of Israel grew out of the body of Jacob. The conception of a possible social resurrection, a transformation that will split the world of history into a spiritual kingdom and a hell, is a part of the gospel teaching itself, though an easy part to misunderstand. I think we do misunderstand it if we assume that everyone in the New Testament period thought that the world was coming to an end at once, and that consequently Jesus himself must have been equally confused about the matter. No doubt there were many for whom the "end of the world" was a simply future event, but we have suggested that a rather subtler notion of time than that seems to be involved in Jesus' teachings.

Seventh Phase: Apocalypse

The Greek word for revelation, *apocalypsis*, has the metaphorical sense of uncovering or taking a lid off, and similarly the word for truth, *aletheia*, begins with a negative particle which suggests that truth was originally thought of as also a kind of unveiling, a removal of the curtains of forgetfulness in the mind. In more modern terms, perhaps what blocks truth and the emerging of revelation is not forgetting but repression. We have noted that the last book in the Bible, the one explicitly called Revelation or Apocalypse, is a mosaic of allusions to the Old Testament: that is, it is a progression of antitypes. The author speaks of setting down what he has seen in a vision, but the Book of Revelation is not a visualized book in the ordinary sense of the word, as any illustrator who has struggled with its seven-headed and ten-horned monsters will testify. What the seer in Patmos had a vision of was primarily, as he conceived it, the true meaning of the Scriptures, and his dragons and horsemen and dissolving cosmos were what he saw in Ezekiel and Zechariah, whatever or however he saw on Patmos.

The general material of the vision is the familiar material of prophecy: there is again a *culbute générale* in which the people of God are raised into recognition and the heathen kingdoms are cast into darkness. There are portentous events in both social and natural orders: plagues, wars, famines, great stars falling from heaven, and an eventual transformation, for those who persist in the faith, of the world into a new heaven and earth. We are greatly oversimplifying the vision, however, if we think of it simply as what the author thought was soon going to happen, as a firework show that would be put on for the benefit of the faithful, starting perhaps next Tuesday. For him all these incredible wonders are the inner meaning or, more accurately, the inner form of everything that is happening now. Man creates what he calls history as a screen to conceal the workings of the apocalypse from himself.

St. John the Divine sees all this "in the spirit" (1:10), with his spiritual body, and the spiritual body is the most deeply repressed element of experience. The *culbute* he describes is political in only one of its aspects. The chief enemy, symbolized as a "Great Whore," is "spiritually" called Babylon, but she is also called "Mystery" (17:5). The word "mystery" is extensively used in the New Testament in both a good and a bad sense: there is a mystery of the kingdom (Matthew 13:11 and elsewhere) and a mystery of iniquity (II Thessalonians 2:7). Nothing is more mysterious to the world than the half-esoteric beliefs of the primitive Christians, and nothing more obvious and apparent than, say, the power of the Emperor Nero. But the mystery turns into a revelation of how things really are, and the obvious power of Nero rolls into the darkness of the mystery of the corrupted human will from whence it emerged. The vision of the apocalypse is the vision of the total meaning of the Scriptures, and may break on anyone at any time. It comes like a thief in the night (Revelation 16:15, cf. I Thessalonians 5:2: this phrase is one of the few links between Revelation and the rest of the New Testament). What is symbolized as the destruction of the order of nature is the destruction of the way of seeing that order that keeps man confined to the world of time and history as we know them. This destruction is what the Scripture is intended to achieve.

There are, then, two aspects of the apocalyptic vision. One is what we may call the panoramic apocalypse, the vision of staggering marvels placed in a near future and just before the end of time. As a panorama, we look at it passively, which means that it is objective to us. This in turn means that it is essentially a projection of the subjective "knowledge of good and evil" acquired at the fall. That knowledge, we now see, was wholly within the framework of law: it is contained by a final "judgment," where the world disappears into its two unending constituents, a heaven and a hell, into one of which man automatically goes, depending on the relative strength of the cases of the prosecution and the defense. Even in heaven, the legal vision tells us, he remains eternally a creature, praising his Creator unendingly.

Anyone coming "cold" to the Book of Revelation, without context of any kind, would probably regard it as simply an insane rhapsody. It has been described as a book that either finds a man mad or else leaves him so. And yet, if we were to explore below the repressions in our own minds that keep us "normal," we might find very similar nightmares of anxiety and triumph. As a parallel example, we may cite the so-called Tibetan Book of the Dead, where the soul is assumed immediately after death to be going through a series of visions, first of peaceful and then of wrathful deities. A priest reads the book into the ear of the corpse, who is also assumed to hear the reader's voice telling him that all these visions are simply his own repressed mental forms now released by death and coming to the surface. If he could realize that, he would immediately be delivered from their power, because it is his own power.

If we take a similar approach to the Book of Revelation, we find, I think, that there is a second or participating apocalypse following the panoramic one. The panoramic apocalypse ends with the restoration of the tree and water of life, the two elements of the original creation. But perhaps, like other restorations, this one is a type of something else, a resurrection or upward metamorphosis to a new beginning that is now present. We notice that while the Book of Revelation seems to be emphatically the end of the Bible, it is a remarkably open end. It contains such statements as "Behold, I make all things new" (21:5); it describes God as the Alpha and Omega, the beginning and end of all possibilities of verbal expression; it follows the vision of the restoring of the water of life with an earnest invitation to drink of it. The panoramic apocalypse gives way, at the end, to a second apocalypse that, ideally, begins in the reader's mind as soon as he has finished reading, a vision that passes through the legalized vision of ordeals and trials and judgments and comes out into a second life. In this second life the creator-creature, divine-human antithetical tension has ceased to exist, and the sense of the transcendent person and the split of subject and object no longer limit our vision. After the "last judgment," the law loses its last hold on us, which is the hold of the legal vision that ends there.

We suggested earlier that the Bible deliberately blocks off the sense of the referential from itself: it is not a book pointing to a historical presence outside it, but a book that identifies itself with that presence. At the end the reader, also, is invited to identify

himself with the book. Milton suggests that the ultimate authority in
the Christian religion is what he calls the Word of God in the heart,
which is superior even to the Bible itself, because for Milton this
"heart" belongs not to the subjective reader but to the Holy Spirit.
That is, the reader completes the visionary operation of the Bible by
throwing out the subjective fallacy along with the objective one. The
apocalypse is the way the world looks after the ego has disappeared.

   In our discussion of creation we were puzzled by the paradox in
the word when applied to human activity. God, we are told, made a
"good" world; man fell into a bad world and the good one vanished;
consequently *human* creativity has in it the quality of *re*-creation, of
salvaging something with a human meaning out of the alienation of
nature. At the end of the Book of Revelation, with such phrases as "I
make all things new" (21:5) and the promise of a new heaven and
earth, we reach the antitype of all antitypes, the real beginning of
light and sound of which the first word of the Bible is the type.

METAPHOR II
Imagery

In this chapter I begin a summary of the Bible as it appears to practical criticism, starting with its imagery. The natural images of the Bible are a primarily poetic feature of it, and we have already seen something of the general structure underlying them. There are two levels of nature: the lower one, expressed in God's contract with Noah, presupposes a nature to be dominated and exploited by man; the higher one, expressed in an earlier contract with Adam in Paradise, is the nature to which man essentially belongs, and the Eden story prefigures the redemption which takes him back to this upper level. On the way from the lower level to the higher one we meet the images of the world of work, the pastoral, agricultural, and urban imagery that suggest a nature transformed into a humanly intelligible shape. The Bible's structure of imagery, then, contains, among other things, the imagery of sheep and pasture, the imagery of harvest and vintage, the imagery of cities and temples, all contained in and infused by the oasis imagery of trees and water that suggests a higher mode of life altogether.

These images constitute part of what I call the apocalyptic world, the ideal world (looking at it from one point of view) which the human creative imagination envisages, which human energy tries to bring into being, and which the Bible presents also as a form of "revelation": the vision, the model, the blueprint that gives direction and purpose to man's energies. We have next to set this apocalyptic structure in its context. In the first place, there is the problem that the nations outside Israel—Egypt, Babylon, Assyria, Phoenicia—are as a rule more wealthy, prosperous, and successful than Israel. They possess the power and domination that the Israelites themselves desperately longed to possess, and would certainly have regarded as a signal mark of divine favor if they had possessed it. The only recourse is to show this heathen success in a context of demonic parody, as a short-lived triumph that has all the marks of the real thing except permanence. It follows that there must be two forms of demonic imagery: the parody-demonic, attached to temporarily successful heathen nations; and the manifest, or you-just-wait demonic, the ruins and wasteland haunted by hyenas and screech owls that all this glory will eventually and inevitably become. In between the demonic and the apocalyptic come the Old Testament types, which the Christian Bible regards as symbols or parables of the existential form of salvation presented in the New.

As an example of this structure, let us look at a group of female figures in the Bible. We may divide them into two groups: the maternal and the marital, mother figures and bride figures. Apocalyptic mother figures include the Virgin Mary and the mysterious woman crowned with stars who appears at the beginning of Revelation 12, and who is presented also as the mother of the Messiah. Bridal figures include the central female character of the Song of Songs and the symbolic Jerusalem of Revelation 21 who descends to earth prepared "like a bride adorned for her husband" and is finally identified with the Christian Church. Intermediate maternal figures include Eve and Rachel, the latter being thought of as the typical wife of Jacob or Israel and hence as the symbolic mother of Israel (Matthew 2:18). Eve in particular is the intermediate female maternal figure, "our general mother," in Milton's phrase, going through the cycle of sin and redemption.

There seems to be no demonic maternal figure, which means that later legend will probably supply one. Later legend obliged by constructing the figure of Lilith, a night-monster probably of Sumerian origin mentioned in Isaiah 34:14. (She is called a "screech owl" in the AV; one of the chief weaknesses of the AV is its overfondness for rationalized translations.) Lilith was said to have been the first wife of Adam, partly in an effort to reconcile the Priestly account of the creation of woman in Genesis 1:27 with the older Jahwist account which begins in Genesis 2:4 and tells of the creation of Eve from

Adam's body. Lilith was allegedly the mother of the demons or false spirits, and in consequence had a flourishing career in the Romantic period, appearing in Goethe's *Faust* and as the heroine of a romance by George MacDonald.

The demonic counterpart of the Bride who is Jerusalem and the spouse of Christ is the Great Whore of Revelation 17 who is Babylon and Rome, and is the mistress of Antichrist. The word "whoredom" in the Bible usually refers to theological rather than sexual irregularity. The term was adopted not simply as abusive, but because of the practice of maintaining cult prostitutes in Canaanite temples. In Deuteronomy 23:18 the Israelites are forbidden to have anything to do with this practice, but the story in Genesis 38 of Tamar, who disguises herself as a cult prostitute to help her gain recognition from her father-in-law Judah, indicates that it was familiar to them. Later on, male prostitutes, the "sodomites" of I Kings 14:24 and elsewhere, seem to have flourished as well. Jezebel, Ahab's queen, is treated as a whore not because she was believed to have cuckolded Ahab—the narrator of Kings could hardly have cared whether she did or not—but because she introduced the worship of Baal into northern Israel.

But, of course, Israel itself is symbolically the chosen bride of God, and is also frequently unfaithful to him. This infidelity comes into Ezekiel 16 and the story of Aholah and Aholibah in Ezekiel 23, as well as into the story in Hosea 1 of that prophet's marriage to two unfaithful women, symbolically north and south Israel. Thus the forgiven harlot, who is taken back eventually into favor despite her sins, is an intermediate bridal figure between the demonic Whore and the apocalyptic Bride, and represents the redemption of man from sin. She appears in the Gospels as the "sinner" of Luke 7:37-50, often identified with the Mary Magdalen who appears in the next chapter. There is also the woman taken in adultery who has firmly established squatter's rights on the beginning of John 8, despite the efforts of nervous editors, ancient and modern, to get her out of there. In most paintings of the Crucifixion the Virgin Mary and Mary Magdalen, one in blue and the other in red, stand beside the cross. The word "eros" does not occur in the New Testament, but the woman whose sins were forgiven because she "loved much" (Luke 7:47) is there to remind us that if there is anything in human nature worth redeeming, it is inseparable from Eros. Rahab, the harlot of Jericho who admitted the Israelite spies (Joshua 6:17), also figures prominently in this category, largely, in Christianity, by virtue of the reference to her in Hebrews 11:31. Thus:

	Demonic	Analogical	Apocalyptic
Maternal	[Lilith]	Eve; Rachel	Virgin Mary; Woman of Revelation 12
Marital	Great Whore (Babylon); Jezebel	Forgiven Harlot (Ezekiel 23; Hosea 1; John 8; Luke 7:37ff; Rahab)	Bride of Song of Songs; Jerusalem

The Bible begins with man in a paradisal state, where his relation to nature was of an idealized kind suggesting a relation of identity on equal terms. The imagery of the garden of Eden is an oasis imagery of trees and water. For a people who were originally desert dwellers, the oasis is the inevitable image of providential order, a garden directly created and sustained by God, a habitation that makes sense in human terms without human transformation, the visible form of the invisible divine creation. This paradisal imagery overlaps to some degree, as it does all through later literature, with idealized pastoral imagery. The Old Testament writers used the imagery of a seminomadic life of a shepherd following and protecting his sheep as they go to pasture, often straying and getting lost in the process, to represent a people in a state of constant though often confused loyalty to their God. The lovely twenty-third Psalm is the most famous expression of this, and the symbolism of the "Good Shepherd" attached to Jesus is its New Testament counterpart. The pastoral metaphors of "pastor" and "flock" survive in language about the Church.

We spoke of the sequence of pastoral, agricultural, and urban phases of imagery in the history of Israel. The archetypes of all three are established much earlier in the Biblical narrative. Directly following the expulsion of Adam and Eve from Eden, we have the story of the farmer Cain and the shepherd Abel. Disputes between a farmer and a shepherd are found centuries earlier in Sumerian literature, but there the farmer scores off the shepherd, as is natural for a country dependent on irrigation and a rotation of crops. But the Biblical writers tended to idealize the pastoral stage of Israelite life, in contrast to the agricultural stage, where contamination by the neighboring cults of Canaan was so frequent and pervasive. Hence Abel's pastoral offering to God of the sacrifice of a lamb, "not without blood" (Hebrews 9:7), was accepted, and Cain's bloodless offering of firstfruits was not. Abel's sacrifice was the type of the primary festival of the Jewish Passover, and the murdered shepherd Abel was also, for Christianity, a type of Christ, whose passion coincided with the Passover, a human victim identified with the Passover Lamb, just as Abel, by his death, is identified with his sacrifice.

One reason Cain's offering was not accepted was, apparently, that God had cursed the ground after Adam's fall (Genesis 3:17). But after the Deluge this curse was removed, the reason being, we are told, that the deity was in a good mood because Noah had just made a tremendous massacre of animals as a burnt offering in his honor, and he highly approved of the smell (Genesis 8:21). So a contract with Noah, already mentioned, was made that seems to have something to do with the establishing of an agricultural economy. Noah is promised the regularity in the cycle of nature that is the basis of farming life:

While the earth remaineth, seedtime and harvest, and cold and heat, and summer and winter, and day and night shall not cease. (Genesis 8:22)

So Noah becomes a farmer, whose first agricultural feat, human nature being what it is, is to discover wine and get drunk.

After the patriarchal pastoral period, the Israelites descend to Egypt, and there, at the beginning of Exodus, they are promised "a land flowing with milk and honey" (Exodus 3:8), neither of which is a vegetable product. But the first symbol of Canaan (the name is derived from the purple murex dye, suggesting "Red Land," and Phoenicia is its Greek equivalent) was an enormous bunch of grapes (Numbers 13:24). After Joshua's conquest the Israelites settled down, with some reluctance, to a farming life:

And they did eat of the old corn of the land on the morrow after the Passover, unleavened cakes, and parched corn in the selfsame day.

And the manna ceased on the morrow after they had eaten of the old corn of the land; neither had the children of Israel manna any more; but they did eat of the fruit of the land of Canaan that year. (Joshua 5:11-12)

The agricultural festivals of harvest and vintage were added to the Passover, and expanded later into Pentecost and the feast of "booths," respectively. But the contact with Canaanite customs added to the law many regulations that might be called negative rituals, things the Israelites were forbidden to do because their neighbors did them. Thus the commandment not to seethe a kid in its mother's milk (Exodus 34:26 and elsewhere), the basis for the present kosher rule about separating milk and meat dishes, probably alludes to a Canaanite fertility rite, as the notion of boiling a kid in its mother's milk would hardly occur to anyone off the top of his head. The Old Testament is consistently edgy and hostile about the vegetative dying-god symbolism that became so central in Christianity, and we notice that the story of Noah ends in an incident that rationalizes the subjection of Canaanites to Israel (Genesis 9:25).

Cain is said to have built a "city" (Genesis 4:17), when the context seems to imply that there were at most only half a dozen people alive in the world. The identity of Cain's wife, in particular, was a puzzle to readers before it was realized that the Cain stories came from a variety of sources. What is interesting is the narrator's evident assumption that cities, not villages or hamlets or individual dwellings, were the oldest historical forms of human settlement. Similarly, Abraham and Moses are represented, not as originally pastoral or desert dwellers, but as having come from the cities of Mesopotamia and Egypt, respectively. There may even be evidence that the word "Hebrew," which appears to be a somewhat pejorative term when used by outsiders, originally meant something more like "proletariat" than a conventional name for a people.

We proceed now to examine in greater detail the structure of five bodies of imagery in the Bible: the paradisal, the pastoral, the agricultural, the urban, and the imagery of human life itself.

In the description of Eden at the beginning of the Bible the emphasis in imagery falls on trees and water:

And out of the ground made the Lord God to grow every tree that is pleasant to the sight, and good for food; the tree of life also in the midst of the garden, and the tree of knowledge of good and evil. (Genesis 2:9)

There are also four rivers: three are identified as the Nile, the Euphrates, and the Tigris; the fourth, "Pison," is the Ganges according to Josephus, though he may have meant the Indus. These rivers all spring from one source (the "mist" of the AV's rendering of Genesis 2:6 is *pege*, fountain, in the Septuagint). A source common to these four rivers, which would stretch from mid-Africa to mid-Asia, could only be a sea of fresh water under the ground, different from the salt sea but coming to the surface in springs and wells. This "fountain" is not explicitly called the water of life in the Genesis account, but symbolically that is clearly what it is. Adam and Eve, then, when they are expelled from Eden, lose the tree and water of life, and at the very end of the Bible it is the tree and water of life that are restored to redeemed mankind (Revelation 22:1-2). These two images are thus the clearest indications of a beginning and an end to the Biblical narrative, as the images of the world that man has lost but is eventually to regain.

In the middle of the Bible comes the prophecy of Ezekiel, represented as having been written during the Babylonian captivity and as looking forward to a return of the Jews from exile to their homeland, where their first achievement will be the rebuilding of the Temple and the restoration of centralized worship there. As soon as the Temple is completed, we are told, a spring of water bubbles up from its threshold and becomes a great river, flowing to the east with many trees along its banks (Ezekiel 47:1-17). Similarly, Zechariah (13:1: the book of Zechariah consists of two quite different prophecies stuck together, and this is from the second one) prophesies the opening of a "fountain" in Jerusalem.

Both prophets speak also of rain and "showers of blessings" (Ezekiel 34:26), though the context of rain is agricultural rather than paradisal; rain at the wrong time can be destructive, and consequently the statements about it are more guarded. Zechariah (14:17-19) says that, once centralized worship at the Temple is restored, those Jews who do not come up to Jerusalem once a year will have no rain. It then occurs to him that some Jews will be living in Egypt, where there is no rain anyway, but a vigilant God will take care of the delinquents there by giving them the plague. In any case the distinction between living water and dead water is of primary importance in the Bible. The AV's "springing water" in Genesis 26:19 is "living water" in the original. In the New Testament "living water" is identified with the gospel (John 4:10) and almost the last thing said in the Bible (Revelation 22:17) is an invitation to the redeemed to drink of the water of life.

We said that each apocalyptic or idealized image in the Bible has a demonic counterpart, and that there are two varieties of demonic imagery: the parody-demonic, associated with the temporary prosperity of heathen kingdoms, and the manifest demonic, the wasteland of drought that lies in wait for them. The water imagery of the parody-demonic includes the Nile, Euphrates, and Tigris of history, the rivers giving life and strength to Egypt, Babylon, and Assyria respectively, as well as the Mediterranean Sea and the Persian Gulf with all their heathen shipping and commerce. It was particularly the Phoenicians who were sea traders; and as Tyre, the chief city of Phoenicia, is one of Ezekiel's denunciatory targets, we hear a good deal about the eventual downfall of its prosperity and its turning into a barren rock (the words "Tyre" and "rock" are close enough together in Hebrew to make a pun). Similarly the Great Whore of Revelation who is Babylon and Rome will lose her shipping trade (Revelation 18: 19).

The most dramatic image of the manifest demonic is the Dead Sea, so full of salt that nothing can live in it or around it. We notice that the spring bubbling up from the threshold of the rebuilt Temple in Ezekiel flows eastward, into the Dead Sea, thereby bringing it to life ("and the waters shall be healed," Ezekiel 47:8; similarly in Zechariah 14:8). The author of Revelation, who is heavily indebted to Ezekiel for the details of his vision, says that in the last day of time "there was no more sea" (Revelation 21:1), i.e., no more Dead Sea, i.e., no more dead water, i.e., no more death. Traditionally, though not explicitly in Genesis 19, the demonic cities of Sodom and Gomorrah are sunk beneath the Dead Sea, and Ezekiel prophesies a similar fate for Tyre (Ezekiel 26:19).

The chaos or abyss that meets us at the opening of Genesis is also closely related to the demonic sea. We remember that the Eden story seemed to assume a fresh-water sea under the earth, from which the four rivers of Eden sprang. There is also apparently a fresh-water sea above the sky, much higher up than the rain clouds (Genesis 1:7; cf. Psalm 148:4). Only once in history did these two bodies of fresh water prove destructive, when they broke through both the sky and the deep to reinforce the Deluge (Genesis 7:11). The Deluge was thus in a sense the annulling of Creation, a return to chaos. In the Babylonian creation hymn *Enuma elish* the god of the fresh-water sea, Apsu, was killed and his widow Tiamat, goddess of the "bitter" or salt waters, threatened the gods with destruction. Marduk, the champion of the gods, killed her and split her in two, creating heaven out of one half and earth out of the other. Similarly, the creation in Genesis begins with a "firmament" separating the waters above from the waters below, but succeeding a world that was waste (*tohu*) and void, with darkness on the face of the deep (*tehom*). The Hebrew words are said to be etymologically cognate with Tiamat, and there are many other allusions in the Old Testament to the creation as a killing of a dragon or monster which we shall come to later. Tiamat is not said explicitly to be a monster, but she breeds monsters, and they must have got their heredity from somewhere.

The Deluge itself is either a demonic image, in the sense of being an image of divine wrath and vengeance, or an image of salvation, depending on whether we look at it from the point of view of Noah and his family or from the point of view of everyone else. The same double context recurs in the crossing of the Red Sea by the Israelites, where the pursuing Egyptian army was caught by the returning waters and drowned. This episode suggests an additional symbolic dimension to the Deluge story, in fact to water imagery in the Bible in general. The question of what happened to the fish in the Deluge is an old puzzle: in one aspect of the symbolism, the flood has never receded and we are all fish in a symbolically submarine world of illusion. Similarly, the drowned Egyptian army is the continuous symbolic Egypt of darkness and death. Hence both Noah's flood (I Peter 3:21) and the Red Sea crossing (I Corinthians 10:2) are regarded in the New Testament as types of the sacrament of baptism, where the one being baptized is symbolically drowned in the old world and awakens to a new world on the opposite shore. Similarly, there is a dimension of the symbolism in which the redeemed, after the apocalypse, are able to live *in* the water of life, as they now live in the air.

For desert dwellers the water supply is a matter of life and death, and the forty-year sojourn of Israel in the desert is punctuated by many references to water, notably the story of Moses' striking a rock and bringing water from it (Numbers 20:11), which he did with so much arrogance as to be prevented from entering the Promised Land. A quaint legend to the effect that a rock followed the Israelite encampments, stopping to disgorge water wherever they stopped, is glanced at by Paul (I Corinthians 10:4), who did not care about the historical facts but was anxious to make the rock a type of the body of Christ, which also gave out water when his side was pierced on the cross (John 19:34). A well-known eighteenth-century hymn, "Rock of Ages, Cleft for Me," is based on this typology.

Tree imagery follows the same general patterns. Two trees are mentioned in Genesis 2:9, the tree of life and the forbidden tree of the knowledge of good and evil. Metaphorically they would be the same tree, and as the forbidden tree clearly has something to do with the discovery of sexual experience as we now know it, the tree of life is one of the myths of what has been called the "lost phallus," a giver of life in a way that is now lost to us. The forbidden tree has a cursed serpent crawling limply away from it on its belly, so the tree of life, if the same imagery applied, would have an erect serpent of wisdom and knowledge climbing up through its branches, as in the Indian symbolic system known as Kundalini Yoga. This is not given in Genesis, but we should keep in mind the fact that no image is inherently good or bad, apocalyptic or demonic: which it is depends on the context. Because of its role in the Eden story, the serpent is usually a sinister image in the Biblical tradition; but it could also be a symbol of genuine wisdom (Matthew 10:16) or of healing (Numbers 21:9), just as it was in Greek mythology. In fact King Hezekiah's fear of serpent worship (II Kings 18:4) may be reflected in the "subtle" treachery assigned the serpent in Genesis.

It is easier to apply the principle of the royal metaphor to trees than to water, and the tree of life is, like Wordsworth's, "a tree of many one." It appears as "very many trees" in Ezekiel 47:7 and as twelve trees in Revelation 22:2, or at least a tree bearing twelve kinds of fruit, which is also a royal metaphor. It would thus be, on the same principle, all the trees of Eden, except in its other aspect as a tree or forest of forbidden knowledge. Because of the association of the latter with sex as we know it, both trees were probably thought of as figs or date palms or some tree that possesses sexual differentiation, but in the Middle Ages, when there was only a Latin Bible, the forbidden tree was assumed to be an apple tree, because *malum* in Latin means both evil and apple. It is still an apple tree in *Paradise Lost*. In any case it was a fruit tree, and it was evidently assumed that, before his fall, Adam lived entirely on tree fruits. The tree of life is thus a provider of food, that is, symbolically, of life itself, and of healing (Revelation 22:2).

The word "sap" occurs only once in the AV (Psalm 104:16), but in animal imagery there is a strong emphasis on the blood as the "life" of the animal (Genesis 9:4 and elsewhere). The corresponding image for trees would be the resins or gums or oils or similar substances that seem to represent the life or inner essence of the tree. These would include bdellium (Genesis 2:12), the "balm of Gilead" (Jeremiah 8:22), again a healing potion, and the frankincense and myrrh presented to the infant Christ by the Magi (Matthew 2:11), which are evidently thought of as being to the plant world what gold is to the mineral world. Both of these, especially myrrh, are also images of the passion of Christ (Mark 15:23). The very central image of "anointing," associated with the Messiah or Christ, seems to imply a metaphorical identification of the body of Christ with the tree of life. (This assumes that some vegetable oil such as olive oil was used—at least it is difficult to think of petroleum in such a connection.) Hence it was easy for the Church to identify the tree and water of life of Revelation 22 symbolically with the sacraments of the Eucharist and of baptism respectively.

The Bible often parodies images and motifs from other mythologies when the context is one of demonic parody. Mythologies all over the world have, not only a tree of life or symbol of a food provider, but a "world tree," sometimes identified with the tree of life and sometimes not. This world tree represents a kind of *axis mundi*, the vertical perspective of the mythical universe, in which the earth is so often a middle earth between a world above and a world below. The Scandinavian Yggdrasil and the beanstalk of a famous nursery tale are relatives of this world tree, whose roots are in the lower world but whose branches rise into or beyond the sky (in more sophisticated versions the planets are its fruits). In Ezekiel 31 there is a vivid description of the power of Assyria, associated with Egypt, in the figure of a great tree of this sort; but the tree is eventually to be cut down by a stronger enemy, and "all the trees of Eden . . . shall be comforted in the nether parts of the earth" (31:16). A later tree in Daniel, doubtless derived from Ezekiel's, which reached to heaven and was visible to the ends of the earth, is identified with Nebuchadnezzar and the short-lived power of Babylon (Daniel 4:10ff.).

The cross of Christ, like the Red Sea, is both a demonic image and an image of salvation, depending on the point of view from which it is regarded. As an image of what man does to God, it is purely demonic, and it is said in Deuteronomy 21:23 that "he that is hanged [on a tree] is accursed of God." Paul refers to this passage (Galatians 3:13) in a way that associates it not simply with the Crucifixion, but with Christ as the universal scapegoat of human sin, of which more later. Perhaps the association of hanging on a tree with a divine curse may, as Blake suggests, point to a metaphorical extension of the imagery of the trees of Eden. Adam before his fall would have been metaphorically himself a tree of life; similarly, Adam after his fall would be attached to the tree of frustrated sex he chose instead—bound down upon the stems of vegetation, as Blake says. This may be one reason that the cursing of a barren fig tree is associated with Jesus (Matthew 21:19). A modulation of the same image, by way of a Greek pun on *anthropos* and *anatrope*, gives us the image of man as an "inverted tree," his hair corresponding to the roots. This image is not of

Biblical origin but survived the Middle Ages despite the general ignorance of Greek at the time, and is still going strong in Andrew Marvell's "Upon Appleton House" and the "Preludium" to Blake's *Europe*. Not impossibly the Hanged Man of the Tarot pack, upside down and tied by one foot with his legs forming a cross but still not seeming to suffer unduly, is related to the same complex of imagery.

The paradisal imagery of trees and water recurs in the individual life. The righteous man, according to the first Psalm, is "like a tree planted by the rivers of water," and the imagery of good and corrupt fruit trees is prominent in the Sermon on the Mount. In the Song of Songs the extension of the imagery to the body of the Bride, who is described as "a garden enclosed, a fountain sealed" (4:17), must wait until a few more categories of images are understood. In Solomon's temple, the two free-standing pillars Jachin and Boaz, and the mysterious "molten sea" (I Kings 7:21-23) may indicate the incorporating of the imagery of the tree and the water of life into a building. Another image of the tree of life which associates it with history is the "branch," the epithet of the Messiah as a lineal descendant of David. This appears in Isaiah 11:1 as a "rod out of the stem of Jesse," David's father, and the tree of Jesse thereby became a favorite design with medieval cathedral builders, especially in stained glass.

Pastoral and agricultural imagery naturally overlap with the oasis imagery of paradise. The green pastures and still waters of Psalm 23 belong equally to both. Herds of cattle are no less pastoral than sheep, and there is no reason in pure metaphor why a herd of cattle should not be as central an image for the Church, say, as a "flock." But the bull was so common a fertility emblem throughout Western Asia (there were bull images in Solomon's temple) that the Biblical preference for sheep is probably in part a matter of negative ritual again. The "golden calf" of Aaron's idolatry and Jeroboam's schism, already mentioned, was actually a bull, and in New Testament times the Christian Lamb "slain from the foundation of the world" (Revelation 13:8) had its rival in the bull of Mithraism, whose sacrifice also repeated a creation myth. On the demonic side of animal imagery are, as a rule, beasts of prey, like the wolf, the enemy of the sheepfold. Near the beginning of the Bible we meet the sinister Nimrod, founder of Babylonia and Assyria, who is described as "a mighty hunter before the Lord" (Genesis 10:8). What he probably hunted, more as a ritual duty than for necessity, was the lion. Later on, the story of Esau the hunter, whose inheritance was taken over by Jacob, marks the superseding of a hunting or food-gathering economy by a ranching one, and the detailed prescriptions of "clean" and "unclean" animals in the Pentateuch suit the latter mode of life much better.

The horse is the central image of a warrior aristocracy, and as such it remains in the background among Biblical animals. The ass, the beast of burden, often stupid and obstinate but often patient and humble as well, carries a much higher symbolic rating. As the symbol for the protesting but usually acquiescent physical body—the "Brother Ass" of St. Francis of Assisi—it is associated with the physical side of the Incarnation, and as such it was the appropriate animal to carry Jesus in triumph into Jerusalem. The law of Exodus 34:19 which prescribes that every firstborn male animal, including human beings, is potentially a sacrificial offering to God, to which we shall return, specifically exempts the ass along with the human being as to be "redeemed" by a lamb instead. Later medieval celebrations of the ass, whatever they may owe to parody or to some pre-Christian ass cult, contain also a tribute to the symbol of toiling and oppressed labor which is the lot of most human lives in the world. The wise men of Matthew 2:1, traditionally three kings, depended like other kings on such service:

> Aurum de Arabia,
> Thus et myrrham de Saba,
> Tulit in ecclesia
> Virtus asinaria.

The animals of the manifest demonic include the jackals and hyenas, which are associated with destroyed and abandoned kingdoms, many of them on the border of a shadow world in which it is difficult to know where animals stop and evil spirits begin. Thus in Isaiah's prophecy of Babylon's ruin:

> But wild beasts of the desert shall lie there; and their houses shall be full of doleful creatures; and owls shall dwell there, and satyrs shall dance there.
>
> And the wild beasts of the islands shall cry in their desolate houses, and dragons in their pleasant palaces: and her time is near to come, and her days shall not be prolonged. (Isaiah 13:21-22)

Many of these terms are translated very approximately: the "wild beasts" are the *tziim*, the dwellers in the *tziyya* or dry places (see Luke 11:24). In the background is the imagery of the parched, waterless world of late summer presided over, in pre-Biblical mythology, by Mot, the god of death. There are also various dragons, both of sea and of land. The dragon seems to be a consistently sinister animal in the Bible, again perhaps because it was a fertility emblem in other mythologies. More important for Biblical imagery are those two hulking brutes Behemoth and Leviathan, who appear at the end of the Book of Job (40-41), but we are not ready for them yet.

In the Old Testament, agricultural symbolism, which finds its focus in bread and wine, is in the main area of antagonism toward the surrounding Canaanite cults. It seems almost a symbolic necessity in mythology to think of nature, more particularly vegetable nature, as female, a mother whose fertility brings all life into being. Hence the widespread myth in the ancient world of a mother goddess attended by a subordinate male figure who is her son, her lover, or sacrificial victim, depending on the phase of the cycle of growth and death that is being stressed. One object of attack in the Bible is the magic that attempts to grease the wheel of the cycle of fertility. Magic of this sort, sympathetic magic as it is called, is founded on the principle of imitation, bringing about rain, for instance, by pouring water on the ground. The denunciations of such practices by the prophets are a part of their effort to de-idolize nature, to suggest that there is no numinous presence or personality in nature that responds to such gestures, except something evil and treacherous.

The main features of the cults of the mother goddess and her dying god are well known. The birth, marriage, and sacrificial death of the male figure represents, and is contained within, the cycle of the growth and gathering of grain and grapes. His death is mourned by a chorus of women who represent the continuing but latent fertility of the earth, dormant but still there in the dead season of the year following the harvest and vintage. Ezekiel in Babylon has a vision of women lamenting Tammuz or Adonis in the deserted temple in Jerusalem (Ezekiel 8:14), and Zechariah speaks of such a ritual mourning in connection with a fertility god named Hadad-Rimmon, linking it to the disasters accompanying the fall of heathen power, and contrasting it with a spirit of compassion among the regenerated Jews, who, it is said, "shall look on him whom they have pierced" (Zechariah 12:10). The quotation of this phrase in John 19:37 indicates how clearly aware the gospel writers were of the dying-god imagery surrounding Jesus, who is also accompanied by a mourning female chorus of "daughters of Jerusalem" (Luke 23:28). The originally magical element in the mourning was perhaps to indicate some sensitivity toward the "killing" of the crop by reaping it.

The magical motivation is stronger in the rite known as the "gardens of Adonis," where plants brought along by forced growth in pots were flung into water, again by a group of women, as a rain charm. The pots are said to have a symbolic association with female sexual organs; if so, they would be thought to stimulate the fertility of the women as well as of the soil. Isaiah 17:10-11 takes a predictably dim view of this practice:

Because thou hast forgotten the God of thy salvation, and hast not been mindful of the rock of thy strength, therefore shalt thou plant pleasant plants, and shalt set it with strange slips:

In the day shalt thou make thy plant to grow, and in the morning shalt thou make thy seed to flourish: but the harvest shall be a heap in the day of grief and of desperate sorrow.

Again, it is a natural extension of magical belief to feel that the more painful or sensational the act, the more likely it is to attract the attention of whatever deity is concerned in the matter. For rain charms, cutting oneself with a knife until the blood flows is not only a dramatic way of expressing a desire for rain, but also identifies the worshiper's body with that of the rain-god. Elijah makes fun of the priests of the fertility god Baal for engaging in this practice (I Kings 18:28), and Hosea also condemns those who "gash themselves for corn and wine" (Hosea 7:14; the AV's "assemble" is wrong).

In the Gospels harvest and vintage are frequently used as symbols of the apocalypse, and the Eucharist rite, identifying the bread and wine of the vegetable world with the body and blood of the animal world, and both with the body of Christ, is established at the beginning of the Passion (Matthew 26:26-29 and elsewhere). The Synoptics represent Jesus as speaking of drinking "new wine" in his kingdom, and the image of new wine appears in the account of the wedding of Cana in John 2. John does not include the instituting of the Eucharist in his account of the Last Supper, but Jesus' discourse there speaks of himself as the "true vine" (John 15:1). The Eucharist is, among other things, the antitype of the covenant of blood between Israel and God (Exodus 24:6-8), and the provision of manna in the desert (see John 6:49-50). Identifying wine and blood unites animal and vegetable worlds; identifying wine and water (John 2:9) or blood and water (I John 5:6) unites both worlds with the paradisal.

In the Old Testament, symbolic meals featuring bread and wine, though not always exclusively, appear in the entertainment of Abraham by Melchizedek (Genesis 14:18), in the banquet of wisdom in Proverbs 9:5, in the feast ordained by David celebrating the entry of the ark into Jerusalem (II Samuel 6:19). The typological significance of these occasions will meet us later. Demonic imagery symbolizes the disasters befalling the hostile and unfaithful in the last day by a harvest and vintage of wrath, in which mankind is, so to speak, made into food to be eaten by death. The most famous of these images is that of the treading of the winepress of Edom in Isaiah 63, where, as usual, wine is identified with blood. The New Testament counterpart of this is the extraordinary vision of a harvest and vintage of wrath in Revelation 14:14ff. A parallel demonic image of communion in excrement appears in the Assyrian Rabshakeh's speech in II Kings 18:27, where it is contrasted with his own version of a Promised Land "of bread and vineyards" (32).

Urban imagery in the Bible is easier to explain if we take the human category itself first. We have suggested that pastoral, agricultural, and urban life represent the apocalyptic or idealized transformations of the animal, vegetable, and mineral worlds respectively into environments with a human shape and meaning. What is the apocalyptic or idealized image for human life itself? As soon as we ask this, we are thrown back on the royal metaphor. It is impossible to think of an ideal human life except as an alternation of individual and social life, as equally a belonging and an escape. However, human imagery, like Greek nouns, has a dual as well as a singular and a plural, a sexual as well as an individual and a social form, and this affords a means of reconciling the two. The individual member of the royal metaphor, the invisible king, is related to the social member, the kingdom he rules, as a bridegroom to a bride. The sexual union of man and woman, which is symbolically an identifying of two bodies as one flesh, becomes the image for the full metaphorical relationship of God and man. Thus:

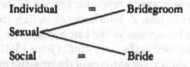

We should notice that symbolically this makes the Messianic figure of Christ not merely the only individual, the only person who really has the right to say "I am," but the only male. All "souls" of his people, whether of men or of women, are symbolically female, making up the Church, which is identified with the Bride in Revelation 21:2. "The male is Christ, the female is the Church," says an early Christian writer (II Clement 14:2), and wedding imagery is a favorite with Jesus himself in his parables about his kingdom.

The love songs in the Song of Songs perhaps referred originally to young villagers in the role of something analogous to the Lord and Lady of the May in rural England. But the association of the poem with Solomon expands it symbolically into a wedding between a king and the "black but comely" bride who represents his fertile land, and whose body is compared to parts of it. "Thy nose is as the tower of Lebanon which looketh toward Damascus" (Song of Songs 7:4) might seem a doubtful compliment to a bride whose charms were less symbolic. Typologically it was not difficult for Christianity to read the poem as an expression of Christ's love for his Bride the Church, the main difference being that Christianity, an urban religion that spread from city to city, did not have the immediate associations with a land and a country that Israel possessed with its "Promised Land." The same figure of the land married to its ruler (that is, its true ruler or God) appears late in Isaiah (62:4):

Thou shalt no more be termed Forsaken; neither shall thy land any more be termed Desolate: but thou shalt be called Hephzibah, and thy land Beulah; for the Lord delighteth in thee, and thy land shall be married.

The imagery of the bride who has not kept her own vineyard because she is searching for her beloved (Song of Songs 1:6) overlaps with that of Psalm 45, which describes what is apparently a royal marriage in which a bride from a strange land is adjured to forsake her homeland and cling to her new home. Another bride from a strange land—on a lower social scale even though her great-grandson is King David—is Ruth, whose delightful story is closely linked to the imagery of harvest.

The demonic parody of Bridegroom and Bride figures is of course the Great Whore who is Babylon and sits on the seven hills of Rome and is the mistress of Antichrist. She would normally be identified only with the ruling class of the heathen kingdom, but the implied distinction between tyrants and the victims of tyrants, apart from Christians, is not explicit. The Whore of Revelation holds in her hand a golden cup full of the blood of saints and martyrs, a figure derived from Jeremiah 51:7. We note the metaphorical identification of blood and wine and the sexual image of the cup: its apocalyptic counterpart would be the cup held by Jesus when instituting the Eucharist (I Corinthians 11:25), where again blood and wine are identified. Later legend expanded this cup into the Holy Grail, which was also said to have been held against the side of Jesus on the cross when blood came out of the spear thrust.

The two symbolic women in the life of Christ, the virgin mother and the bride who is the body of his people, are closely associated in imagery. The bride of the Song of Songs is also the Virgin who is impregnated by the Holy Spirit, the wind blowing over the enclosed

garden (Song of Songs 4: 12-16; *hortus conclusus* in the Vulgate) which
is the body of the Virgin. The scene so common in medieval painting,
the coronation of the Virgin by her Son, also associates the images of
mother and bride. At the same time the death of Christ is explained in
later theology as the appeasing of the wrath of the Father against the
sin of man. If one wanted to construct a demonic form of this, one
would get something very like the basis of the Oedipus legend, the
story of the king who killed his father and married his mother. There
are traces of this Oedipal version in the story of Adam, whose
"mother," so far as he had one, was the feminine *adamah* or dust of the
ground, to whose body he returned after breaking the link with his
father (Genesis 2:7; 3:19).

Yeats constructed an elaborate cyclical theory of history out of the
contrast between the Oedipal and Christian myths, but this seems to
me a red herring. It is true that Oedipus belongs to tragedy and
Christ to a divine comedy, but tragedy reflects the human situation as
it is, and comedy normally attains its happy ending through some
mysterious and unexpected twist in the plot. Hence it is simpler to
think of the Christian myth as the comic (which in this context means
apocalyptic or ideal) version of the Oedipal one. From a Christian
point of view the Oedipal myth, in its Sophoclean form at least, is not
a demonic parody but a secular or extra-Biblical type. The Old
Testament gives us the story of Reuben, who, though the eldest son
of Jacob or Israel, lost the inheritance because he committed the worst
crime conceivable in a patriarchal society, of approaching one of his
father's women—not his own mother, though the Oedipal outline of
the story is clear enough (Genesis 35:22).

Urban imagery is naturally focused on Jerusalem, and cities are apt
to be symbolically female, as the word "metropolis" (mother city)
reminds us. In sexual imagery the relation of male to female is
expressed in two ways, depending on whether the two bodies or only
the sexual organs themselves are taken as the basis. In one the male is
above and the female below; in the other the male is at the center and
the female surrounds him. No general trend is without many exceptions in mythology, but we have seen that throughout Mediterranean
and Near Eastern countries, apart from Egypt, there was a general
tendency to associate the sky with a male principle and the earth with
a female one. The metaphorical kernels of the all-male Christian
Trinity of Father, Son, and Spirit are probably the sky, the sun, and
the air. The other relation is illustrated by the temple of the (usually
male) god in the midst of the bridal city. The Jerusalem Temple (I am

not concerned with historical accuracy here but with the typological use made of it in the New Testament, more particularly in the Epistle to the Hebrews) had an outer court that was a marketplace, an inner court where the believers gathered, and the inmost Holy of Holies, a space representing the presence of God, covered with a veil and entered once a year by the High Priest (Hebrews 9:7). The sacrilege of placing a statue or altar of a heathen god in the temple has been mentioned: the coming of a visible God in the flesh was its apocalyptic opposite. Hence at Jesus' death the veil of the Temple of Jerusalem was torn from top to bottom (Matthew 27:51); Jesus is said by Paul to have broken down the middle wall of partition (Ephesians 2:14); and his act of cleansing the outer temple is of such symbolic importance that John places it at the very beginning of his ministry.

The typical healing act of Jesus is the casting of "devils" out of the bodies of those possessed by them. As each body is a temple of God (I Corinthians 3:16), and as all of us are born with devils in the possession of it, the casting out of devils is symbolically the same act as cleansing the temple. The process is completed in the apocalypse: the author of Revelation is emphatic that there is no temple in the new Jerusalem, as the body of Christ has replaced it (Revelation 21:22). The final consummation of Bridegroom and Bride is thus a total mingling of bodies, and is no longer symbolized, as Blake remarked, by "a pompous high priest entering by a secret place."

Within the same metaphorical construct, Christ is not only the temple but the cornerstone of the temple, and each member of the Christian community is a stone in the same temple. The verse from Psalm 118:22, "the stone which the builders rejected is made the head of the corner," is quoted several times in the New Testament (Acts 4:11 among others), and we are also reminded that in a world where there is no death, stones are as much alive as anything else:

To whom coming, as unto a living stone, disallowed indeed of men, but chosen of God, and precious,
Ye also, as lively stones, are built up a spiritual house, an holy priesthood. . . . (I Peter 2:4-5)

The same metaphor is labored with great prolixity in an early Christian writing known as the Shepherd of Hermas, in marked contrast to the crisp incisiveness of the above. The Book of Revelation has also many suggestions of an imagery of living stones, of the type later elaborated in the symbolism of alchemy. The "white stone" of 2:17 could be metaphorically the "white raiment" of 3:5; later on, an angel

(15:6) is said in the AV to be clothed in "linen" (*linon*), but there is better textual authority for *lithon* (stone), and this translation may be rationalizing again.

Jerusalem is on top of a hill, and symbolically it is therefore the highest point in the world. It is "Jerusalem, whither the tribes go up" (Psalm 122:4), and its temple thus touches heaven, as its demonic parody the Tower of Babel also tried to do (Genesis 11:4). The building of Babel ended in the confusion of tongues, in contrast to the "pure speech" promised to the restored Israel in Zephaniah 3:9. The model of Babel was the ziggurat temple of Mesopotamian cities, which was also thought of as a link between heaven and earth. Some of the later Psalms are called psalms of "ascents" or "degrees," and seem to be connected with ritual processions up the hill to the temple. The ascent is not said to be a winding or spiral ascent, but if it were it would be an interesting addition to a very widespread symbolic pattern, extending in literature through Dante's *Purgatorio* to the winding stairs of Eliot and Yeats and Pound. The most notable example in the Bible is the "ladder" of Jacob's vision in Genesis 28:12, which, as angels were going both up and down on it, was clearly a staircase rather than a ladder.

A city or building so situated would also be a kind of keystone for the world, so that its removal would release the forces of chaos. In the Psalms there is a frequent symbolic connection between the temple or city of God and the control of the "floods" below it. Psalm 24, for example, associates a vision of the world founded on chaos with a procession into the temple. Jesus, who emphasizes the importance of founding buildings on rocks, says that his Church will also be founded on a rock, and that "the gates of hell shall not prevail against it" (Matthew 16:18), a phrase that incorporates the same imagery of the control of the chaotic world. As "a city set on a hill cannot be hid" (Matthew 5:14), the Church is probably thought of as on a hill too, and Augustine was later to see an Old Testament type of the Church in Noah's ark resting on Ararat. The apocalyptic contrast with the tower of Babel and its confusion of tongues is the coming of the gift of tongues to the apostles at Pentecost (Acts 2): the law of Sinai was also given from a mountain, according to tradition also at Pentecost. Whatever is struck by fire from the sky, whether benevolently or in wrath, is symbolically at the highest point in the world.

We notice that, as the Bible goes on, the area of sacred space shrinks. If the garden of Eden stretched from Egypt to India, it provided a fair amount of room for two people to wander in: that is, it was a complete world, of society without crowding and of solitude without loneliness. Abraham's Promised Land was much smaller but still spacious enough for a pastoral economy; Joshua's Promised Land was smaller still, and even at that the map of Canaan divided among twelve tribes which appears in the back of most AV Bibles was a map of what the Israelites wished to possess rather than of what they permanently held. The division of the kingdom and the conquests that followed cut the sacred space down to Judah, then Jerusalem, then the Temple, and finally to the Holy of Holies within the Temple. With the sacrilege of Antiochus, perhaps repeated in intention by Caligula, the last vestige of sacred space disappears.

For Christianity this was an indication that a central sacred place could no longer exist. The Messiah himself was a wanderer (Luke 9:58), and Christianity was not centered symbolically on Jerusalem as Judaism was, even though Jesus accepted the centering on a temporary basis (John 4:20ff.). Later the headquarters of Christianity was Rome, but, very typically of Christianity, what became sacrosanct about Rome was the administration. The diffusion of Christianity is symbolically connected with the progress of man back to the garden of Eden and the wandering but guided pastoral world of the twenty-third Psalm, and its type is the figure, frequent in the Psalms, of referring to the temple as the "tabernacle," the portable temple of the wilderness.

The conception of the violation of the sacred space is a very ancient one: it appears, for instance, in the elaborate precautions taken to baffle thieves in the construction of the royal tombs of Egypt. In an Ugaritic myth the fertility god Baal demands a temple, on the ground that he is the only god without one: the supreme god El finally gives permission, and an architect, Kothar-wa-Hasis (cunning and skillful) says he will build him a spanking new temple full of the latest thing in temples—windows. Baal, an old-fashioned type, says he doesn't want any windows, and the architect is on no account to put any in. If the reader has ever been on a building committee he will know who won that argument: Baal's palace got windows, and it was through a window that the death-god Mot climbed to pull Baal out of his temple into the lower world. The image of death coming through the window survives in Jeremiah 9:21.

Naturally there will be parody mountains where rivals of God have their temples. We are told that Solomon, after spending seven years building the temple on Zion and thirteen years building his own palace, amiably built other temples to Moloch and Chemosh on a hill facing Zion, at the suggestions of his seven hundred wives (I Kings 11:7). Solomon's reputation for wisdom was a little tarnished by this, but the Solomon portrayed in the Book of Kings is as many-layered as a character in a dream, and the historical Solomon may not have been a monotheist at all. In any case the image of the demonic rival mountain, like the image of the demonic city and temple, appears in connection with Babylon, Tyre, and other centers of false gods. It is in connection with Babylon that Isaiah gives us his famous oracle of the fall of Lucifer:

> For thou hast said in thine heart, I will ascend into heaven, I will exalt my throne above the stars of God: I will sit also upon the mount of the congregation, in the sides of the north. (Isaiah 14:13)

Ezekiel expands the prince of Tyre to the same cosmological dimensions, and speaks of him as having been "upon the holy mountain of God" (Ezekiel 28:14). The Great Whore of Revelation sits on seven hills identified with those of Rome (Revelation 17:9). The apocalyptic or idealized mountain is similarly treated, both in the Bible and in later imagery. The garden of Eden must also have been the highest point in the world: Dante puts it at the antipodes, on top of the mountain of purgatory, and Milton contrasts Eden in the upper air with the "subjected plain" below it. The apocalyptic counterpart of the demonic seven hills of Nero's Rome appears in II Esdras:

> . . . seven mighty mountains, whereupon there grow roses and lilies, whereby I will fill thy children with joy. (II Esdras 2:19)

Another body of imagery closely connected with the urban is the imagery concerned with highways and roads, the skeletons of empire, of which the antitype is the "way" or path of redemption, so central in the imagery of Christianity as in that of most religions (Matthew 7:13-14). There is, in the first place, the miraculous highway, the path opened through the Red Sea, the original type of all paths of salvation. A passage in Isaiah (11:16) foretells the extension of this miraculous path to bring the lost people of Israel back from Assyria. In the account of the Exodus the Red Sea crossing was followed by a long period of wandering in labyrinthine and frustrated directions. This image remains in the background, set against a contrasting image of a straight highway of God through the desert (Isaiah 40:3). At the beginning of the gospel of John, John the Baptist quotes this verse from Isaiah and applies it to Christ.

The building up of a pathway through the desert into a straight highway is connected with fertility imagery about bringing the desert to life in Isaiah 35:18ff. The prologue to Blake's *Marriage of Heaven and Hell* is based on this passage, and expands it into an image of the growth of civilization as it develops from a pioneering "voice crying in the wilderness" into a broad and crowded trade route. Both Isaiahs are fascinated by the imagery of highways (perhaps it was one reason for putting their prophecies together), and the second one (the main author of Isaiah 40-55) shows what can only be called an engineering imagination in 40:4. The demonic labyrinth of lost direction is transformed into the random wanderings of grazing sheep in a restored pastoral world in Psalm 23:3 (where "right paths" is perhaps more accurate than the AV's "paths of righteousness").

"Above" the human world is a world of spiritual beings or angels, metaphorically associated with the sky. Angels are also creatures of God, fellow servants of man, and several warnings appear in the New Testament against angel worship (Colossians 2:18; Revelation 22:9). Two kinds of angels are mentioned especially in the Old Testament: seraphim (Isaiah 6 and elsewhere) and cherubim (Ezekiel 1 and elsewhere). Later theology developed a more elaborate structure of nine orders of angels, but retained these two as spirits of love and contemplation respectively, and medieval painters colored them respectively red and blue. The colors suggest the origin of angelic imagery from the two levels of the sky. On the upper level are the fiery bodies of the sun and stars; on the lower level is the blue sky with its clouds and birds. On the principle of the royal metaphor all spirits are one Spirit, the Holy Spirit of the later Trinity, and the Holy Spirit is associated with both bodies of imagery: with birds, specifically the dove, with wind, and with lightning-like flame descending on the apostles and bringing them the gift of tongues (Matthew 3:16; John 3:8; Acts 2:3). The Old Testament type of the descending tongue of flame is the hot coal, applied to Isaiah's mouth by a seraph, which gave him the power of prophetic speech (Isaiah 6:7). The demonic parody, the fire tongue of slander, appears in James 3:6. All this implies a special connection between angelic messengers and verbal communication: in Galatians 3:19 and elsewhere angels are said to be the agents of the giving of Scripture.

Man in his present state cannot live in fire, but, as with water, there is a fire of life and a fire of death. The fire of life burns without burning *up*: there is light and heat but no pain or destruction. This fire appears in the burning bush of Exodus 3:2, which "burned with fire, and the bush was not consumed." On metaphorical principles all the categories of apocalyptic existence can be thought of as burning in the fire of life. The bird is an image of the Holy Spirit, and the burning bird is the phoenix, whose story was regarded later as a type of the Resurrection. There is no phoenix in the canonical Bible, unless the word rendered "sand" by the AV translators in Job 29:18 is the phoenix, but it appears as early as III Baruch among the Pseudepigrapha. The Old English poem on the phoenix, a paraphrase of Lactantius, begins with a beautiful description of the earthly paradise or Eden which is the phoenix's home. We have mentioned the possibility that the tree of life was originally thought of as a date palm, which in Greek is also called *phoinix*.

The tree of life would similarly be a tree burning in the fire of life: it is represented not only in the burning bush of Moses but in the seven-branched candlestick or "lampstand" of Exodus 25:31ff. Human beings burning in the fire of life include the three Jews in Nebuchadnezzar's furnace, miraculously transformed from a destructive fire into a living one (Daniel 3:25). They include also the saints of medieval paintings with their glowing haloes, and the "burning babe" of the Elizabethan Jesuit Southwell's wonderful Christmas poem. The chariot of fire in which Elijah went up to heaven is metaphorically his own transformed body, however the original narrator thought of it, and is a rising movement corresponding to the fire descending from God to his altar on Carmel (I Kings 18:38). Similarly, a fire rises on the altar in the temple in response to a fire descending from God (II Chronicles 7:1). As late as Eliot's "Little Gidding" we have the same imagery: descending fire from the flames of the Holy Spirit and ascending fire on the funeral pyre of Hercules, set over against a demonic parody of fire bombs falling in London and fires breaking out of the streets in response. Blake also borrows Elijah's chariot of fire for building Jerusalem, which is seen by John of Patmos as a city glowing with gold and gems—in other words, a city burning in the fire of life.

Spiritual beings are the "gods" of heathen kingdoms in the parody-demonic category, and devils in the manifest-demonic. Hence the conception of heathen gods as fallen or rebel angels is quite consistent with the symbolic language the Bible uses, however fragmentary the textual evidence for it may be. In the Old Testament there is a frequent tendency to reduce the heathen "god" to the secular ruler of the country. Thus the cosmological "covering cherub" of Ezekiel 28 is identified with the Prince of Tyre, and the planet Venus, or "Lucifer son of the morning," of Isaiah 14 with the King of Babylon, as explained. There is also the curious Psalm 82, which appears to be an address by God to an assembly of "gods," whose divinity is not denied, but who are being cut down to human size:

> I have said, Ye are gods; and all of you are children of the most High.
> But ye shall die like men, and fall like one of the princes. (Psalm 82:6-7)

Jesus refers to this passage (John 10:34) to show that the conception of the divine man is established in the Scriptures, even though in a negative category.

Like angels, devils are associated with the imagery of the sky. On the lower level they are demons of storm and tempest, and their chief is described as "the prince of the power of the air" in Ephesians 2:2. Satan falls like lightning from heaven (Luke 10:18), and the abode of evil spirits is traditionally a prison of heat without light, though false lights are associated with them, by implication in the Bible and explicitly in later imagery, as in Milton's *Comus*. The whole complex of such demons and their human agents survives now only in the playful form of Halloween imagery, but in earlier years the perversions of "literal" meaning, in the hands of hysteria and sadism, produced all the horrors of witch-burning and the like.

In the divine world the royal metaphor appears again in the doctrine of the Trinity, where three "persons" are said to be one God. The Trinity, though a logical enough inference from Biblical language about God as a Father, a Son, and a Spirit, does not explicitly appear in the Bible except in I John 5:7:

> For there are three that bear record in heaven, the Father, the Word, and the Holy Ghost: and these three are one.

This verse is not in the early Greek manuscripts of the New Testament, but was inserted into some Latin copies, and so entered the Vulgate: then, by further efforts of devout faking, it was translated into Greek and thereby got into Erasmus' edition of the Greek New Testament, into the so-called *textus receptus* of the mid-sixteenth century, and into the AV. Modern translators not only omit the verse, but do not show in the verse numbering that anything has been omitted, which, considering the historical importance the verse has had, seems a trifle self-righteous. The human tendency to feel that, if one accepts both the authority of the Bible and the doctrine of the Trinity, the way to make the latter true is to get it somehow into the Bible, is too subtle and insidious a tendency to be swept under the rug.

No demonic God, of course, can exist as such, but the chief of the devils, usually Satan (whose name means enemy or adversary; see Numbers 22:22) may set himself up as God and be incarnated in various agents of Antichrist. It is interesting that Paul, although he gives one of the clearest descriptions of Antichrist, runs counter to the general tendency to associate false gods with human rulers. He tends to think that the most formidable enemies of God and man alike are the *stoicheia tou kosmou*, the powers of nature, whenever they are taken by man to be, not creatures of God and therefore fellow creatures of himself, but to be charged with numinous and mysterious power independent of man. When they are assigned this power, they invariably become enslaving agents, inspiring beliefs, derived from the permanence of the natural order, about cyclical fatality and the like. This leads to the mindless observance of rituals out of superstition, or the inorganic persistence of obsolete customs out of habit, along with a vague anxiety that breaking with them will lead to disaster:

> Howbeit then, when ye knew not God, ye did service unto them which by nature are no gods.
> But now, after that ye have known God, or rather are known of God, how turn ye again to the weak and beggarly elements, whereunto ye desire again to be in bondage?
> Ye observe days, and months, and times, and years. (Galatians 4:8-10)

Consequently it is a waste of time to attack human societies, however hostile, because they derive their real strength from demonic forces that would have no power if power were not conceded to them by human ignorance:

> For we wrestle not against flesh and blood, but against principalities, against powers, against the rulers of the darkness of this world, against spiritual wickedness in high places. (Ephesians 6:12)

If this is not Paul, it is quite consistent with Paul's point of view.

The rather simpleminded polemics against idolatry that we sometimes find in the Bible, for instance in the Epistle of Jeremy in the Apocrypha, seem to keep missing their own point. They concentrate on the question: How can man bring himself to worship something that he knows he has made himself? As Vico says, *Verum factum:* man understands only what he has made (and that only up to a point). The *stoicheia tou kosmou* are the mysterious natural forces that, originally local, tend to retreat from man until, by Paul's time, most of them were in the stars. It is precisely because man has not made them and does not understand them that he is impelled to worship them. They do not, however, exist as objects of worship, hence when they become such they are filled up with human projections. Man made the wheel, and when he interprets the stars as constituting a wheel of fate or of fortune, he is projecting something he has made on something he has not made, and this is when idolatry really becomes dangerous. For in due course he becomes assimilated to his projection: becomes what he beholds, as Blake says, or, as the Psalmist says, "They that make them [idols] are like unto them" (Psalm 115:8).

We may illustrate the structure of imagery in the Bible by a double table, as is shown on pages 166 and 167.

We tend to think of the first table as a hierarchy of being, which is what it became in later Western thought. This hierarchy is the basis of the famous "chain of being" polarized by form and matter, which lasted from early Greek times until the eighteenth century at least. But in its apocalyptic context it is not a hierarchy but a vision of plenitude, in which everything is equal because identical with everything else. Such a world cannot be perceived, or even comprehended theoretically, by what is usually called the ego: we have described it as the way reality looks after the ego has disappeared. The most difficult part of it, perhaps, is the role of the two elements of water and fire, which are essential to life but which we cannot live *in*, without drowning or burning. We find it hard to imagine a life in which all four elements are equally a part of human existence; in which man has passed the ordeals of water and fire, like Tamino in *The Magic Flute*. Nor does the Bible give us much help, except in the astounding conclusion of the Book of Wisdom. Most of this book is given over to a "spiritual" commentary on the Exodus, and it ends with a vision of the newly created Israel on the opposite shore of the sea of death:

For the elements were changed in themselves by a kind of harmony, like as in a psaltery notes change the name of the tune, and yet are always sounds; which may well be perceived by the sight of the things that have been done.

For earthly things were turned to watery, and the things that before swam in the water, now went upon the ground.

The fire had power in the water, forgetting his own virtue; and the water forgat his own quenching nature.

On the other side, the flames wasted not the flesh of the corruptible living things, though they walked therein; neither melted they the icy kind of heavenly meat, that was of nature apt to melt. (Wisdom 19:18-21)

Table of Apocalyptic Imagery

Category	Class or Group Form	Individual
Divine	[Trinity]	God
Spiritual or Angelic	1) Fire-spirits (Seraphim) 2) Air-spirits (Cherubim)	Spirit as Flame Spirit as Dove or Wind
Paradisal	Garden of Eden	Tree of Life Water of Life
Human	People as Bride (Israel)	Bridegroom
Animal	Sheepfold or Flock	1) Shepherd 2) Lamb (Body and Blood)
Vegetable	Harvest and Vintage	Bread and Wine (First Fruits)
Mineral	City (Jerusalem) Highway	Temple; Stone

(All individual categories metaphorically identified with Christ)

The apocalyptic vision, in which the body of Christ is the metaphor holding together all categories of being in an identity, presents us with a world in which there is only one knower, for whom there is nothing outside of or objective to that knower, hence nothing dead or insensible. This knower is also the real consciousness in each of us. In the center of our table is the identification of the body and blood of the animal world, and the bread and wine that are the human forms of the vegetable kingdom, with the body of Christ. This identification forms the basis of the Eucharist rite instituted by Jesus at the Last Supper. The statements about this in the New Testament are too explicit for historical Christianity to avoid the question of what identity means in these categories and in that context. But there is a recurrent tendency in Christianity to ignore or even resist the extension of such a sense of identity beyond the specific rite.

Isaac Watts, in the eighteenth century, has a poem on the metaphors attached to Christ in Scripture, and his phrasing makes it clear that for him as many as possible of these metaphors are to be

Table of Demonic Imagery

Category	Manifest Demonic	Parody Demonic	
		Group	Individual
Divine	[Satan]	Stoicheia Tou Kosmou	Antichrist
Spiritual or Angelic	1) Fire-spirits 2) Demons of Tempest	False gods	Moloch, Baal, Dagon, etc.
Paradisal	Waste Land and Sea of Death	Tree and Water of Heathen Power	
Human	Those Cast Out	"Great Whore" (Heathen Kingdoms)	Nero, Nebuchadnezzar, Antiochus
Animal	Dragons of Chaos (Leviathan, Rahab; etc.)	Beasts of Prey or Fertility	Deified Animal (Bull, Serpent)
Vegetable	Harvest and Vintage of Wrath	Vegetation Gods and Earth-Mothers	
Mineral	Ruins	Heathen City (Babylon, Rome)	Tower of Babel

regarded as "just" metaphors, rhetorical expressions of pious emotion but not of the meaning of the Bible. The New Testament itself is rather reserved in its metaphorical language, and it is interesting to note that the scattered sayings of Jesus recorded outside it are sometimes more uninhibited in expression. One of them reads "He who is near to me is near unto the fire," and the Oxyrhynchus Papyri represent him as saying: "Raise the stone and thou shalt find me; cleave the wood and I am there."

Once again, my interest is not in doctrines of faith as such but in the expanding of vision through language. In particular, I am interested in seeing what happens if we follow a suggestion made earlier in this book and turn the traditional form of the metaphorical structure inside out. Instead of a metaphor of unity and integration we should have a metaphor of particularity, the kind of vision Blake expressed in the phrase "minute particulars" and in such lines as "To see the world in a grain of sand."

This would lead us to something like the notion of interpenetration in Buddhism, a type of visionary experience studied more systematically in Oriental than in Western traditions. The great Buddhist philosopher D. T. Suzuki gives an account of it in his study of the Avatamsaka or Gandavyuha Sutra, the Buddhist scripture that is most fully devoted to it. Suzuki speaks of it as "an infinite mutual fusion or penetration of all things, each with its individuality yet with something universal in it." As he goes on to speak of the "transparent and luminous" quality of this kind of vision, of its annihilating of space and time as we know them, of the disappearance of shadows (see Song of Songs 2:17) in a world where everything shines by its own light, I find myself reminded more and more strongly of the Book of Revelation and of similar forms of vision in the Prophets and the Gospels.

We touch here on a principle we have mentioned before, and will return to at the end of the book. Metaphors of unity and integration take us only so far, because they are derived from the finiteness of the human mind. If we are to expand our vision into the genuinely infinite, that vision becomes decentralized. We follow a "way" or direction until we reach the state of innocence symbolized by the sheep in the twenty-third Psalm, where we are back to wandering, but where wandering no longer means being lost. There are two senses in which the word "imperfect" is used: in one sense it is that which falls short of perfection; in another it is that which is not finished but continuously active, as in the tense system of verbs in most languages. It is in the latter sense that "the imperfect is our paradise," as Wallace Stevens says, a world that may change as much as our own, but where change is no longer dominated by the single direction toward nothingness and death.

CHAPTER SEVEN

MYTH II
Narrative

We referred earlier to the structure of the Book of Judges, in which a series of stories of traditional tribal heroes is set within a repeating *mythos* of the apostasy and restoration of Israel. This gives us a narrative structure that is roughly U-shaped, the apostasy being followed by a descent into disaster and bondage, which in turn is followed by repentance, then by a rise through deliverance to a point more or less on the level from which the descent began. This U-shaped pattern, approximate as it is, recurs in literature as the standard shape of comedy, where a series of misfortunes and misunderstandings brings the action to a threateningly low point, after which some fortunate twist in the plot sends the conclusion up to a happy ending. The entire Bible, viewed as a "divine comedy," is contained within a U-shaped story of this sort, one in which man, as explained, loses the tree and water of life at the beginning of Genesis and gets them back at the end of Revelation. In between, the story of Israel is told as a series of declines into the power of heathen kingdoms, Egypt, Philistia, Babylon, Syria, Rome, each followed by a rise into a brief moment of relative independence. The same U-narrative is found outside the historical sections also, in the account of the disasters and restoration of Job and in Jesus' parable of the prodigal son. This last, incidentally, is the only version in which the redemption takes place as the result of a voluntary decision on the part of the protagonist (Luke 15:18).

It would be confusing to summarize all the falls and rises of the Biblical history at once. In honor of the days of creation, let us select six, with a seventh forming the end of time. The first fall, naturally, is that of Adam from Eden, where Adam goes into a wilderness that modulates to the heathen cities founded by the family of Cain. Passing over the story of Noah, which adds the sea to the images of disaster, the first rise is that of Abraham, called out of the city of Ur in Mesopotamia to a Promised Land in the west. This introduces the pastoral era of the patriarchs, and ends at the end of Genesis, with Israel in Egypt. This situation again changes to an oppressive and threatening servitude; Israel again passes through a sea and a wilderness, and under Moses and Joshua reaches its promised land again, a smaller territory where the main images are agricultural. There succeed the invaders in the Book of Judges, of whom the most formidable were the Philistines, probably a Greek-speaking people from Crete (if that is the "Caphtor" of Amos 9:7) who gave their name to Palestine. They held the mastery of Israel after the defeat and death of Saul and his son Jonathan. The third rise begins with David and continues with Solomon, where the imagery is urban, concerned with cities and buildings. After Solomon, however, another disaster begins with the splitting of the kingdom. The northern kingdom was destroyed by Assyria in 722 B.C.; the southern kingdom of Judah had a reprieve until after Assyria was destroyed in its turn (Nahum 2:3ff.); but with the capture of Jerusalem by Nebuchadnezzar in 586 the Babylonian captivity began.

The fourth rise in the fortunes of the Israelites, now the Jews, begins with the permission—perhaps the encouragement—given the Jewish captives in Babylon by Cyrus of Persia to return and rebuild their temple. Two returns are prominently featured in the Old Testament, and there were probably more, but symbolically we need only one. Some flickering hopes of a restored Israel clustered around the chief figure of the first return, Zerubbabel of the line of David. After several changes of masters, the next dramatic descent was caused by the savage persecution of the non-Hellenized Jews by Antiochus Epiphanes of the Seleucian empire, which provoked the rebellion of the Maccabees, five brothers of a priestly family who finally gained independence for Judea and established a royal dynasty. This lasted until the Roman legions under Pompey rolled over the country in 63 B.C., and began the Roman domination that lasts throughout the New Testament period. At this point Jewish and Christian views of the sixth deliverance of Israel diverge. For Christianity, Jesus achieved a definitive deliverance for all mankind with his revelation that the ideal kingdom of Israel was a spiritual kingdom. For Judaism, the expulsion from their homeland by the edict of Hadrian in 135 A.D. began a renewed exile which in many respects still endures.

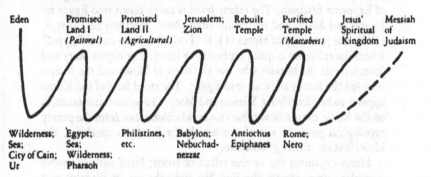

| Eden | Promised Land I (Pastoral) | Promised Land II (Agricultural) | Jerusalem; Zion | Rebuilt Temple | Purified Temple (Maccabees) | Jesus' Spiritual Kingdom | Messiah of Judaism |

| Wilderness; Sea; City of Cain; Ur | Egypt; Sea; Wilderness; Pharaoh | Philistines, etc. | Babylon; Nebuchadnezzar | Antiochus Epiphanes | Rome; Nero | | |

This is a sequence of *mythoi*, only indirectly of historical events, and our first step is to realize that all the high points and all the low points are metaphorically related to one another. That is, the garden of Eden, the Promised Land, Jerusalem, and Mount Zion are interchangeable synonyms for the home of the soul, and in Christian imagery they are all identical, in their "spiritual" form (which we remember means metaphorically, whatever else it may also mean), with the kingdom of God spoken of by Jesus. Similarly, Egypt, Babylon, and Rome are all spiritually the same place, and the Pharaoh of the Exodus, Nebuchadnezzar, Antiochus Epiphanes, and Nero are spiritually the same person. And the deliverers of Israel—Abraham, Moses and Joshua, the judges, David, and Solomon—are all prototypes of the Messiah or final deliverer.

Of all the upward movements on our chart, the primary and model form is the deliverance from Egypt, and the creation of the nation of Israel that formed part of this deliverance. As the various declines of Israel through apostasy and the like are not acts so much as failures to act, it is only the rises and restorations that are real events, and as the Exodus is the definitive deliverance and the type of all the rest, we may say that mythically the Exodus is the only thing that really happens in the Old Testament. On the same principle the resurrection of Christ, around which the New Testament revolves, must be, from the New Testament's point of view, the antitype of the Exodus. The life of Christ as presented in the Gospels becomes less puzzling when we realize that it is being presented in this form.

Like that of many gods and heroes, the birth of Jesus is a threatened birth: Herod orders a massacre of infants in Bethlehem from which Jesus alone escapes. Moses similarly escapes from an attempt to destroy Hebrew children, as they in turn escape later from a slaughter of Egyptian firstborn. The infant Jesus is taken down into Egypt by Joseph and Mary, and his return from there, Matthew (2:15) says, fulfills the prophecy of Hosea (11:1) "I called my son out of Egypt," where the reference is quite explicitly to Israel. The names Mary and Joseph recall the Miriam who was the sister of Moses and the Joseph who led the family of Israel into Egypt. The third Sura of the Koran appears to be identifying Miriam and Mary; Christian commentators on the Koran naturally say that this is ridiculous, but from the purely typological point of view from which the Koran is speaking, the identification makes good sense.

Moses organizes the twelve tribes of Israel; Jesus gathers twelve disciples. Israel crosses the Red Sea and achieves its identity as a nation on the other side; Jesus is baptized in the Jordan and is recognized as the Son of God. The baptism is the point at which Mark and John begin, the infancy stories of Matthew and Luke being probably later material. Israel wanders forty years in the wilderness; Jesus, forty days. Miraculous food is provided for Israel and by Jesus for those gathered around him (see John 6:49-50). The law is given from Mount Sinai and the gospel preached in the Sermon on the Mount. A brazen serpent is placed on a pole by Moses as preservation against the fatal bites of "fiery serpents" (Numbers 21:9); this brazen serpent was accepted by Jesus as a type of his crucifixion (John 3:14), with an underlying association between the lethal serpents and the serpent of Eden. Moses dies just outside the Promised Land, which in Christian typology signifies the inability of the law alone to redeem man, and the Promised Land is conquered by Joshua. The hidden link here is that Jesus and Joshua are the same word, hence when the Virgin Mary is told to call her child Jesus or Joshua, the typological meaning is that the reign of the law is over, and the assault on the Promised Land has begun (Matthew 1:21).

This is the longer version of the parallel: the shorter one is still more important typologically. The core of the Exodus story is the interval between the last plague and the crossing of the Red Sea, and it contains three main events. First is the destruction of the Egyptian firstborn by a destroying angel, which the Israelites escaped by smearing the blood of a lamb on their doorposts. This is the archetype of the Passover festival. Second is the drowning of the Egyptian army in the Red Sea, and third is the crossing of the Red Sea by the Israelites to the desert beyond. The life of Christ also has a longer version in the upper air, so to speak, in which he comes "down" from heaven, metaphorically the sky ("descendit de coelis," as the Creed says) to be born on the earth, goes through his ministry on the earth, and goes back into the sky with the Ascension. This movement is repeated on a lower level in the Passion, where Jesus dies on the cross on Good Friday, is buried, descends to the lower world during what from the Christian point of view was the last Sabbath, and returns to the surface of the earth in the Resurrection on Easter Sunday morning.

It follows that the crossing of the Red Sea, leaving the Egyptians still in it, is the type, not merely of Jesus's baptism in the long version, but of the Resurrection in the short one. Hence the imagery of such Easter hymns as this fourth-century one of St. Ambrose:

For these are our paschal solemnities, in which the very lamb is slain, by whose blood the doorposts of the faithful are made holy.

This is the night in which thou, Lord, didst first lead our fathers, the children of Israel, out of Egypt and make them cross the Red Sea on dry foot.

This is the night in which Christ broke the bonds of death and rose again as a victor from hell.

O truly blessed night, which alone was worthy of knowing the time and the hour at which Christ rose from the dead!

The Gospels could hardly be more careful than they are to synchronize the Crucifixion with the feast of the Passover, to make it utterly clear that the Passion, as they saw it, was the antitype of the Passover sacrifice.

The contrast with the birth date of Jesus is curious. There is no evidence in the New Testament about the time of year at which he was born, and in celebrating Christmas the Church was apparently content to take over the winter solstice festival from other religions. The most important event in the Mithraic ritual calendar was the birthday of the sun, celebrated on December 25. In Christian typology too Christ was a rising "sun of righteousness" (Malachi 4:2), and Milton's *Nativity Ode* will serve as an example of hundreds of poems that testify to the appropriateness of the winter solstice date. There was perhaps some influence too from Hanukkah, the Jewish feast of the Dedication of the Temple, observed by Jesus when he was in Jerusalem (John 10:22). This was not a winter solstice festival, but it does feature lights and celebrates the birth of a new and purified temple on the anniversary of its pollution by Antiochus Epiphanes (II Maccabees 10:5). This makes it a type of the birth of Christ in the physical body of Adam (John 2:19). Hanukkah was celebrated on the twenty-fifth of Chislev, which is not the twenty-fifth of December, but the coincidence of numbers is interesting.

Mythical and typological thinking is not rational thinking, and we have to get used to conceptions that do not follow ordinary distinctions of categories and are, so to speak, liquid rather than solid (not gaseous: they tend to keep their volume if not their form). In the later commentary on the Exodus story known as the Book of Wisdom we read:

For while peaceful silence enwrapped all things, and night in her own swiftness was in mid course, thine all-powerful Word leaped from heaven out of the royal throne. (18:14ff.)

This refers, in its own context, to something totally different from the birth of Christ, but it is the only type we have of the birth story recorded in Luke, which has Jesus born at midnight. Similarly, in the Church calendar the forty days of wilderness wandering by Jesus are commemorated in Lent, which is immediately followed by Good Friday and Easter, although in the Gospels the whole ministry of Jesus intervened. T. S. Eliot's "Ash-Wednesday" is based on a structure of parallels between the Church calendar, Dante's *Purgatorio*, and various elements in the Bible:

	Old Testament	New Testament	Dante	Church Calendar
1	Promised Land	Resurrection	Eden	Easter
2	Wilderness Wandering	Wilderness Wandering	Purgatory	Lent
3	Red Sea	Baptism (Jordan)	Sea	(Ash Wednesday)

The Christian Bible, considered as a narrative, has for its hero the Messiah, who emerges, as frequently happens in romances, with his own name and identity only near the end. Being the Word of God that spoke all things into being, he is the creator of Genesis, and the secret presence in Old Testament history—the rock that followed the

Israelites with water, as Paul says in a passage (I Corinthians 10:4) already referred to. He enters the physical world at his Incarnation, achieves his conquest of death and hell in the lower world after his death on the cross, and, according to later legend, "harrows hell," extracting from limbo the souls destined to be saved, from Adam and Eve through to John the Baptist. Then, as noted, he reappears in the physical world at his Resurrection and goes back into the sky with Ascension. Thus:

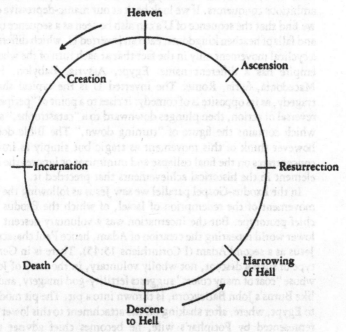

There is a considerable foreshortening of time in the thousands of years between the first two intervals and the "three days and three nights" in the lower world—two nights and one day, according to our reckoning. We also see the working of a principle we have met before: that what fills out a scheme and is not mentioned, or is only doubtfully referred to, in the Bible is very apt to be supplied by later legend. The New Testament evidence for the descent into hell is weak, and the "harrowing of hell," though extremely popular in the Middle Ages, is purely apocryphal, deriving from a work known as the Gospel of Nicodemus or the Acts of Pilate.

It may seem inconsistent to show the Messianic quest as a cycle when the anticyclical bias of the Bible has been so stressed, but this is one more example of the fact that every apocalyptic image has a demonic parody or contrast, and vice versa. The quest of Christ can be thought of as a cycle, because, however important for man, it involved no essential change in the divine nature itself. The nearest suggestion of such a change is the liturgical metaphor that places Christ in the middle of the Trinity before his quest and on the right after it. There is also a demonic cycle caused, not by an impersonal fate, but by the fate deliberately generated out of the pride and folly of ambitious conquerors. If we look back at our manic-depressive chart, we find that the sequence of U's can also be seen as a sequence of rises and falls of heathen kingdoms, each an inverted U, which differs from a cyclical movement only in the fact that at each turn of the wheel the empire has a different name: Egypt, Assyria, Babylon, Persia, Macedonia, Syria, Rome. The inverted U is the typical shape of tragedy, as its opposite is of comedy: it rises to a point of "peripety" or reversal of action, then plunges downward to a "catastrophe," a word which contains the figure of "turning down." The Bible does not however think of this movement as tragic but simply as ironic: it concentrates on the final collapse and minimizes or ignores the heroic element in the historical achievements that preceded it.

In the Exodus-Gospel parallel we saw Jesus as following the rising movement of the redemption of Israel, of which the Exodus is the chief prototype. But the Incarnation was a voluntary descent into a lower world repeating the creation of Adam, hence Paul characterizes Jesus as a second Adam (I Corinthians 15:45). There is in Genesis a type of such a descent, not wholly voluntary, in the story of Joseph, whose "coat of many colors" suggests fertility-god imagery, and who, like Burns's John Barleycorn, is thrown into a pit. The pit modulates to Egypt, where, after shaking off the attachment to this lower world represented by Potiphar's wife, he becomes chief adviser to the Pharaoh through his skill in interpreting dreams. A related story is told of Daniel, who performs a similar service for Nebuchadnezzar and also undergoes tests of faith. Both dreams have to do with historical cycles. Pharaoh's is of a seven-year cycle of alternating plenty and famine, connected with the great importance of seven-year cycles in the Near East that is also reflected in the "jubilee" regulations in Leviticus 25. Nebuchadnezzar's is of a statue representing a sequence of world empires, beginning with his own, which are destroyed by a stone rolling downhill, representing in turn the Messianic kingdom that puts an end to all cycles of power in history.

The four empires in Daniel, we are told, are the Babylonian,

Median, Persian, and Macedonian: there seems to have been no Median empire, but evidently the author of Daniel thought there was. It was more natural for later readers to see the sequence as Babylonian, Persian, Greek, and Roman. In the Reformation period, we saw, some Protestant polemic extended to the Roman Catholic Church the allusions to the Roman Empire in the Book of Revelation, and declared the Pope to be an Antichrist figure. In seventeenth-century England a sect of "fifth-monarchy men" identified them-selves with the stone of Nebuchadnezzar's dream, the image of the final kingdom putting an end to the tyranny of Rome, which in their view had lasted since New Testament times. They formed part of a quite significant counterculture in their time, one brilliantly satirized in Ben Jonson's play *The Alchemist*, but very difficult to understand without some knowledge of Biblical typology.

In the Gospel the emphasis naturally falls on the end of all cyclical movements and the coming of a final separation between apocalyptic and demonic worlds. For all that, a new historical cycle was begin-ning, though in the New Testament itself it was thought to extend only from the first to the second coming of Christ, and its duration (so far as it was in time) was assumed to be very short. In any case there appears to be an intermediate cyclical movement in Biblical history which runs, in the phrase of Robert Graves, "from ark to ark." Here translations make a connection that the Hebrew does not: the Hebrew words for Noah's ark (*thebah*) and the ark of the covenant ('*aron*) are quite different; but the Septuagint uses the same word (*kibotos*) for both, the Vulgate uses *arca* for both, and the AV's "ark" follows suit. Noah's ark, floating on a drowned world and coming to rest on top of a mountain, a gigantic seed of a new world with all future human and animal life in it, completes the first great cycle of human existence. Another, on a smaller scale, begins when the infant Moses escapes the fate of the other Hebrew children by being concealed in an ark. The Israelites carry the ark of the divine presence through the dry land they reach after their pursuers are drowned in the sea; and the ark is eventually brought into Jerusalem, where it rests at symbolically the highest point of the world, as Noah's ark did before it.

Two versions of the Nativity are given in Matthew and in Luke: tradition has never had any difficulty in adding Matthew's wise men to Luke's shepherds, but has adopted Luke's "manger" in preference to Matthew's "house" (2:11). If the antitype of the temple is the body of Christ, the antitype of the ark of the covenant could be the infant Christ. The manger, with its fertility overtones, contains a vestige of

Noah's ark in the animals inhabiting it. An ox and an ass invariably appear in paintings of the scene: they come ultimately from Isaiah 1:3:

> The ox knoweth his owner, and the ass his master's crib: but Israel doth not know, my people doth not consider.

The word "crib" in the Septuagint is *phatne*, the same word translated as "manger" in Luke. There is nothing in the Old Testament to connect the ark of the covenant with Bethlehem, except for a curious Psalm that appears to be based on some ritual of searching for the ark, a ritual with many parallels in extra-Biblical cults, and which contains the line: "Lo, we heard of it at Ephratah [Bethlehem]" (Psalm 132:6). The end of this "ark" sequence in the Bible is the appearance, in Revelation 11:19, of the ark of the covenant in heaven, where what has been a hidden presence is now manifest to everyone.

As the hero of the entire Biblical narrative, Christ unites within himself all the types of authority, specifically those of prophet, priest, and king. As king, and recognized as such by the wise men, he is the antitype of Solomon in particular, the legendary king of wisdom and the composer of proverbs and fables (I Kings 4:32). The visit of the wise men to Christ is the antitype of the Queen of Sheba's visit to Solomon, the connecting link being Isaiah 60:6. It is obvious from the extended prayer ascribed to Solomon at the consecration of his temple that he was thought to have priestly functions as well, but the figures of king and high priest were not combined until Simon, the third brother of the priestly Maccabee family to rise to power in Judea, was made high priest, like his predecessors Judas and Jonathan, and added to this some attributes of royalty (I Maccabees 14:43), his successors taking the title of king. The king-priest figure is represented mainly in the Bible by the mysterious "Melchizedek" of Genesis 14:18, described as priest of El Elyon in Salem, who brings bread and wine and the blessing of his God to Abraham when the latter was returning from a successful foray. If El Elyon means the most high God, and if Salem means Jerusalem, this episode appears to have the object of establishing Israel's original right to the city of Jerusalem, along with a god readily identifiable with its own.

Melchizedek appears again in Psalm 110, one of the two Psalms—the other is Psalm 2—that seemed especially significant to Christian readers in defining the royal nature of the Messianic figure. Psalm 2 makes the king the begotten (i.e. adopted) Son of God, who is to rule the whole heathen world. Psalm 110 calls him a priest after the order of Melchizedek, a fact which has made some scholars think that this psalm originally referred to Simon Maccabaeus. Both psalms deeply impressed the author of Hebrews in the New Testament, who makes a good deal of Jesus as a Melchizedek figure, etymologizing the latter's name as "king of righteousness in the city of peace" (Hebrews 7:2).

As the antitype of the prophets, Jesus is related to two great figures in particular, Moses and Elijah. In Jesus' day what was then Scripture was thought of essentially as "the law and the prophets," and Moses and Elijah respectively personified these elements, though Moses, we noticed, was a prophet as well as the secretary of the law (Deuteronomy 34:10). In the AV arrangement of Old Testament books, which follows the Septuagint order but puts the Apocrypha in a separate section, the Old Testament ends with Malachi, so that the closing words of the Old Testament are Malachi's formal exhortation (4:4-6) to remember the law of Moses and wait for the return of Elijah. In the Gospels the prophecy of the return of Elijah is regarded as fulfilled by John the Baptist (Matthew 11:14), though when John himself is asked if he is Elijah he denies it (John 1:21). There is no great difficulty here, but we should note again the implied rejection of the wrong kind of literal meaning. In particular, reincarnation, in its "literal," or there's-that-man-again, form, is not a functional doctrine in the Bible, although, for instance, Nebuchadnezzar and Nero are "spiritually" the same person, ruling over what is "spiritually" the same city of Babylon-Rome. In any case it is appropriate that Moses and Elijah, representing the summary of the Word of God as it was up to that point, should be the figures flanking Jesus in the Transfiguration (Mark 9:2ff.).

This image of a Messianic figure flanked by two others has a type in Zechariah 4, where two olive trees, identified with the spiritual and temporal leaders of the return from Babylon—Zerubbabel of the line of David and Joshua the high priest—are portrayed as flanking a candlestick. This image has a demonic parody in the Crucifixion, with Jesus crucified between two thieves. In Revelation 11 the calamities of the last days include the martyrdom of two "witnesses" ("witness" is the literal meaning of "martyr") who are identified with the symbolic olive trees of Zechariah and apparently with Moses and Elijah as well:

> These have power to shut heaven, that it rain not in the days of their

prophecy: and have power over waters to turn them to blood, and to smite the earth with all plagues, as often as they will. (Revelation 11:6)

In Biblical tradition two men are said not to have died: Enoch (Genesis 5:24), and Elijah, who was carried up to heaven in a chariot. These were associated with, respectively, the first judgment by water, Enoch being a direct ancestor of Noah, and the last judgment by fire. It was this association that gave the books ascribed to Enoch so much authority in the early Church (see Jude 14). But some mysterious features in the death of Moses (Deuteronomy 34:6) led to a pseudepigraphic tradition that his death was an illusion (see Jude 9), and that he was a third person who did not actually die. One of the early sketched outlines for *Paradise Lost* begins with some speculations on this point. Evidently the author of Revelation feels that anyone who did not go through the process of death must return to do it before the end of all death, though he seems to have merged Enoch with Moses.

Prophet, high priest, and king are all figures of authority, but prophets are often martyred and even kings, as we saw, have scapegoat and victim imagery attached to them. Joshua was a type of Christ as the conqueror of the Promised Land: his enemies included five kings who were hung on trees and then buried in a cave with great stones rolled against it (Joshua 10:16ff.). Solomon, the king who succeeded David, is a type of Christ as a temple builder and wise teacher: Absalom, equally a son of David, rebelled against his father and was caught in a tree, traditionally by his golden hair, hanging there "between heaven and earth" until David's general Joab came up and thrust darts into his side (II Samuel 18:14). Absalom's curious helplessness in what seems a relatively easy situation to get out of suggests a ritual element in the story of his death. The writers of the Gospels found that in telling the story of Jesus they needed the imagery of the executed kings and Absalom quite as much as that of the figures of glory and triumph. Similarly, Zechariah's vision of God sold by his people for thirty pieces of silver (11:12), the type of Judas' betrayal of Jesus (Matthew 26:15), turns on the fact that God's value is the symbolic price of a slave (Exodus 21:32).

In this connection there is one theme that recurs frequently in the early books of the Bible: the passing over of the firstborn son, who normally has the legal right of primogeniture, in favor of a younger one. The firstborn son of Adam, Cain, is sent into exile, and the line of descent goes through Seth. Ham, the rejected son of Noah, is not said to be his eldest son, but the same pattern recurs. Abraham is told to reject his son Ishmael because a younger son (Isaac) is to be born to him. Isaac's eldest son Esau loses his birthright to Jacob through some rather dubious maneuvers on Jacob's part, some of them backed by his mother. Jacob's eldest son Reuben loses his inheritance for the reason given in Genesis 49:4. Joseph's younger son Ephraim takes precedence over the elder Manasseh. The same theme is extended, though not essentially changed, in the story of the founding of the monarchy, where the first chosen king, Saul, is rejected and his line passed over in favor of David, who is practically his adopted son (I Samuel 18:2). In later literature the theme is carried much farther back: if we look at the fifth book of *Paradise Lost*, for instance, we see an archetype of the jealousy of an older son, Lucifer or Satan, at the preference shown to the younger Christ.

The Bible is not very friendly to tragic themes: except for the Passion itself, its approach to victim figures tends to be ironic only. Job is a special case, but even Job is hardly a tragic figure in the Greek sense. The Bible does not accept the Greek conception of the hero, the figure of greater-than-ordinary human size, power, descent, and articulateness, who so often seems to have a divine destiny almost within his grasp. But the nodes of tragedy, for a sympathetic reader, are present in some of these passed-over Biblical figures: in Cain's bewilderment at the non-acceptance of his (so far) bloodless sacrifice; in Ishmael's near-starvation with his mother in the desert, and his father's lament: "O that Ishmael might live before thee!" (Genesis 17:18); in Esau's bitter cry when he discovers how callously he has been cheated: "Bless me, even me also, O my father" (Genesis 27:34).

Saul is the one great tragic hero of the Bible: not only physically taller than any of his subjects (I Samuel 9:2), he is an able ruler and by his standards a fair-minded one. But he seems to do nothing right. He spares his enemy King Agag out of human decency, only to be told that in not killing him he is cheating Samuel's ferocious god out of a sacrifice, and that this will never be forgiven by a deity who "is not a man, that he should repent" (I Samuel 15:29). One can of course rationalize this episode, or any other episode, if one is interested in rationalizing. It seems to me that the narrator has not simply made the elementary though very common error of identifying God with the devil, but, by a kind of inspired blundering, has managed to add the one element that makes the story of Saul genuinely tragic. This is the suggestion of malice within the divine nature, a suggestion that is perhaps essential to all great tragedy. Saul becomes a doomed man from then on, with intermittent fits of melancholy and of frantic but futile efforts to rid himself of the threat from David. In the Witch of Endor scene he finally turns to the occult powers that he himself had forbidden consultation with, and disaster and death follow. The terrible and inevitable degeneration will remind the modern reader that Shakespeare must have studied the account of Saul with considerable care before writing *Macbeth*.

With the Romantic movement there comes a large-scale renewal of sympathy for these rejected but at least quasi-tragic Biblical figures, who may be sent into exile and yet are in another context the rightful heirs. Cain, Ishmael, Esau, Saul, even Lucifer himself, are all romantic heroes. The significance of this has to do partly with the change in outline of the mythological universe derived from the Bible by Western culture, which will occupy us in a later part of this study. It is possible too that the theme of the rejected rightful heir is linked to a nostalgia for aristocracy, not so much for itself as for representing some kind of glamour or splendor that has vanished from human life. Certainly Byron, who owed much of his popularity to his combination of aristocratic rank and melancholy attitude, portrays in his *Vision of Judgment* a Lucifer who is an icily polite aristocrat: the younger son, Christ, naturally does not appear, but he is running what is clearly a much more bourgeois establishment, where such inmates as George III feel at home.

The theme of the passed-over firstborn seems to have something to do with the insufficiency of the human desire for continuity which underlies the custom of passing the inheritance on to the eldest son. All human societies are anxious for a clear and settled line of succession: the intensity of this anxiety is written all over Shakespeare's history plays, and if Shakespeare's particular form of it is no longer with us, the anxiety itself is. In such things as the doctrine of apostolic succession we see how strong the need for a sense of unbroken continuity is in the Church as well. Hence the deliberate choice of a younger son represents a divine intervention in human affairs, a vertical descent into the continuity that breaks its pattern, but gives human life a new dimension by doing so. A closely related theme is that of the birth of a son to a mother so late in her life that the birth is a miracle, or at least an act of special grace. This theme appears in the birth of Isaac from the old Sarah (Genesis 21), and is suggested in the birth of Samuel from Hannah. What is interesting in the latter story is that Hannah's song of triumph on the birth of her son makes that birth a symbol of God's revolutionary activity in upsetting and reversing the normal standards of continuous human society:

> The Lord maketh poor, and maketh rich: he bringeth low, and lifteth up.
>
> He raiseth up the poor out of the dust, and lifteth up the beggar from the dunghill, to set them among princes, and to make them inherit the throne of glory. . . . (I Samuel 2:7-8)

This song of Hannah has clearly influenced the Magnificat, or song of Mary, in Luke, which adopts the same theme of revolutionary upheaval:

> He hath put down the mighty from their seats, and exalted them of low degree.
>
> He hath filled the hungry with good things; and the rich he hath sent empty away. (Luke 1:52-53)

The theme of miraculous birth enters the stories of the birth of John the Baptist, whose father, like Sarah, doubts that such a birth can happen, and of the birth of Jesus from a virgin mother, which, as suggested earlier, breaks the line of continuity of descent through David. Jesus is also a second Adam superseding the first one, as well as a second Israel.

But the eldest son, whenever born, and whether naturally or miraculously born, is in either case the first gift of God, and so is technically a "firstfruit" to be given back to God with other firstfruits. This takes us back to the law of Exodus 34:19 already referred to, which stipulates that every firstborn male, whether animal or human, belongs to God, but that human beings are to have a lamb substituted for them. The pattern for this was established when Abraham was commanded to sacrifice his son Isaac, a command which at the last moment was recalled and a ram substituted (Genesis 22). It was confirmed by the redemption of Hebrew children with lambs at the first Passover. The antitype of this is God's sacrifice of his son, where the human and animal or lamb victim are identified. The theme of the sacrifice of Isaac in medieval miracle plays owes much of its moving eloquence to the audience's framework: what is going on is a type of a sacrifice that God carries through to the end with no reprieve.

The original motive behind human sacrifice was doubtless a *do ut des* bargain: I give that you may give. It is assumed that the god, like the ghost in Yeats, lives off the smell of offerings. So if the god is fed by sacrifices he will respond by giving good weather for crops or increased fertility among animals. And he must be fed first, with the "firstfruits" of vegetable and animal produce. However, giving up what is of greatest value to the sacrificer becomes irksome after a while, and objects of lesser value are likely to be substituted. This can happen not only with human but with animal sacrifices: one of the Greek myths tells us that the real sin of Prometheus consisted in his persuading mankind that when they made burnt offerings to the gods they could eat all the real meat themselves, and that the gods would be fully satisfied with the offal. They were not. So, sooner or later, some exceptional disaster will remind us that the deity still wants full payment without cheating. When the Israelites were besieging the king of Moab, Mesha, the Moabite king, placed in a desperate situation, made a desperate effort to attract the support of his god Chemosh:

> Then he took his eldest son that should have reigned in his stead, and offered him for a burnt offering upon the wall. And there was great indignation against Israel: and they departed from him, and returned to their own land. (II Kings 3:27)

The last sentence reads like a somewhat clumsy editorial effort to conceal the fact that in the original story the maneuver worked and the Israelites were in fact driven off. Archaeologists have discovered an inscription by this Mesha which indicates that his devotion to Chemosh was quite as genuinely pious as that of a "good" king of Judah to Jehovah.

The Exodus law specifically rules out human sacrifices, though, as the stories of Agag and Joshua's conquests show, the killing of captives and enemies or of criminals could be thought of as not merely an acceptable but a demanded sacrifice. And Micah seems to imply that the ultimate sacrifice of a firstborn son as payment for some sin (whether the sacrificer's own sin would not matter: see Job 1:5) was a genuine moral problem among his people:

> . . . Shall I give my firstborn for my transgression, the fruit of my body for the sin of my soul? (Micah 6:7)

This is followed by a verse often regarded as one of the great moral breakthroughs in history. The sacrifices of children to the god Moloch, probably connected with breaking the summer drought, are naturally condemned (II Kings 16:3 and elsewhere), but the Old Testament writers are more neutral on the question of sacrifices of children made to fulfill a curse, a vow, or a revenge.

When Jericho was destroyed a curse was laid upon it (Joshua 6:26) to the effect that any rebuilder of the city would have to sacrifice his eldest son to lay the foundation, and his youngest son to set up the gates. But trade routes are more important than children, and Jericho seems to be one of the oldest inhabited human sites in the world, so the sacrifices were duly made and the city rebuilt (I Kings 16:34). When a drought struck in the reign of David, it was broken by the hanging of seven sons of Saul at a carefully specified time of the year:

> And he [David] delivered them into the hands of the Gibeonites, and they hanged them in the hill before the Lord: and they fell all seven together, and were put to death in the days of harvest, in the first days, in the beginning of barley harvest. (II Samuel 21:9)

And while female animals, human or otherwise, are loftily ignored in the Exodus law, Jephthah sacrifices his daughter in fulfillment of a vow (Judges 11:34ff.). Two points are stressed: her virginity, which made her an untouched and hence acceptable sacrificial figure, and the fact that she became the center of a local female cult, doubtless originally on the principle mentioned earlier that virgin goddesses, like Artemis, are often the protectors of childbirth.

Jesus is obviously the eldest of his family (in the New Testament he is explicitly said to have had brothers; see Matthew 13:55 and elsewhere), and was consequently exposed to the two fates of firstborn males. One is that of a sacrificial victim; the other is that of isolation and exile. The type of this double tragedy is given in some of the regulations in the Mosaic law. If there is an outbreak of leprosy, we are told, the priest is to take two birds, kill one over running water, dip the other in its blood, and then let it go (Leviticus 14:4-7).

The meaning of this rite becomes clearer later on, in the ritual prescribed for the Day of Atonement (Leviticus 16). Here there are two goats: one is killed and the other, who has all the sins of the people transferred to him ritually, is driven out and sent to the devil, or more precisely to Azazel, a demon of the wilderness. The AV's ingenious mistranslation of "scapegoat" for Azazel has given an essential word to the language. In the trial of Jesus the same pattern recurs. There are two prisoners, Jesus and Barabbas, a robber whose name means "son of the father": one, Pilate proposes, is to be killed and the other released according to the custom on a feast day. It is, however, abundantly clear that Jesus has both roles: that is, he is also a scapegoat who after his death on the cross, according to tradition, descends into the world of devils. The demonic parody of such a rite would be an offering *to* the demon, Azazel or whomever, which the scapegoat ritual perhaps originally was (see Leviticus 17:7). In some of the early Christian efforts to explain the doctrine of the Atonement this notion of an offering to the devil recurs.

With all this it seems clear that God's statement "Israel is my son, even my firstborn" (Exodus 4:22) confers a highly ambiguous honor, raising the possibility that Israel is being chosen either as a sacrificial victim, or to be passed over and sent into exile, or even both. And this is precisely the inference that Paul does draw in Galatians 4:22ff., where he interprets the story of Abraham's two wives and sons to mean that Ishmael represents Judaism and the accepted Isaac, with his line of descent, Christianity. From the point of view of Judaism this interpretation could hardly be more preposterous, but it is consistent with the Pauline, and in general the Christian, conception of the "new testament." The word "testament" (Hebrew *berith*, Greek *diatheke*) means a covenant or contract, specifically the contract between God and Israel. It also means treaty, and the language of ancient treaties, with their curses on the party who is the first to break it, parallels many Old Testament passages. God, who takes the initiative in drawing up this contract, can break it but will not; Israel cannot really break it but is forever trying to.

We are told that, because of the disobedience of the Israelites who left Egypt, their entire generation would have to die before their descendants could enter the Promised Land: "Unto whom I sware in my wrath that they should not enter into my rest" (Psalm 95:11). The quotation of this passage in Hebrews 3:11 forms part of an argument in which the author of Hebrews is making much the same point about Christianity as the legitimate heir of Judaism that Paul is making with his "allegory" in Galatians. At the time of the Babylonian captivity, Jeremiah expands this conception of the destruction of an older generation and a granting of the promise to a new one into a conception of a new covenant or testament. This new covenant is to be made with a new generation of Israel following the captivity, and will be more individualized and "spiritual" than the old one (Jeremiah 31:31-33). Christianity promptly identified this new covenant or testament with its own teachings, and the new Israel with its own Church.

This structural theme in the Biblical narrative reminds us of folktales where a great quest is to be achieved and a number of older brothers fail to do so before a younger one succeeds. It reminds us chiefly by contrast, it is true, because here it is not any human hero who achieves a quest: the hero, Israel, is merely granted a promise.

But the narrative parallel is still significant. In the folktales we know best it is usually the third son or hero who succeeds, as the rhythm of three seems to provide the most satisfying balance between tension and resolution in a story. If we ask what the hero is supposed to do, we have to make a slight digression from the Biblical narrative in order to re-enter it at another point.

The central expression of human energy is the creative work that transforms the amorphous natural environment into the pastoral, cultivated, civilized world of human shape and meaning. The other side of this is the struggle against the enemy, who has two aspects. The enemy is, first, the human enemy encountered in warfare, and, second, the unshaped and chaotic element in nature, usually symbolized as some kind of monster or beast of prey, and identified with drought, floods, and natural sterility of all kinds. The hero of most human traditions is not the worker but the leader against the human enemy, and no ancient king felt that his record was adequate unless he was portrayed with his foot on the necks of cowed and beaten enemies, most of them prisoners. The second enemy was more mysterious and powerful, usually to be propitiated with sacrifices. But there remained the hope that some hero would prove strong enough to tackle him too. Thus the Athenians were forced to send tributes of youths and maidens to feed the Minotaur in the Cretan labyrinth, until the great hero Theseus went to Crete, descended into the labyrinth, and killed the monster at its heart.

We spoke of Nimrod's exploits as a "mighty hunter" as probably connected with a ritual duty of hunting the lion, a symbol of a greater heroism than a purely military one. In the Tutankhamen collection there is a superb golden statue of the Pharaoh engaged in a similar ritual act of hunting the hippopotamus, identified with the evil god Set, the enemy of Osiris. The youthful Pharaoh looks very resolute, whether or not in practice he could have distinguished a hippopotamus from a zebra. The general form of the myth connected with such rites is given us in the legend we know as that of St. George and the dragon, associated in Classical myth with the story of Perseus.

In this legend an old and impotent king rules over a wasteland oppressed by a sea monster who demands human victims. Already we see a cluster of metaphorical identifications. The land is waste because the king is impotent, the fertility of the land and the virility of the king being linked by sympathetic magic. The monster from the sea inevitably turns up when the land and the king have lost their power, because he is another aspect of sterility. The victims provided for his dinner are chosen by lot, and eventually the lot falls on the king's daughter. At that point the hero arrives, also from over the sea; he kills the dragon, releases the daughter, and becomes the next king by marrying her—the story being old enough to assume a mother-right custom in society. As a myth of renewal, its general shape is clear enough: the hero is the reviving power of spring and the monster and old king the outgrown forces of apathy and impotence in a symbolic winter. It is an easy step from here to a creation myth, and there are many myths in which the creation takes the form of killing some amorphous monster or power of darkness. They belong to a family of myths older than the Bible, and are incorporated into the Old Testament as a form of poetic imagery. We have already noticed that a dragon-killing story like that of the Akkadian *Enuma elish* lies close behind the Genesis creation of the "firmament" out of the chaos of the deep. In the Old Testament this dragon that symbolizes the original chaos is usually called either Rahab or Leviathan.

The creation results from the dragon's death because the dragon *is* death, and to kill death is to bring to life. In contrast to many other mythological systems, in the Bible the dragon seems to be a consistently sinister image. This is not only because of its antisocial habits of breathing fire and eating virgins, but because, of all sinister animals, it has the unique advantage of not existing, and so admirably symbolizes the paradox of evil, which is a powerful and positive force in our present mixture of things in time, but which by itself is pure negation or non-being. The author of Revelation calls him "the beast that was, and is not, and yet is" (17:8; "is" translates the Greek *parestai*, with its overtones of "continuing for the time being"; see v. 10).

The Psalms are full of praises to God as creator, and among these there are frequent references to the act of creation as a victory, as though there were some kind of malignant force that opposed the creation. Thus:

> Thou rulest the raging of the sea: when the waves thereof arise, thou stillest them.
> Thou hast broken Rahab in pieces, as one that is slain; thou hast scattered thine enemies with thy strong arm. (Psalm 89:9-10)

This passage is, among other things, an Old Testament type of one of the attributes ascribed to Christ: the ability to command the raging sea (Mark 4:41 and elsewhere). The sense of a malevolent force of darkness, that wants to bring everything back to formless chaos, and still operates through black magic and similar self-destructive impulses in man, appears in Job's reference to those "that curse the day, who are ready to rouse up Leviathan" (Job 3:8; the AV is wrong). The mythical complex goes back in some measure to the ancient Egyptian myth of a sun-god who descends to the lower world of darkness each night, having to fight his way through evil creatures until his victory the next morning.

Given the strong political slant of the Bible, it is not surprising that these dark mythological forces should be identified with the heathen empires. Thus Isaiah calls Egypt "Rahab that sits still" (Isaiah 30:7; again the AV will not do). Egypt is called Rahab in Psalm 87:4, and its Pharaoh is identified with "the great dragon that lieth in the midst of his rivers" in Ezekiel 29:3. Hence the imagery of the creation myth can be extended to the Exodus and to the "Day of the Lord" in the future when Israel is to be redeemed:

Awake, awake, put on strength, O arm of the Lord; awake, as in the ancient days, in the generations of old. Art thou not it that hath cut Rahab, and wounded the dragon?

Art thou not it which hath dried the sea, the waters of the great deep; that hath made the depths of the sea a way for the ransomed to pass over? (Isaiah 51:9-10)

God has shown his power over Rahab at the creation, and for a second time when he drowned the Egyptian army in the Red Sea and allowed the Israelites to pass through it. He is now being appealed to to make a third and final demonstration of his power.

The leviathan is thought of as a sea monster, and this final effort is symbolized as the hooking and landing of the leviathan. Isaiah says:

In that day the Lord with his sore and great and strong sword shall punish leviathan the piercing serpent, even leviathan that crooked serpent; and he shall slay the dragon that is in the sea. (Isaiah 27:1)

Ezekiel is even more explicit: here the leviathan is the Nile as well as the sea, and as the Nile is the source of the life of Egypt, the catching of the leviathan will be followed by the fertilizing of the desert he is thrown into:

But I will put hooks in thy jaws, and I will cause the fish of thy rivers to stick unto thy scales. . . .

And I will leave thee thrown into the wilderness; thee and all the fish of thy rivers: thou shalt fall upon the open fields; thou shalt not be brought

together, nor gathered: I have given thee for meat to the beasts of the field
and to the fowls of the heaven. (Ezekiel 29:4-5)

But, if the symbolism is to be complete, it will not be only birds and
animals that will eat the flesh of the leviathan but the people of Israel
as well. This is an element in later Jewish Messianic myth, and
appears in the Psalms:

Thou didst divide the sea by thy strength: thou brakest the heads of the
dragons in the water.
Thou brakest the heads of leviathan in pieces, and gavest him to be meat
to the people inhabiting the wilderness. (Psalm 74:13-14)

The text of the last phrase is not beyond dispute, but the symbolic
theme is clear: in the "Day of the Lord" the leviathan, the devouring
monster who swallows everything, will himself be swallowed: a
reversal of perspective we encountered earlier, for example in harvest
and vintage imagery. Metaphorically, a monster in the sea *is* the sea;
hence the landing of the leviathan is much the same thing as the
abolition of the sea of death in Revelation 21:1 already glanced at.

Now if Leviathan and Rahab are also Babylon and Egypt, it follows
that Israel in Egypt, or the Jews in captivity in Babylon, have already
been swallowed by the monster, and are living inside his belly:

I will make mention of Rahab and Babylon to them that know me:
behold Philistia, and Tyre, with Ethiopia; this man was born there. (Psalm
87:4)

But what is true of Israel in Egypt is typologically true of the human
situation generally. All of us are born, and live our natural lives,
within the leviathan's belly. In the political aspect of the leviathan,
we live in subjection to secular powers that may become at any time
actively hostile to everything except their own aggressiveness, the
leviathan being "king over all the children of pride" (Job 41:34).
Cosmologically, the leviathan is the element of chaos within creation:
that is, it *is* creation as we see it now, the world of time and space that
extends away from us indefinitely, the limitless expanse that is the
most secure and impregnable of all prisons.

This suggests a modulation of the St. George-Perseus story in
which the heroine (Andromeda in the Perseus version) is already
inside her leviathan, and the hero has to go down the brute's throat to
rescue her. Here we have the structural pattern behind any number of
displaced versions in romance, in which a hero has to make a perilous
journey into a place of great danger where the heroine is held.

Descending a monster's throat reminds us of Jonah, who is told to prophesy against Nineveh, and, having no taste for martyrdom, sets off in a ship in the opposite direction. The ship is nearly wrecked in a storm: the sailors, discovering by lot that Jonah is responsible, throw him overboard and he is swallowed by a great fish, who eventually disgorges him on dry land. We should have enough training in metaphorical thinking by now to realize that the sea, the sea monster, and the foreign island he lands on are all the same place and mean the same thing. Jesus accepted the Jonah story as a type of his own Passion (Matthew 12:40), and in medieval paintings of the descent to hell he is shown walking into the throat of a large toothy monster representing hell. Again, metaphorically, his redemption ("harrowing") of the subterranean world is identical with his redemption of the world above it, the latter being symbolically subterranean as well. The heroine, or Andromeda, of the gospel story is the "bride" Jerusalem, the total body of redeemed souls who are symbolically a single female.

Toward the end of the Book of Job we are introduced to two monsters, a land monster and a sea monster, Behemoth and Leviathan. The poetic kernels out of which they developed may have been the hippopotamus and the crocodile, both Egyptian animals, as marginal notes in many editions of the AV suggest. But this is as irrelevant as any other rationalizing: it would be interesting but unlikely to see a crocodile of whom it could be said that "by his sneezings a light doth shine, and his eyes are like the eyelids of the morning" (Job 41:18). The New English Bible, apparently taking "behemoth" to be the intensive plural of the Hebrew word for beast, reduces the two animals to the leviathan only. But whatever may be textually true of Job, traditionally there have always been two monsters. Behemoth and Leviathan are mentioned in II Esdras 6:49 as two creatures; a land beast and a sea beast appear in Revelation 13, and Daniel's story of Nebuchadnezzar's turning into a variety of the behemoth is clearly a parallel to Ezekiel's earlier identification of the leviathan with the Pharaoh of Egypt.

The symbolic reason for the importance of having two animals is that if we all live inside the belly of the leviathan, our habitat can be thought of symbolically as either subterranean or submarine, in comparison with the reality of the world of the restored Israel. The wonderful cave drawings of the paleolithic period may have been connected with an earth-mother cult in which the cave was identified with her womb. This symbolism may have persisted into historical times in the form of the labyrinths of Crete and the like. Later, as mythologies, especially the Biblical one, broke away from earth-mother symbolism, the subterranean world became associated with the bowels of a sinister monster. This monster belongs to a *lower* world, and may be thought of as under the earth, as in Dante. If we turn, however, to the sea monster that is metaphorically the sea, we remember what we said earlier, that in one dimension of the Deluge story the Deluge has never receded, and we still live in a submarine world of reality.

We can now, perhaps, understand why there should be so much about fishing in the Gospels, and why Jesus himself should be so often associated in later legend with a fish or dolphin. The identification of Jesus with a fish has been traditionally assisted by an acronym: the initial letters of "Jesus Christ, Son of God, Saviour" in Greek spell out the word *ichthys*, fish. In any case the theme of redemption out of water follows in the sequence that includes the story of Noah's ark, the crossing of the Red Sea by the Israelites, the symbolism of baptism in which the person baptized is separated into a mortal part that symbolically drowns and an immortal part that escapes, and such occasional uses of the image as the cry to God from the depths of the waters in Psalm 69. The figure of the wise teacher or culture hero as fish goes back to the undoubtedly ancient myth of Oannes in Babylonian legend.

Further, if the monster that swallows us is metaphorically death, then the hero who comes to deliver us from the body of this death (the phrasing is from Romans 7:24) has to be absorbed in the world of death—that is, he has to die. Even the St. George plays make a point of this, as in these plays St. George usually dies along with the dragon, and has to be brought to life by a "doctor." In the story of Jesus there is a scapegoat theme, already referred to, in which the hero is driven from his society into a world of demons. We suggested that originally the scapegoat rite may have been an offering *to* the demons; and in the gospel story too sin and death are symbolically transferred by the hero to the demonic world, hence the Resurrection, including the harrowing of hell of later legend, effects a total separation of the world of life from the world of death.

To summarize: If we follow the narrative of the Bible as a sequence of events in human life, it becomes a series of ups and downs in which God's people periodically fall into bondage and are then rescued by a leader, while the great heathen empires rise and fall in the opposite rhythm. At a certain point this perspective goes into reverse, and what we see is something more like an epic or romantic hero descending to a lower world to rescue what is at the same time a single bride and a large host of men and women. In this perspective the *sequence* of captivities and redemptions disappears and is replaced by a unique act of descent and return. But the act, if in itself unique, has many symbolic settings.

Traditionally man lives in four elements—earth, water, air, and fire—and in Christian typology we have seen something of the imagery of resurrection in connection with the first two. Subterranean imagery, or something very close to it, also enters Ezekiel's vision of the valley of dry bones and the opening of the graves at the time of Jesus' death on the cross (Matthew 27:52). Deliverance out of fire comes into the references to Egypt as a "furnace of iron" (I Kings 8:51 and elsewhere) and in the story of Nebuchadnezzar's fiery furnace. We may note that the song of celebration for this latter deliverance, reproduced in the Apocrypha as the "Song of the Three Holy Children," is a paean of praise to God for his creation, as seen from the perspective of a wholly awakened mind. In the story of the Ascension (Acts 1), the "literalness" of the account of Jesus' rising through the air until "a cloud received him out of their sight" seems curious at first. But, again, the image is not really one of Jesus' floating upward into what we call outer space, but of the deliverance he achieves for mankind *out of* the natural air, an image most appropriately placed just before the descent of the true or spiritual air (and fire), the Holy Ghost, in the next chapter. The same imagery is glanced at by Paul when he speaks of meeting the Lord "in the air" at the time of the apocalypse (I Thessalonians 4:17).

We may take the Book of Job, perhaps, as the epitome of the narrative of the Bible, as the Book of Revelation is the epitome of its imagery. The order of Old Testament books in most copies of the AV, following the Septuagint but keeping the Apocrypha separate, seems very arbitrary at first, but it makes its own kind of sense. The books from Genesis to Esther are concerned with history, law, and ritual; those from Job to Malachi with poetry, prophecy, and wisdom. In this sequence Job occupies the place of a poetic and prophetic Genesis. It is again a U-shaped story: Job, like Adam, falls into a world of suffering and exile, "repents" (i.e., goes through a *metanoia* or metamorphosis of consciousness), and is restored to his original state, with interest. In contrast to Genesis, there is no breach of contract to attract theological lawyers, and Job's ordeal is not a punishment but a testing.

His friends come to see him in his misery: they may be "miserable comforters" (16:2), but they are neither foolish nor malignant. They have nothing to gain from coming to see him, and their motivation seems decent enough (see 2:13). The discussion naturally focuses on a question of causality: What has brought about Job's disasters? The friends struggle hard to contain the issue within the rather simpleminded Deuteronomic framework of law and wisdom that they understand, or feel that they understand. Job must somehow have disturbed the balance of divine justice, and the balance must right itself. If that is not the answer, there is no human answer, and we must resign ourselves to the mystery of God's ways, with the hope that they make better sense than they appear to do. At first glance Job's final acquiescence (42:3) seems to be agreeing with this, which implies that the friends have been right all along, even though they are expressly said not to be (42:7).

Job is "righteous in his own eyes" (32:1) only from the point of view of his friends: he is not protesting innocence but saying that there is a vast disproportion between what has happened to him and anything he could conceivably have done. In other words, the situation cannot be contained within the framework of law and wisdom, and no causal explanation is good enough. All four speakers, or five counting Elihu (who is thought to be a later addition), are deeply pious men, and the one type of explanation that cannot occur to them is the one that has already been given to the reader: that God had made a kind of wager with Satan on Job's fidelity. Such a notion would have seemed to them not only frivolous but blasphemous, suggesting as it does that God has a stake and a concern of his own in the matter.

The fact that God's speech at the end of Job makes no reference to the pact with Satan, and that Satan disappears totally from the action after the second chapter, is not a real difficulty, as we see if we look at our table of demonic images. Behemoth and Leviathan are metaphorically identical with Satan; what is different is Job's perspective. We noted that the Biblical account of creation is ambiguous in the sense that darkness and chaos are at first outside the created order and are then dialectically incorporated into it, with the separation of land from sea and the division of light from darkness. Hence Leviathan and Satan may be thought of either as enemies of God outside his creation, or as creatures of God within it. In the Book of Job, and consistently only there, the latter perspective is adopted:

Satan the adversary is a tolerated visitor in God's court, and Leviathan is a creature of whom God seems to be rather proud.

At the beginning, however, the role of Satan is the traditional one of cynical accuser, and his appearance in the poem sets up the whole legal framework of prosecution, defense, trial, and judgment which is the "fallen" or Satan-initiated vision of the human situation. Job is confident that he has a defender on his side (19:25; the AV's "redeemer" is perhaps over-Christianized, but the general sense of Job's word *go'el* is not too different from this), but he also wishes, like the hero of Kafka's *Trial*, which reads like a kind of "midrash" on the Book of Job, that his accuser would identify himself, so that Job would at least know the case against him. He wishes for his accuser to write a book (31:35) and we have suggested that Byron may have been right in calling history "the devil's scripture." The case against Job is simply that he lives in a world in which a good deal of power is held by Satan. Job, like the good Samaritan in Jesus' parable, comes from the country of an *Erbfeind* of Israel (assuming that Uz is in Edom), and, however genuine his piety, he is, like Israel in Egypt, in a world exposed to an arbitrary process of nature and fortune. If a soldier is asked why he kills people who have done him no harm, or a terrorist why he kills innocent people with his bombs, they can always reply that war has been declared, and there are no innocent people in an enemy country during a war. The answer is psychotic, but it is the answer that humanity has given to every act of aggression in history. And Job lives in enemy territory, in the embrace of heathen and Satanic power which is symbolically the belly of the leviathan, the endless extent of time and space.

The magnificent conclusion of Job's summarizing speech (29-31) is the climax of the poem, and nowhere in literature is there a more powerful statement of the essence of human dignity in an alien world than we get from this miserable creature scraping his boils with a potsherd. One issue in the great test is that of identity or property: how much can a man lose of what he has before the loss begins to affect what he is? God had previously drawn a rough line between Job's possessions and his "life" (2:6), but here we begin to see what "life" means for humanity: a consciousness that is neither proud nor abased, but simply responsible, and accepts what responsibility is there. God has clearly won his wager. The imagery suggests a man in the prime of his life: Job is no aged and impotent king whose daughters can be appropriately swallowed by a monster. The friends, who are old, have spoken; Elihu, who is young, has yet to speak: they are the continuing cycle of the voice of law and wisdom. Job lets Elihu's speech go by without comment on either its cocksureness or its genuine if not altogether original eloquence. He has heard it all before: it is all true, and all nonsense. He is waiting for a different kind of voice altogether. And suddenly, out of the whirlwind, it comes.

At first we are very disappointed. God seems to be only echoing Elihu, saying that he made the world and that Job did not, and that consequently Job has no right to be questioning his ways. We begin to wonder if some quaking later editor has decided to botch the whole enterprise, in order to justify the ways of man's superstition and slave morality to God. But even if such an editor exists, he has left too much of the original poem for us to come to terms with him: he is, in short, too facile a hypothesis. The fact that God's speech is thrown into a series of rhetorical questions to which "no" is the only answer seems to give it a bullying and hectoring quality, and certainly there is no "answer" to Job's "problem." But did we ever seriously think that so great a poem would turn out to be a problem with an answer? To answer a question, we suggested at the beginning, is to accept the assumptions in it, and thereby to neutralize the question by consolidating the mental level on which the question was asked. Real questions are stages in formulating better questions; answers cheat us out of the right to do this. So even if we remain dissatisfied with God's performance, a God who was glibly ready to explain it all would be more contemptible than the most reactionary of divine bullies.

We remember that Job himself was groping toward a realization that no causal explanation of his alienated plight was possible. In a sense God is speaking out of Job's own consciousness here: any causal explanation takes us back to a First Cause, that is, the creation. The rhetorical questions really mean, then, in this context: don't look along the line of causes to the creation: there is no answer there, and no help there. How Job got into his position is less important than how he is to get out of it; and it is only because he was not a participant in creation that he can be delivered from the chaos and darkness within it. God's speech, if we are right about its general meaning, makes no sense without the vision of Behemoth and Leviathan at the end, which is the key to it. The fact that God can point out these monsters to Job means that Job is outside them, and no longer under their power.

The Book of Job is usually classified among the tragedies, but it is technically a comedy by virtue of its "happy ending," with Job restored to prosperity. In its conventional comic form of renewal, this kind of conclusion is seldom very convincing: people who lose their daughters are not really consoled with new daughters; conditions that cause suffering can be changed, but the scars of the suffering remain. Once again, a renewal or future restoration is most intelligible as a type of a present transcendence. But the transcendence can hardly be to a different state of being altogether, as in waking from a dream: if the restored world were discontinuous with the world of the boils and uncomprehending friends, there would be no point in the poem.

The sequence of resolutions at the end follows the usual Biblical pattern. First is the restoration of the human community: we are told that God turned the captivity of Job when he prayed for his friends (42:10), even though what the friends have said "in God's behalf," to use Elihu's phrase, is not acceptable. The reintegration of the human community is followed by the transfiguration of nature, in its humanized pastoral form. One of Job's beautiful new daughters has a name meaning a box of eye shadow. Perhaps if we were to see Job in his restored state we should see, not beautiful daughters or sixteen thousand sheep, but only a man who has seen something that we have not seen, and knows something that we do not know.

For all the conventional Oriental formulas of self-abasement, some kind of confidential message seems to pass between God and Job, of which we overhear only such fragments as "I abhor myself" and "I have heard of thee by the hearing of the ear; but now mine eye seeth thee" (42:5-6). The first statement seems to mean primarily that what we should call Job's egocentric perception has disappeared along with its objective counterpart, the leviathan. The second one, even though it continues to use the first personal pronoun, makes the shattering claim to a direct vision of God that the Bible, even in the New Testament, is usually very cautious about expressing. A previous statement to the same effect (19:26-27) seems to have been retouched by an editor. The one reference to Job in the New Testament: "Ye have heard of the patience of Job, and have seen the end of the Lord" (James 5:11) carries on the same figure of a leap from hearing to seeing, but puts it in a Christian setting: what the readers of James have "seen" is the coming of Christ. But Job seems to have gone the entire circuit of the Bible's narrative, from creation and fall through the plagues of Egypt, the sayings of the fathers transmitting law and wisdom, the flash of prophetic insight that breaks the chain of wisdom, and on to the final vision of presence and the knowledge that in the midst of death we are in life.

We have somewhat expanded our earlier remark that the Book of Job, though classified as wisdom literature, needs the prophetic perspective to understand it. Job follows, not the horizontal line of precedent and prudence, but the U-shaped progression of original prosperity, descent to humiliation, and return. The prophetic element in the book is thus connected with its narrative shape. This in turn reminds us of the Bible's concern for narrative or *mythos* generally, which may be fictional, as here or in the parables of Jesus, or closer to the historical categories vaguely called "non-fiction." The emphasis on narrative, and the fact that the entire Bible is enclosed in a narrative framework, distinguishes the Bible from a good many other sacred books. The Buddhist sutras employ relatively little narrative, and the Koran consists of revelations gathered up after Mohammed's death and arranged in order of length, with no discernible narrative principle in their sequence. The narrative framework of the Bible is a part of its emphasis on the shape of history and the specific collision with temporal movement that its revelation is assumed to make. In a sense, therefore, the deliverance of Job is a deliverance from his own story, the movement in time that is transcended when we have no further need of time. Much the same thing would be true of the relation of Jesus to the Passion narrative, which is the kernel of the Gospels. The inference for the reader seems to be that the angel of time that man clings to until daybreak (Genesis 32:36) is both an enemy and an ally, a power that both enlightens and cripples, and disappears only when all that can be experienced has been experienced.

CHAPTER EIGHT

LANGUAGE II

Rhetoric

So far we have devoted most of our attention to the unity of imagery and narrative to be found in the Bible. Some aspects of this unity are clear enough, such as the care taken to indicate a beginning and an end. It would hardly be possible to start off a sacred book more logically than the opening words of Genesis do. The Book of Revelation, difficult as it may be for "literalists," becomes much simpler when we read it typologically, as a mosaic of allusions to Old Testament prophecy. The writer seems to have been closer to the Hebrew text of the Old Testament than most New Testament writers, and he seems to have little explicit awareness of other New Testament books. But the more one studies his book, the more convinced one feels that it was deliberately composed as a coda or finale to the whole canon. It ends with the adjurations which are conventional in this type of writing, not to remove or add anything from or to "this book," with appropriate curses on anyone who tries to do so. The primary reference of "this book" is to the Book of Revelation itself, but it is hardly possible to see these words at the end of the entire Bible without giving them a wider application, and one perhaps also intended. It has Old Testament prototypes in Deuteronomy 4:2 and elsewhere.

In the middle of the book (11:1ff.) the author is exhorted by an angel to take a "reed" and measure the temple of God. The source of this is Ezekiel 40:3 (see also Zechariah 2:1), where the word for reed is *qaneh*, from which our word "canon" is ultimately derived. Remembering that in Christian typology the antitypical temple is the body of Christ or the Word of God, one wonders whether the figure of measuring the temple does not have something to do with establishing a canon of writings. At any rate the two "witnesses" Moses and Elijah, the two pillars of Scripture as the author of Revelation knew it, turn up immediately afterward in the text.

The Israelites seem to have been a rather unhandy people, not distinguished for architecture or sculpture or even pottery; and their one great building achievement, Solomon's temple, besides being built by foreigners, was of rather modest dimensions, though the more enthusiastic Chronicler, writing centuries later, transforms it into a fairytale confection glittering with something like twenty tons of gold. But in general it was the heathen kingdoms that produced the really impressive temples and palaces, while the Israelites produced a book. This doubtless seemed at best only a consolation prize to people who thought of buildings as more substantial than words, but history has long since reversed such a perspective. The irony expressed in Shelley's sonnet "Ozymandias" was familiar to ancient writers also. Nineveh was the greatest city of the ancient world, and it was a three-day's journey, the author of Jonah assures us (3:3), to cross it: an impressive tribute to the size, if not of Nineveh, at least of the Nineveh legend. Yet it quite suddenly disappeared under the sands, where it remained until the mid-nineteenth century.

In the Book of Jeremiah (36:20ff.) there is a superb scene in which the prophet's secretary sits in the king's palace reading from a scroll to the king a prophecy which consists mainly of denunciations of his foolish and obstinate policy of resistance to Babylonia. Every so often the infuriated monarch cuts off a piece of the scroll with a knife and throws it into the fire. This must have been a papyrus scroll: parchment, besides being out of the prophet's price range, would have been tough enough to spoil the king's gesture. The king's palace totally disappeared in a few years, whereas the Book of Jeremiah, entrusted to the most fragile and combustible material produced in the ancient world, remains in reasonably good shape. The supremacy of the verbal over the monumental has something about it of the supremacy of life over death. Any individual form of life can be wiped out by the smallest breath of accident, but life as a whole has a power of survival greater than any collection of stones.

Some ancient nations showed little interest in recording their mythologies in writing. The Egyptians must have been familiar with the myth of Isis and Osiris for thousands of years, but there is apparently no consecutive or full account of it before Plutarch. The Semitic peoples, including the Assyrians, took much greater documentary care of their mythological traditions, but the Hebrew devotion to a canonical body of writing seems to be a unique development, whatever the partial parallels. It is possible that another Old Testament scene catches the moment of its birth. During the reign of Josiah, one of the last kings of Judah, repairs are made in the temple and a document is discovered by accident there which is brought to the king and read to him. The king says:

Go ye, enquire of the Lord for me, and for the people, and for all Judah, concerning the words of this book that is found: for great is the wrath of the Lord that is kindled against us, because our fathers have not hearkened unto the words of this book, to do according unto all that which is written concerning us. (II Kings 22:13)

The most interesting feature of this is the king's obvious conviction that it was a matter of the highest importance for the people as a whole to know the contents of a written document. Inevitably such a document would be a law book: the primary social elements to be committed to writing are the laws. But considering that contemporary democracy is really based on the principle of access to public documents, we can perhaps see history turning a decisive corner here.

Many scholars have accepted as likely the possibility that the scroll thus discovered was, or was closely related to, the existing Book of Deuteronomy. In the present arrangement of the first five Old Testament books, Deuteronomy (the word means "second [or repeated] law") is placed last, where it looks like a summary or addendum to the preceding four. But if this conjecture is right, Deuteronomy was the germ out of which the whole canon eventually developed. In continuing the process, the ancient materials in the first four books were re-edited; writings of prophets older than the discovery of Deuteronomy were collected; histories were written under Deuteronomic influence, and so on until the New Testament canon was established around the first law of Christianity to love God (Matthew 22:37), which is a quotation from Deuteronomy 6:5. This historical theory is not essential to my present approach, except that it gives a dimension of time and growth to the assumption of the imaginative unity of the Bible. The closing of the canon is a more mysterious process, but by Jesus' time, while the status of a few books was still undetermined, there was a general feeling that the law was complete and that the voice of prophecy had ceased. A large body of post-prophetic writing, known as apocalyptic, was produced by both Jewish and Christian writers, but except for Daniel in the Old Testament and Revelation in the New, none of it got into the canon as we know it.

In most scholarly fields there is a central body of data so generally accepted as to be treated, for all practical purposes, as established facts. The historical scholarship of the Bible has produced a smaller body of such data than its bulk would naturally suggest. Most of the established principles are negative, and many of them have to do with questions of traditional authorship. There is a body of writings, apart from the Apocrypha and dating mostly from the last century or so before Christ, which are called Pseudepigrapha, meaning "false writings," because some of them, such as the Book of Enoch, are ascribed to venerated figures who assuredly did not write them. Most of the generally accepted data of Biblical scholarship are connected with demonstrating that many if not most books of the Bible are pseudepigrapha in the same sense.

This fact seldom affects the text of the Bible, only the captions it has been traditionally festooned with. Nevertheless even a century ago many people were rather scandalized to hear that Moses could not have written any part of the Pentateuch, that David and Solomon did not write the Psalms and the Wisdom literature, that "the Book of Isaiah" is not a book by Isaiah but a collection of oracles extending over several centuries; that the Book of Daniel turns into Aramaic halfway through, and could no more be written by a contemporary of Nebuchadnezzar than a book that turned from Latin into Italian could be Julius Caesar's; that it is unlikely that any of the twelve disciples mentioned in the Gospels wrote any part of the New Testament, and that some of Paul's most typical and personal letters may not be wholly his.

A great deal of learning and ingenuity is still employed in resisting these conclusions, and revisionist arguments based on the as-we-now-have-them formula still appear. The anxieties in such arguments are based on modern assumptions about bookmaking and writing which are irrelevant to the Bible. The assertion that Jesus' beloved disciple John wrote the Gospel of John, the three epistles of John, and perhaps the book of Revelation as well, even if it turned out to be true, would still not be a defense of the "authenticity" of these works. Similarly with the conception of "inspiration" often invoked in this connection, that is, a semi-trancelike state in which an author is a kind of sanctified tape recorder writing from the immediate dictation of what appears to be an external source. This again, we see, is an author-centered conception, which grew up in later times after it was assumed that revelation had ceased. But the Bible is not what people whose taste in style differs from mine would call an "authored" book at all: authorship is of too little importance in the composition of the Bible for such conceptions as "inspiration" to have any real function. The word "author" is used only for convenience, and should really be kept in quotation marks.

For example: tradition has unanimously assigned to the third Gospel the name of Luke. This means that he is usually spoken of as its author, or even its inspired author. But there is hardly a word in that Gospel, beyond perhaps the first four verses, of which Luke is likely to have been in any modern sense the author. Luke's Gospel, like the majority of Biblical books, is an edited compilation of a variety of documents. According to what is still the prevailing view, he used Mark and a collection of sayings of Jesus called *Q* by scholars (from the German *Quelle*, source), which he shares in common with Matthew. *Q* was for a long time a scholar's hypothesis only, but since the discovery of the so-called Gospel of Thomas we have had tangible evidence that such documents as *Q* did exist. There is also a certain amount of material peculiar to Luke, including the "Magnificat" and "Nunc Dimittis" hymns at the beginning, of which he is unlikely to have been the composer. Editing and compiling of this sort are highly conscious and deliberate activities, and if the conception of "inspiration" is going to be stretched far enough to include them, it cannot add much to an argument.

Similarly with the Pentateuch, generally regarded as edited from four or five major documents differing widely in date and character. Even discounting the complexities of editorial scholarship in this field, which sometimes suggest a schizophrenic working with scissors and paste, one point is clear: if the Bible is to be regarded as "inspired" in any sense, sacred or secular, the editing and conflating and redacting and splicing and glossing and expurgating processes all have to be taken as inspired too. There is no way of distinguishing the voice of God from the voice of the Deuteronomic redactor.

It is futile also to try to distinguish what is "original" in the Bible, the authentic voices of its great prophetic and poetic geniuses, from the later accretions and corruptions sometimes alleged to surround them. The editors are too much for us: they have pulverized the Bible until almost all sense of individuality has been stamped out of it.

There are, of course, many different rhetorical styles in the Bible, and here and there we find glints of a writer's personality: in Ecclesiastes, in Jeremiah, in Paul. But the author of Ecclesiastes was an editor too: he "set in order many proverbs" (12:9) that are not claimed to be his; and with Paul we often cannot be quite sure where Paul stops and someone else begins. We are so possessed by the modern notion that all the qualities we admire in literature come from the individuality of an author that it is hard to realize that this relentless smashing of individuality could produce greater vividness and originality rather than less. But so it seems to be.

Typology may sometimes provide a tentative explanation of why the material in the Bible is as it is. In the Gospel of Thomas we find most of the beatitudes, but they are not gathered together in one place as they are in Matthew. In the usual count there are ten beatitudes, corresponding to the ten commandments of the older dispensation, parodied in the demonic world by the plagues of Egypt, also usually counted as ten. The Sermon on the Mount, in which the beatitudes appear, is in great part a commentary on the ten commandments. Perhaps the idea of a Sermon on the Mount itself is editorial and originated with Matthew, as the Christian counterpart to the giving of the law from Mount Sinai; if so, the idea of collecting the beatitudes may also have originated with Matthew, or a predecessor (Luke has a less complete series). Such notions may seem startling to our normal expectations in reading, guided as they are by certain assumptions that belong to modern formalism, and to cultural conditions that we have no reason to suppose Matthew understood or shared. In any case, what the gospel writers were doing clearly will not fit into the usual conventions of modern authorship, whether of fact or of fiction.

Whatever the truth about the antiquity of writing as compared to the oral tradition—a question considerably fogged up in recent times—an oral tradition is normally anonymous, and a fully developed writing tradition tends toward identified authorship. Pseudonymous authorship, which we find both inside and outside the Bible, is a halfway stage between the two, and is even more difficult for the modern mind to understand. It is in a sense more primitive than either, and descends from the primitive habit of regarding everything sacred as secret, to be communicated only orally. In this process the "author" is the first person who delivered the secret, and he is a legendary figure lost in the mists of time. Occult literature is closely related to this tradition. In occult writing there normally is, or is assumed to be, a long oral tradition preceding, which does not commit itself to writing until the tradition has begun to break down. Hence in written occultism some identification with a legendary figure is very frequent. For example, the "hermetic" literature that had such a vogue in the fifteenth century was ascribed to the legendary Hermes Trismegistus, and regarded as incorporating the wisdom of ancient Egypt in which Moses himself was instructed. What we possess of hermetic literature, however, are Alexandrian and Neoplatonic works dating from the early centuries of the Christian era.

Eventually pseudonymous identification begins to clash with the ethos of a developed writing culture, which says that pseudonymous authorship must be either purely imaginative or else fraudulent. The Epistle of Jude (14) accepts the Enoch of Genesis as the author of the book of that name, but others realized that that was impossible, and the book fell out of favor, disappearing from the Western world until the end of the eighteenth century. In a work of literature such identification is purely imaginative, as when Browning identifies himself with Fra Lippo Lippi, or Ezra Pound with Simon Zelotes. We recognize that we are very near this imaginative area in the Book of Ecclesiastes, where the writer says, "I the Preacher was king over Jerusalem," thereby identifying himself with Solomon. There is also in early Christianity a story called the Clementine Recognitions, where the narrator is said to be Clement, a well-known figure of the early Church, and the chief character Peter. This work has affinities with late Greek romance, and is on the borderline between the pseudonymous and the imaginative.

Tertullian, writing around 200 A.D., tells us of a priest who wrote a fraudulent book about Paul, and says that when his authorship was discovered he was degraded from his office. His superiors must have felt, quite reasonably as it seems to us, that, even though his book was not written in the first person, anyone who suggests he is the Apostle Paul when he is not the Apostle Paul is a liar, and the truth is not in him. But the unlucky priest thought he was doing honor to Paul by associating his book with him. I say "unlucky" advisedly, because the second Epistle of Peter in the New Testament, perhaps not so far removed from him in time, says that it was written by Simon Peter the Apostle of the Lord, and not many New Testament scholars would accept that statement. One can of course work out conceivable connections with Peter in various ways, but the smell of rationalization is over them all, and II Peter is probably best described, in terms of the ethos of a writing culture, as a pious fraud. But to infer that it should not be in the canon because it is pseudonymous would indicate a very undeveloped historical imagination, besides starting a process that logically could not stop until most of the Bible had been thrown out with it.

Certainly such aids to faith as the conception of inspiration are easier if we have an identifiable author, such as we have in the Koran. The Koran, like most sacred books, has its origin in dictation and secretarial recording, but there is only one intermediary: nothing would ever be added to the Koran that had not come from (or, theologically, through) Mohammed. But the Koran is both a later and a vastly more homogeneous book than the Bible. The Bible is, first of all—to use a word no less accurate for being a fashionable term—a mosaic: a pattern of commandments, aphorisms, epigrams, proverbs, parables, riddles, pericopes, parallel couplets, formulaic phrases, folktales, oracles, epiphanies, *Gattungen*, *Logia*, bits of occasional verse, marginal glosses, legends, snippets from historical documents, laws, letters, sermons, hymns, ecstatic visions, rituals, fables, genealogical lists, and so on almost indefinitely. All these elements are, to use Milton's phrase in *Areopagitica*, contiguous and not continuous, and it is no good looking for continuous consistency of the sort that we get in verse or prose controlled by a single mind.

Once we have got rid of the fetish of individual authorship, and recognize that we are in a more objective world, we can see many unities of a different kind. Homeric criticism has passed through a similar development. First it was unquestioned that a man named Homer wrote both the *Iliad* and the *Odyssey*; then the poems were torn into fragments by analytical critics; and now scholarship is back to the notion of a "Homer." But this new "Homer" is not a man but a metaphor for the fact that once more we read both poems as unities. Similarly, the Book of Isaiah is not a unity of authorship, but it is a unity for all that: a sequence of oracles grouped around three major foci that carry us through the three great narrative stages of Israel's descent, bondage, and return with warnings. Or, again, the Hebrew arrangement of Old Testament books, which is much more schematic than the Christian one derived from the Septuagint, divides them into the Law, the Former Prophets or Histories, the Latter Prophets, and a more miscellaneous group called the "Writings," which includes Daniel and the later Chronicle history. The New Testament shows a greatly foreshortened but curiously parallel sequence, the Gospels corresponding to the law, the Acts to the histories, the

Epistles to the prophecies, and Revelation, which owes so much in spirit to Daniel and the Chronicler's romanticized story of the temple, to the Writings.

In the Hebrew arrangement the Old Testament canon ends with II Chronicles, where the last words are an exhortation to the Jews in Babylon by Cyrus of Persia to return to their homeland. As a type of the future restoration of Israel, this makes a logical and effective conclusion to the Bible from the point of view of Judaism. Christianity had no interest in making a dramatic conclusion to a story which it regarded as having a sequel, but the opening of John's Gospel, we saw, was intended to be the Christian antitype of the Genesis account of creation. It seems likely then that this Gospel was intended to stand first in the New Testament canon. By a historical accident, however, it was the last Gospel to be admitted, and so was placed fourth, where it interrupts the narrative flow from Luke into its sequel Acts.

It is remarkable that the Bible displays as much interest as it does in unifying its material, and the anxiety reflected in Judaism about closing the canon of law and prophets, and similar anxieties in Christianity, are connected with that interest. But unity, a primary principle of works of art since Plato's time, also indicates the finiteness of the human mind, the *care* that works toward transforming the "imperfect" or continuous into the "perfect," the form achieved once and for all. The Bible, however unified, also displays a carelessness about unity, not because it fails to achieve it, but because it has passed through it to another perspective on the other side of it. We have now to try to get a glimpse or two of that wider perspective.

By themselves verse and prose are both normally continuous, and the Old Testament at least is a mixture of verse and prose. The AV translators knew very little about Hebrew poetry, and do not distinguish verse from prose typographically as modern translations do. But most copies of the AV in general circulation do something else of considerable interest: they print each verse as a separate paragraph, so that normally the sentence and the paragraph are the same unit. This gives the rhythm of the AV a curiously discontinuous quality that is neither verse nor prose but something in between, and that does correspond to something in the original. That something is connected with the paratactical structure of Biblical Hebrew, with its avoidance of qualifying or subordinate clauses and its relentless sequence of short sentence units connected by "and" (*wa*). The AV translators sometimes substitute "hence," "therefore," "accordingly," or other quasi-logical connectives for "and": these may not be mistranslations of sense, because *wa* is a versatile word, but of course the effect on the ear is very different. In no language but Biblical Hebrew, perhaps, would it have been possible to put together so miscellaneous a mass of material. The Hebrew Old Testament, despite the use of the Septuagint, is also the stylistic model of the New Testament, which is as close to it in rhythm as the nature of the Greek language will allow.

Printing each sentence separately, along with numbering the verses, which has no ancient authority but is essential for reference, is a device affected by two factors. One is that it is a convenience to preachers looking for texts; the other is that it is a convenience in public reading. Modern translations assume a culture of rapid and silent individual reading, hence they usually render at least the prose in as continuous a rhythm as possible, with the verse numbers, which in such a context have become something of a nuisance, spattered down the side. The implication is that the AV has stressed one aspect of the Biblical rhythm only, perhaps to the point of exaggeration. But the aspect it stresses is of great importance nonetheless. The clue to the immense literary success of the AV is the clause on its title page: "appointed to be read in churches." The ear of the AV translators for the rhythm of the spoken word, though there are many lapses, was very acute, and it is a sobering thought that it is sensitivity to one's own language, not scholarly knowledge of the original, that makes a translation permanent. A translator with a tin ear, including a translator of the Bible, is continually mistranslating, whatever his scholarly knowledge. The AV renders *Yahweh Tzabaoth* "the Lord of Hosts"; the American Revised Version (1901) renders it "Jehovah of Hosts," which is a greatly inferior translation. Anyone who doubts this has only to try it out on his eardrum.

As for the convenience of preachers, it is worth considering for a moment just what the critical assumption is that underlies the choice of a text for a sermon. The conception of the "text" in this sense implies that the Bible is a collection of authoritative sentences, and that the center of the entire Biblical structure is whatever sentence one happens to be looking at. For the preacher's purpose the immediate context of the sentence is as likely to be three hundred pages off as to be the next or the preceding sentence. Ideally, every sentence is the key to the whole Bible. This is not a factual statement about the Bible, but it helps to explain the practice of preachers who knew what they were doing, like some of those in seventeenth-century England.

In the sermons of John Donne, for example, we can see how the text leads us, like a guide with a candle, into the vast labyrinth of Scripture, which to Donne was an infinitely bigger structure than the cathedral he was preaching in.

We have now two critical principles to go on with. One is that the Bible, in its linguistic conventions, is very close to the conventions of the spoken word and the oral tradition. The other is that, ideally, every sentence in it is a kind of linguistic monad. From one point of view the Bible is as unified and continuous as Dante, which is how we have been looking at it hitherto; from another point of view it is as epiphanic and discontinuous as Rimbaud. It is this decentralized perspective that I want to examine next.

In the history of every literature, poetry develops before prose. In Old English, for example, it is only the prose that sounds at all "primitive": the poetry is as subtle and mature as any other poetry. This is partly because the formulaic devices of verse—meter, rhyme, alliteration, fixed epithets, and the like—make verse the simplest and most direct way of conventionalizing words for communication. They permit ready memorizing and improvising, both essential in days before anything that we think of as "literature" was normally consigned to writing. Such features make some types of verse powerfully continuous, as Homer shows. Other types are more meditative: the rhythm returns on itself, completing one unit at a time. Later examples would be the Latin elegiac and the English stopped couplet. The unit of Biblical verse, parallelism, is of this returning kind. It is a unit of two (more rarely three) members, of which the second completes the rhythm but often adds little if anything to the sense. It is an admirable rhythm for conveying the feeling of a dialogue initiated by God, which the reader completes simply by repetition:

I will say of the Lord, He is my refuge and my fortress,
 my God; in him will I trust.
Surely he shall deliver thee from the snare of the fowler,
 and from the noisome pestilence.
He shall cover thee with his feathers,
 and under his wings shalt thou trust . .
Thou shalt not be afraid for the terror by night,
 nor for the arrow that flieth by day;
Not for the pestilence that walketh in darkness;
 nor for the destruction that wasteth at noonday.
   (Psalm 91:2-6)

It is interesting to see how this antithetical rhythm of Hebrew verse persists in the New Testament, which is neither in verse nor in Hebrew:

> Or what man is there of you, whom if his son ask bread, will he give him a stone?
> Or if he ask a fish, will he give him a serpent? (Matthew 7:9–10)

or:

> If the whole body were an eye, where were the hearing?
> If the whole were hearing, where were the smelling? (I Corinthians 12:17)

The fact that the greater part of the Old Testament is in prose indicates that it achieved its present form at a relatively late cultural stage. Bits of earlier poetry are embedded in the text from Genesis through Kings: they were found in earlier records, and several of these records are identified by name, the most important being the "Book of Jasher" (the word means "upright," but the significance is unknown: perhaps it implies "heroes"). If we turn to Numbers 21, we can see something of the variety of sources that the Pentateuchal documents draw from: this chapter includes, first, a fragment from a source called "The Book of the Wars of Jehovah"; second, a little work-song of celebration after digging a well, and, third, a fragment from a collection of proverbs (the New English Bible reads "bards"). Some of these bits of verse are centuries older than the context in which we find them, and the difference in attitude between early poem and later narrative is often clearly marked. The later poetry of the Psalms and prophets follows the same conventions, though the difference from the early verse is as obvious to Hebrew scholars as the difference between Wyatt and Tennyson is to us. Sometimes the fact that the second half of a parallel couplet is not intended to add to the sense leads to misunderstandings. The Old Testament type of the event celebrated in Christianity as Palm Sunday, the riding of Jesus into Jerusalem on an ass, is the oracle in Zechariah 9:9:

> Rejoice greatly, O daughter of Zion; shout, O daughter of Jerusalem: behold, thy King cometh unto thee: he is just, and having salvation; lowly, and riding upon an ass, and upon a colt the foal of an ass.

Mark, Luke, and John, reading this passage correctly as poetry, realized that only one animal was involved: Matthew, reading it more "literally," tries to get two into the act:

> . . . Go into the village over against you, and straightway ye shall find an

ass tied, and a colt with her: loose them, and bring them unto me. (Matthew 21:2)

Parallelism is a rhythmical unit, but not, so far as scholars can tell, consistently a metrical one: metrical organization certainly occurs in the Old Testament, but probably a good many metrical patterns have been wiped out by an editorial process that had no interest in poetry as such. Continuous prose, as we saw, belongs to a later phase of language, and the prose contemporary with earlier phases falls into a much more discontinuous rhythm, where there is a very little distinction between sentence and paragraph. As we have just seen that this is true of Biblical prose as well, we seem led to the principle that the predominant rhythm of the Bible is one that can extend in the direction of either verse or prose with a minimum of change.

The simplicity of the AV style has often been praised, and this too is a quality that belongs to the original. But there are different kinds of simplicity. A writer of modern demotic or descriptive prose, if he is a good writer, will be as simple as his subject matter allows him to be: that is the simplicity of equality, where the writer puts himself on a level with his reader, appeals to evidence and reason, and avoids the kind of obscurity that creates a barrier. The simplicity of the Bible is the simplicity of majesty, not of equality, much less of naïveté: its simplicity expresses the voice of authority. The purest verbal expression of authority is the word of command, as we have it in the army, where long training in automatically obedient response is fundamental. The rhetoric of command is as paratactical as words can be: soldiers will not charge with fixed bayonets in response to a parenthesis, a subordinate clause, or a subjunctive mood. The higher the authority, the more unqualified the command: if qualifying or adapting to circumstances is essential, it is for subordinates to do it.

God says "Let there be light," and light appears, unable to protest that it might have been more logical to create first a source of light, such as the sun. In the Decalogue God says "Thou shalt not kill" or, in Hebrew, "Kill not." Period, as we say now: there is nothing about judicial execution, war, or self-defense. True, these are taken care of elsewhere in the Mosaic code, because the commandment is addressed to human beings, that is, to psychotic apes who want to kill so much that they could not even understand an unconditional prohibition against killing, much less obey it. Hence in its human and legal context "Don't kill" cannot "really" mean "Don't kill": it means only "Private murder is wrong because it is unpredictable and upsets established social authority." The point is that it is in the unqualified order that we hear the voice of authority most clearly.

The voice of authority, when transmitted by a human being, is impersonal: another reason that individuality is of so little importance in the Bible. In the proverbs of wisdom literature, it expresses the authority of tradition; in the oracles of the prophets, it is normally prefaced by "Thus saith the Lord." The same oracle appears in Isaiah 2:4 and Micah 4:3: it does not matter which of them uttered it. In the Book of Amos the prophet is urged by a nervous official to go somewhere else to prophesy and not to go on attacking the establishment in his own country. Amos responds:

> Now therefore hear thou the word of the Lord: Thou sayest, Prophesy not against Israel, and drop not thy word against the house of Isaac.
>
> Therefore thus saith the Lord: Thy wife shall be an harlot in the city, and thy sons and thy daughters shall fall by the sword, and thy land shall be divided by line; and thou shalt die in a polluted land. (Amos 7:16-17)

The prophet may be right or wrong, reasonable or unreasonable: the thing he does not do is hedge. The lion, unlike the monkey and the squirrel, is not a conversationalist, and the rhetoric of authority is leonine rhetoric: "The Lord will roar," as Amos says (1:2). And the lion risks his authority as king of beasts unless his roar is in the strictest paratactical rhythm. Similarly, Jesus says:

> But I say unto you, That whosoever shall put away his wife, saving for the cause of fornication, causeth her to commit adultery: and whosoever shall marry her that is divorced committeth adultery. (Matthew 5:32)

Some scholars think that the phrase "saving for the cause of fornication" is a later interpolation. One reason why they think so is stylistic: the cautious legal cough of parenthesis has no place in a prophetic style, but is a sign that someone is trying to corrupt the gospel into a new law.

Continuous or descriptive prose has a democratic authority: it professes to be a delegate of experiment, evidence, or logic. More traditional kinds of authority are expressed in a discontinuous prose of aphorisms or oracles in which every sentence is surrounded by silence. The Greek philosophers before Plato—Heraclitus, Pythagoras, Anaximander—uttered their sayings and stopped. It was for the disciple to ponder and meditate, not to argue or question as he might with the more linear Socrates. Or again, suppose we wanted to learn something about yoga, a discipline also founded on oral tradition. There are many books on yoga, written in continuous prose, but they all refer us, as a higher authority, to the Yoga Sutras of Patanjali. We turn to Patanjali and find ourselves, stylistically speaking, in a quite different world. Every sentence is a gnarled, twisted, knotty aphorism demanding a long period of study, able to carry a whole commentary by itself. Again, it is for the subordinate to explain and qualify. Philosophers, who sometimes grow weary of being contradicted or refuted, have always been strongly attracted to this aphoristic style of unquestioned authority: we find it in Spinoza, in Leibnitz, and as late as Wittgenstein. The Bible has less of the dark saying because its primary interest is in ethical action: its style, as noted, is of the battlefield rather than the cloister, but the same principle holds.

The rhythm of the Bible expands from a series of "kernels," as we may call them, units that are very close to the kinds of verse and prose employed in the Bible. In the wisdom literature this kernel is the proverb or aphorism; in the prophets it is the oracle, usually in verse like the Greek oracles; in the Torah it is the commandment; in the Gospels it is the pericope, a term to be discussed later. In the New Testament epistles, especially Paul, with his lively colloquial style and his many business and commercial metaphors, there is more sense of running continuity, but there is an underlying discontinuous rhythm of exhortation that comes out very clearly here:

> Rejoice evermore.
> Pray without ceasing.
> In every thing give thanks. . . .
> Quench not the Spirit.
> Despise not prophesyings.
> (I Thessalonians 5:16-20)

A similar if less staccato rhythm is found in the catalogues of scriptural exempla, as in the "by faith Abel," "by faith Enoch," "by faith Noah," sequence in Hebrews 11.

It is already clear that what has been called the metaphysic of presence meets us at every turn in the Bible, and that the spoken word either takes precedence of the written word or lies closely behind it. In general, the great religious teachers do not write: they talk, and their words are recorded by secretaries or disciples. In the Bible the written word, for all the permanence I have assigned to it, is often associated with transience. God speaks, and his words are described as eternal: writing is not only a far greater condescension, but what is said to be written by God's own hand in Exodus 32:16 is destroyed by verse 19. Jesus says that his words will outlast heaven and earth (Mark 13:31), but is shown only once as writing, and then on the ground

(John 8:6), what he wrote being obviously soon erased. Many of the prophets wrote or had their oracles recorded in writing, but the archetypal prophet is Elijah, who, whatever else he may have been, was clearly not a writer.

In poetry recited to a listening audience a great deal of repetition is needed that a reader does not need. The Old English poem *Beowulf* contains a long recapitulation of a previous narrative, because it is close to and is reflecting the conventions of oral literature. In Shakespeare, too, near the end of a play we sometimes have a summarizing speech of a kind that a theater audience would find helpful. Then again, music, which also addresses a listening audience, is capable of a degree of repetition that a reader would find intolerable. We do not want the singer of a *da capo* aria merely to say "Now I go back to the beginning and do it all over again," although that is all that his score would say. In listening we demand that a certain rhythmical period be filled out, regardless of the repetition involved.

There is one curious episode in the Bible that illustrates this point. In Exodus 25ff. God gives detailed instructions for constructing the ark of the covenant and similar sacred objects, and a craftsman named Bezaleel is appointed for the task. In ordinary written prose we should expect one sentence saying that Bezaleel made all these things as he was commanded to do. We actually get, in Exodus 36ff., a repetition of each detail, with "and thou shalt make" transposed to "and he made." Such repetition is primarily to impress the reader with the importance of what is being done, but the conventions employed are close to those of oral literature.

Traditionally, the Bible speaks with the voice of God and through the voice of man. Its rhetoric is thus polarized between the oracular, the authoritative, and the repetitive on the one hand, and the more immediate and familiar on the other. The more poetic, repetitive, and metaphorical the texture, the more the sense of external authority surrounds it; the closer the texture comes to continuous prose, the greater the sense of the human and familiar. This principle holds even when the context is not one of direct command. Take the account of the killing of Sisera in Deborah's war-song:

She put her hand to the nail, and her right hand to the workmen's hammer; and with the hammer she smote Sisera, she smote off his head, when she had pierced and stricken through his temples.

At her feet he bowed, he fell, he lay down: at her feet he bowed, he fell: where he bowed, there he fell down dead. (Judges 5:26-27)

If we compare this with the later prose account that precedes it (Judges 4), we can see how the prose narrator, simply because he is writing prose, is compelled to be circumstantial, to give details and explain things: in short, suggest that "this is the way it must have happened." Here we have the poetic original, so we know that the Judges 4 account is only one of many possible ways of explaining what happened. Elsewhere we are not so fortunate.

I have hinted that the AV emphasizes, to the point of exaggeration, the oracular and discontinuous rhythms of the Bible: the aspect of its rhetoric that suggests divine authority rather than human action. Every translation is likely (certain if it is a translation of the Bible) to be more homogeneous in style than its original, and the AV is least successful when the human voice is most obvious. It renders, for example, the beginning of Ecclesiastes 2:3 as "I sought in mine heart to give myself unto wine, yet acquainting mine heart with wisdom." What this means is that the Preacher tried to be a sensible epicurean, seeking pleasures without hangovers, drinking without getting drunk. When this is rendered in a style that sounds like something out of an *oraison funèbre* of Bossuet, the reader is badly misled about the emotional tone of the shrewd, humorous, tough-minded attitude behind it. Then again, while the language of the AV, though conservative, was still the language of its time, by our day the antique coloring of "thou hast" and the southern "eth" ending of verbs greatly increases the sense of the oracular and distant. The tone of much of the New Testament, especially Paul, is sometimes better caught by modern translations, simply because they are modern. And yet we often find that the most secular-minded readers are startled and put off by the assimilation of the Bible to the conventions of continuous prose. The rhetorical problem posed by the Bible is insoluble for the translator, who can only do his best and cut his losses; perhaps some aspects of it were insoluble for the original writers and editors as well.

Jesus remarks to Nicodemus (John 3:8) that those who are born of the Spirit are like the wind, in that no one can tell whence it comes or where it goes. How does one present the life of a man who was so obviously one of those born of the Spirit? A continuous biography, such as would be appropriate for someone existing continuously on our own level, would be out of the question: a series of mysterious apparitions by some kind of disembodied phantom would be equally so. The gospel writers solve this problem by the device sometimes called "pericope," the short discontinuous unit normally marked by a paragraph sign in most copies of the AV. Jesus appears in a certain context or situation that leads up to a crucial act, such as a miraculous healing, or to a crucial saying, such as a parable or moral pronouncement. Hence the Gospels are, as one scholar says of Mark, a sequence of discontinuous epiphanies. In the pericope one may distinguish the kernel, as we have called it, the miracle, the parable, or the aphorism, and a "husk," a setting in which it takes place. Similar "husk" material is found in the Old Testament, where the oracles of prophecy are embedded in the context of a prophet's life and career. Perhaps the entire historical aspect of the Bible may be thought of as a husk or context of certain laws, the histories being mainly illustrations of what happens when they are or are not observed.

In Chapter I we saw that the rhetorical style of the Bible was oratorical, a combination of the poetically figured and the concerned, of imaginative and existential appeal. Like Orpheus, it combines poetic with magical influence, a point to which we shall soon return. The twentieth-century guru Gurdjieff is said to have taught his followers that practically everything we consider art is "subjective" art, where the artist is taken over by the conventions and conditions of his art, and whose appeal to his audience is both restricted and haphazard. Beyond this is an "objective" art which sounds like a propagandist's wish-fulfillment dream, where the artist knows exactly what effect he wants to produce and can produce it at will, influencing his public as he wishes. The examples given of objective art are the Sphinx, a statue in India that only Gurdjieff had seen, the objective music that brought down the walls of Jericho, and, in the verbal area, the Gospels. I get a strong impression, which may be quite unfair, that Gurdjieff did not really know what he was talking about, but had derived the notion from someone who did. Yet the questions his distinction raises of the role of the "objective" in the arts, of the degrees of authority and persuasive power in the works of any given cultural heritage, of the meeting point of the sacred book and the work of literature, are worth exploring, however tentatively.

I have often recurred to a distinction of experience in the arts that seems to me a genuine one. If we are listening to music on the level of say, Schumann or Tchaikovsky, we are listening to highly skillful craftsmanship by a distinguished and original composer. If then we listen to, say, the "Kyries" of the Bach B Minor Mass or the Mozart Requiem, a certain impersonal element enters. What we hear is still "subjective" in the sense that it is obviously Bach or Mozart, and could not possibly be anyone else. At the same time there is a sense of listening to the voice of music itself. This, we feel, is the kind of thing music is all about, the kind of thing it exists to say. The work we hear is now coming to us from within its context, which is the totality of musical experience; and the authority of that total context reinforces the individual authority of the composer. Similarly in literature, where I have devoted much of my critical life to attempting to suggest what context within literature individual works of literature belong to. It is the voice of drama itself that we hear in Shakespeare or Sophocles, and the sense of a totality of dramatic experience, of what drama exists to set forth, looms closely behind them.

As we continue to study the "classics" of literature, certain details begin to come loose from their moorings. Characters in Shakespeare or Dickens take on a life of their own apart from their function in the play or the novel they appear in; certain quotations become, not simply familiar, but equipped with a relevance to hundreds of situations in addition to their original one. In Shakespeare's day there was much more emphasis, in studying literature in school, on the importance of *sententiae*, the epigrammatic comments on the human situation in, for example, a comedy of Terence: these were often copied into commonplace books and memorized. What is happening here is that the work of literature is acquiring the existential quality of entering into one's life and becoming a personal possession. The capacity to take on this quality of being quotable in a variety of situations is unpredictable: there is far more of it in *Alice in Wonderland*, for example, than there is in Thackeray or Browning, and it correlates with no system of value. But it indicates that literature can acquire the same decentralizing element that we have been discussing in connection with the Bible. The man who could not enjoy *Hamlet* because it was so full of quotations was responding to this quality in Shakespeare, if not in a very well-informed way.

Returning to the Bible, we soon come to understand the importance of a critical principle we may call *resonance*. Through resonance a particular statement in a particular context acquires a universal significance. Thus the tremendous vision of a blood-soaked deity treading the winepress alone in Isaiah 63 is one that has haunted us ever since with its terrible beauty; through "The Battle Hymn of the Republic" it entered the American consciousness, and a title such as "The Grapes of Wrath" testifies to its continuing power. Yet in its original context it is little more than a ferocious celebration of a prospective massacre of Edomites, who were bitterly hated because in the later Old Testament period they had begun to push into the territory of Judah. The story of Elijah fleeing from the priests of Baal tells how he heard the noises of earthquakes, thunder, and fire, after which "a still small voice" speaks (I Kings 19:12). Again, in its context, the still small voice says only that he is not to worry because all adherents of Baal in North Israel will be slaughtered in due course. But the wonderful phrase has long ago flown away from this context into many new contexts, contexts that give dignity to the human situation instead of merely reflecting its bigotries. The principle of resonance is not confined to phrases. The smallest details of the geography of two tiny chopped-up countries, Greece and Israel, have imposed themselves on our consciousness until they have become part of the map of our own imaginative world, whether we have ever seen these countries or not.

Such resonance would be impossible without, first, an original context, and, second, a power of expanding away from that context. The unity of context that we have been exploring in the Bible, then, is there as a foundation for its real structure. The Bible includes an immense variety of material, and the unifying forces that hold it together cannot be the rigid forces of doctrinal consistency or logic, which would soon collapse under cultural stress, but the more flexible ones of imaginative unity, which is founded on metaphor. Metaphor, we saw, is an identity of various things, not the sham unity of uniformity in which all details are alike. We noticed this earlier in connection with the authority of the prophets of the Old Testament and the apostles of the New. The prophets bring a message that often causes their contemporaries to regard them as traitors, fools, or madmen. Ezekiel may denounce the false prophets who prophesy "out of their own hearts" (13:2), but Ezekiel himself seems to present us with a profoundly neurotic God who keeps desperately punishing his own people in order to reassure himself of the reality of his own existence. He says, for instance, that he deliberately polluted the laws and rituals of Israel, inspiring the Israelites to perform human sacrifices, "that they might know that I am the Lord" (Ezekiel 20:26). Even Ezekiel gives up at this point and protests that his audience will say that he is only a maker of parables (20:49). But the word "parable" is important, because it indicates that we should look for our criteria in a much wider area than consistency of doctrine.

In the New Testament, Paul often calls attention to the outrage on common sense that the gospel represents. It is only superstition or a crank heresy to the conventionally educated, whether Jewish or

Hellenic (I Corinthians 1:23). Similarly with the kind of personal guarantees, so to speak, that we associate with a speaker of authority. "I am not mad," Paul is obliged to say to Festus (Acts 26:25); "We're not drunk," says Peter (Acts 2:15): "after all, it's only nine in the morning." These protests may have something to do with the fact that many quasi-hysterical phenomena, such as "speaking in tongues," seem to have been a feature of early Christian gatherings, and Paul gives a good deal of attention to them. Without condemning them, he remarks caustically that he would rather speak five words that made sense than ten thousand that did not (I Corinthians 14:19), and he speaks, as we noticed, of the "proportion" (Romans 12:6) of faith as a criterion of prophecy. What unity or consistency the gospel has seems to be, for Paul, a provisional defense against a centrifugal development that breaks away from its origin altogether. An example would be the anarchy of "proof-texts," isolated sentences that acquire, so to speak, a cancerous vitality, destroying the integrity of the context in which they are embedded. But, like other forms of the myth of integration, the conception of unity or consistency takes us only so far.

A poem of Blake's entitled "Auguries of Innocence" consists largely of aphorisms of this general type:

> He who to wrath the Ox has mov'd
> Shall never be by Woman lov'd.

We say at once that this is nonsense: perhaps cruelty to animals ought to make one repulsive to women, but there is certainly no evidence that in fact it does. Blake would say that he never intended such statements to be true of ordinary experience: they are precisely what they are said to be, auguries of innocence, statements about an ideal or paradisal world where it would in fact be true that men who abuse animals are no longer loved or admired. This conception of an augury of innocence is a useful one in responding to the discontinuous and aphoristic style of the Bible. We said earlier that while certain provisions about executions and war are made in the Old Testament law, the flat commandment "Thou shalt not kill" is the place where we hear the voice of authority most clearly. It is less important as a law than as a vision of an ideal world in which people do not, perhaps even cannot, kill. Similarly, many of Jesus' exhortations are evocations of a world very different from the one we live in, so that we may find them unpractical or exaggerated as guides to practice. They are not guides to practice directly, however, but parts of a vision of an "innocent" world, and it is that vision which is the guide to practice. The vision is based on the commandments to love God and one's neighbor: if we say that love cannot be commanded, we are speaking out of a different order of existence.

The decentralizing element in Shakespeare, for example, that changes him from simply a poet into an aspect of our own imaginative lives implies that the quality of *care* in literary craftsmanship, the unifying of design that enables art to make its appeal and yet is in itself a manifestation of human finiteness, can at some point be transcended. It may be right for Kierkegaard to contrast the apostle and the genius; and certainly the highly specialized skill of the great poet or composer seems to be in a quite different world from the work of Matthew or John. But however far Matthew and John were from the usual considerations of literary criticism, they were deeply concerned to put across a message; and experience would soon tell them, if they did not know it already, that precision would convey the message and that vagueness or carelessness would not. There is no possibility of going back to the view of a conveyed message as a simple verbal signal, to be accepted on the same level. If we insist that the Bible is "more" than a work of literature, we ought at least to stick to the word "more," and try to see what it means.

What I think it means is that we have to turn again to the traditional but still neglected theory of "polysemous" meaning. One of the commonest experiences in reading is the sense of further discoveries to be made within the same structure of words. The feeling is approximately "there is more to be got out of this," or we may say, of something we particularly admire, that every time we read it we get something new out of it. This "something new" is not necessarily something we have overlooked before, but may come rather from a new context in our experience. The implication is that when we start to read, some kind of dialectical process begins to unfold, so that any given understanding of what we read is one of a series of phases or stages of comprehension.

In the Middle Ages these phases were classified in definite schemata, starting with the literal or immediate sense and going on to a series of further senses, usually three, that is, four including the literal. Dante gives us a concise and useful summary of the most familiar version of the whole scheme:

To elucidate, then, what we have to say, be it known that the sense of this work is not simple, but on the contrary it may be called polysemous, that is to say, "of more senses than one"; for it is one sense which we get through the letter, and another which we get through the thing the letter signifies; and the first is called literal, but the second allegorical or mystic. And this mode of treatment, for its better manifestation, may be considered in this verse: "When Israel came out of Egypt, and the house of Jacob from a people of strange speech, Judaea became his sanctification, Israel his power."

For if we inspect the letter alone the departure of the children of Israel from Egypt in the time of Moses is presented to us; if the allegory, our redemption wrought by Christ; if the moral sense, the conversion of the soul from the grief and misery of sin to the state of grace is presented to us; if the anagogical, the departure of the holy soul from the slavery of this corruption to the liberty of eternal glory is presented to us.

And although these mystic senses have each their special denominations, they may all in general be called allegorical, since they differ from the literal and historical; for *allegory* is derived from *aileon*, in Greek, which means the same as the Latin *alienum* or *diversum*.

Dante gives us a verse from the Psalms (114:1-2) as an example of what he is talking about, which is his own *Commedia*. That is, polysemous meaning is a feature of all deeply serious writing, and the Bible is the model for serious writing. The later reaction against reading the Bible in this way, expressed by Milton in the formula "No passage of Scripture is to be interpreted in more than one sense," indicates a source of possible misunderstanding of the metaphor implied in the word "polysemous." For Dante "polysemous" does not really imply different meanings, suggesting that the chosen meaning of a given passage is purely relative, nor is there any question of a superimposed series of different contents of understanding, where we move from one level to the next like grades in a school. What is implied is a single process growing in subtlety and comprehensiveness, not different senses, but different intensities or wider contexts of a continuous sense, unfolding like a plant out of a seed.

The phrase "deeply serious," which we have just used, is to be connected with the fact that in our critical experience some verbal structures keep responding to progressive critical treatment, while others seem to be more exhaustible, at least within the terms of reference we are using. We may not, for example, want to go on studying a detective story for long after we have discovered the identity of the murderer from the first reading. At this point we may be enticed into the witch's house of value judgments, and tempted to abandon the whole quest. A value judgment is a possible, though not inevitable, inference from our experience of the fact of continuing response, and of the feeling that the work itself keeps growing in reality along with our comprehension of it. But the hierarchy created by value judgments is a mirage based on what we think we already know, an illusory form of the upward path of discovery that we are embarked on.

Polysemous meaning, then, is the development of a single dialectical process, like the process described in Hegel's *Phenomenology*. I mention the *Phenomenology* because it seems to me that the ladder Hegel climbs in that book contains a theory of polysemous meaning as well, and that a new formulation of the old medieval four-level sequence can be discerned in it. The hero of Hegel's philosophical quest is the concept (*Begriff*), which, like Ulysses in the *Odyssey*, appears first in an unrecognized and almost invisible guise as the intermediary between subject and object, and ends by taking over the whole show, undisputed master of the house of being. But this "concept" can hardly exist apart from its own verbal formulation: that is, it is something verbal that expands in this way, so that the *Phenomenology* is, among other things, a general theory of how verbal meaning takes shape. Even the old metaphor of "levels" is preserved in Hegel's term *Aufhebung*. What Hegel means by dialectic is not anything reducible to a patented formula, like the "thesis-antithesis-synthesis" one so often attached to him, nor can it be anything predictive. It is a much more complex operation of a form of understanding combining with its own otherness or opposite, in a way that negates itself and yet passes through that negation into a new stage, preserving its essence in a broader context, and abandoning the one just completed like the chrysalis of a butterfly or a crustacean's outgrown shell.

The process described by Dante is also dialectical, and has also the sense of a continuous movement going into itself, so to speak, at each stage and emerging from it into a new phase. Thus the verse quoted from the Psalms refers, according to Dante, to the historical exodus taking place in the time of Moses. But Old Testament history, for Dante, differs from all other history in that it was intended by God to be a type or symbol of what was clearly revealed by the coming of Christ. Hence our understanding of the historical event expands, by virtue of its context, into an understanding of that event as a type of redemption of the world by Christ, who led mankind out of slavery just as Moses led Israel out of slavery in Egypt. Even so, understanding the relation of the Exodus to the work of Christ is of little use unless we apply it to our own lives, and thereby reach a condition in which those lives can be transformed into the analogy or imitation of Christ known as the Christian life. This takes us into the moral level, the level of action and behavior informed by faith. But such a life, however desirable in itself, is not completely comprehended until its context too is understood, when it is seen sacramentally, as a model of the life we live in eternity after this one.

At each stage of Dante's scheme the understanding of the Bible forms the center of an entire mode of human activity. The literal level, hearing the Word and seeing the text, is at the center of the activity of sense experience, the foundation of all knowledge. The allegorical level is at the center of the contemplative reason which sees the world around it as objective, and hence as a type or image concealing what the reason can interpret. The moral, or third, level is that of the faith that transcends and yet also fulfills the reason, and the anagogic level is at the center of the beatific vision that fulfills faith.

The scheme is a logical and coherent one, but there are two features in it that may give us pause, if we are thinking of adopting it as a basis for contemporary criticism, whether of the Bible or of anything else. In the first place, Dante's scheme assumes the exclusive truth of one interpretation of the Bible, the one that assimilates it to medieval Catholic Christianity. Continuous dialogue with people of quite different world outlooks is not possible on such a basis, and that naturally gives it a restricted usefulness in our time. In Dante's historical context such a view of the Bible was of course inevitable, as well as comprehensible enough in itself. But it was a view that absorbed the study of the Bible into the sacramental system administered by the Church, a system extending over this and every other possible form of human life. The factor of the disinterested cannot exist in such a context. Of course there is a traditional prejudice against the disinterested in Christianity, a strong tendency to feel that at some point the disinterested has to be abandoned for the committed, as in Kierkegaard's either-or dilemma. It is conceivable, however, that here too there may be an *Aufhebung*, that Kierkegaard's either-or dilemma can be transcended too, and thereby essentially preserved.

In the second place, we see that, at each of Dante's four levels, the words of the actual verbal structure being studied, the Bible itself, are being subordinated to something else assumed to be more real. Once again, the more real always turns out to be something external to words, and regarded as superior to them. Thus the literal sense for Dante is what we have called the demotic sense, the "true" representation by words of actual events or things outside them. Dante's phrasing, both here and in a similar passage in the *Convivio*, indicates that he is not quite easy in his mind about this application of the word "literal." The literal sense of his own *Commedia*, he tells us, is the state of souls after death, which can hardly be literal in any descriptive sense. But it was not prudent, perhaps not even possible, to give up this basis for literal meaning when one was dealing with the Bible in his day. In any case the projecting or externalizing of the literal meaning in Dante's scheme carries through on all the other levels. On the allegorical level the words are subordinated to the historical fact of the work of Christ on earth; on the moral level they are subordinated to the actions we perform existentially; on the anagogic level they are subordinated to the actual life we enjoy after this one in heaven. On every level words are treated as instrumental, as servomechanisms of reality, thought, activity, and existence. Once again, this is comprehensible enough in itself, but a book that speaks of the "Word of God" in the way that the Bible does is *a priori* likely to have a different attitude toward the relation of words to things.

A philosopher, like Hegel, would most naturally start this polysemous expansion with the concept, and end with absolute knowledge. A literary critic might well do something closer to what I briefly attempted myself in the *Anatomy of Criticism*: start with a "symbol," or unit of poetic expression, and end with a verbal universe in which the symbol has become a monad, though one that interpenetrates with all the other monads. Dante starts with a verse taken to some extent at random from the Bible, and ends with the whole medieval structure of faith and vision. In summarizing and concluding this part of our study, our present procedure would be closer to Dante's, but would start on a different basis of literal meaning, and would avoid his subordination of words to non-verbal "realities." A book as introductory and tentative as this can hardly have a conclusion, but it must have an end; and a brief sketch of a theory of polysemous meaning, so far as it affects a literary approach to the Bible, will bring us to that end.

The first two levels have been dealt with at some length in the first part of this book. Literally, the Bible is a gigantic myth, a narrative extending over the whole of time from creation to apocalypse, unified by a body of recurring imagery that "freezes" into a single metaphor cluster, the metaphors all being identified with the body of the Messiah, the man who is all men, the totality of *logoi* who is one Logos, the grain of sand that is the world. We also traced a sequence of manifestations of this reality, each one a stage more explicit than its predecessor. First is the creation, not the natural environment with its alienating chaos but the ordered structure that the mind perceives in it. Next comes the revolutionary vision of human life as a casting off of tyranny and exploitation. Next is the ceremonial, moral, judicial code that keeps a society together. Next is the wisdom or sense of integrated continuous life which grows out of this, and next the prophecy or imaginative vision of man as somewhere between his original and his ultimate identity. Gospel and apocalypse speak of a present that no longer finds its meaning in the future, as in the New Testament's view of the Old Testament, but is a present moment around which past and future revolve.

This sequence is connected with one of the most striking features of the Bible: its capacity for self-re-creation. The way that the Pentateuch is constructed, with its different narrative strands woven together, forms, among other things, a highly self-conscious retrospective view of the early history of Israelite culture. We see this very clearly in the use of quotations of early verse, for example. Again, there are such features as the Chronicler's re-creation of Samuel and Kings, the re-creation of the Exodus experience in many of the Psalms (e.g. 78 and 106, AV numbering) as well as the Book of Wisdom, the assimilation of later periods of bondage and exile to early ones, all culminating, for the reader of the Christian Bible, in the complete reconstruction of the Old Testament in the New, some features of which we have tried to touch on. The dialectical expansion from one "level" of understanding to another seems to be built into the Bible's own structure, which creates an awareness of itself by the reader, growing in time as he reads, to an extent to which I can think of no parallel elsewhere. Nor can we trace the Bible back to a time when it was not doing this. The New Testament's "Word of God" is admittedly a special use of "word," but, as we have been insisting all along, it is connected with more ordinary uses of it, and it is thought of as a powerful dialectic (Hebrews 4:12), essential for cutting through all the confusions of experience and reshaping the structure of vision in the mind.

Proverbs 9 presents us with the contrast between a wise and a foolish woman. Both start their sales pitch with the same formula: "Whoso is simple, let him turn in hither." But the wise woman provides a communion of bread and wine, and a community of a temple with its "seven pillars" of wisdom, while the foolish one says "Stolen waters are sweet, and bread eaten in secret is pleasant." I suspect that these metaphorical women, who represent wisdom and folly rather than commonplace warnings against prostitutes, also have a good deal to do with the use and misuse of language respectively. Nothing can be secretly possessed except something stolen, and the simplicity the foolish woman appeals to is the simplistic jargon of panic, anxiety, repression, prejudice, and social conditioning that disintegrates a verbal community. This approach to language sets up prefabricated verbal structures that can turn any attempt to grapple with reality into a facile gabble about doing so. The agility of language in chasing red herrings has caused some religious traditions to make a cult of the wordless, even to the point of writing books by the score about the utter inadequacy of words to convey genuine experience. All this is right so far as it goes, but it is a futile maneuver to retreat from words into some body language of gesture or similar forms of implied understanding that short-circuits the verbal. The wise woman appeals to the primitive impulse of consciousness to connect with reality which is often released by the simplest modes of language, such as metaphor. But, being wise, she knows that a transformation of consciousness and a transformation of language can never be separated.

We start, then, with the "literal" Bible of myth and metaphor, the centripetal body of words that we simply accept as our primary datum. Two principles connected with the fact that the Bible is a written book seem to me of particular relevance here. First, in the theory of criticism, during the past two decades especially, there has been a strong emphasis on the ontological status of the text, on where it is in relation to itself and its reader's mind, on where its meaning is in relation to the author's intention, its explicit statements, its implicit statements, and the interpretations of its readers. If I may pick out of all this the principle most relevant to our present argument, we may perhaps say that every text is the type of its own reading. Its antitype starts in the reader's mind, where it is not a simple reception but the unfolding of a long and complex dialectical process, the winding of the end of a string into a ball, in Blake's figure. I speak of "a" reader, but of course readers form a community, of whom critics and scholars, who work on the second level of meaning only, are a minority.

We said earlier that the great doctrinal structures of the past, the ones that we identify as Catholic or Protestant or the like, have always tended to make themselves the antitypes of Biblical narrative and imagery. They are designed to establish the claim: this is what our central revelation really means, and this is how you have to understand it. Such systems of faith, however impressive and useful still, can hardly be definitive for us now, because they are so heavily conditioned by the phases of language ascendant in their time, whether metonymic or descriptive. A reconsideration of the Bible can take place only along with, and as part of, a reconsideration of language, and of all the structures, including the literary ones, that language produces. One would hope that in this context the aim of such a reconsideration would be a more tentative one, directed not to a terminus of belief but to the open community of vision, and to the charity that is the informing principle of a still greater community than faith. What follows will, I hope, make this clearer.

There are, of course, a good many pitfalls in a reconsideration of language, and the title of a recent critical study, *The Prison-House of Language*, carries a warning of some of these in its title. But the title is from a passage in Nietzsche that goes on to speak of "the doubt which asks whether the limit we see is really a limit." This is the kind of creative doubt that could carry us, wherever Nietzsche wanted it to go, beyond the limits of dialectic itself, into the infinite identity of word and spirit that, we are told, rises from the body of death.

Second, we have often noted, both in this book and elsewhere, the long-standing connection between the written book and the arts of magic, and the way that the poetic impulse seems to begin in the renunciation of magic or, at least, of its practical aims. Without his books, says Caliban, Prospero would be as much of a sot as I am. We referred earlier to the critics of the god Thoth, the inventor of writing according to Plato's *Phaedrus*, and their fear that his art would greatly weaken the function of memory in society. What these critics did not realize was that the written word is far more powerful than simply a reminder: it re-creates the past in the present, and gives us, not the familiar remembered thing, but the glittering intensity of the summoned-up hallucination. The phrase that Elizabethan critics took from Horace, "ut pictura poesis," that poetry is a speaking picture, refers primarily to this quality of voluntary fantasy in writing and reading.

The chief aim of magic is to control spirits, and this takes the form of controlling their time and space. Spirits are controlled in time by the reciting of spells, which forces them to act in certain ways and inhibits them from acting in others; they are controlled in space by a charmed circle that keeps them at a distance. When we subtract the practical side of this procedure, we see that such magic attempts to realize more intensely the "now" and "here" centers of time and space respectively; and when the same procedure is applied to a reader's re-creation of a text, the controlled spirits are his own functions.

This "literal" Bible of myth and metaphor then combines with its opposite, or secular knowledge, the world of history and concept which lies outside the Bible, but to which the Bible continually points. It points to it because it grows out of that world, not because it regards it as establishing criteria for itself. And yet the Bible comes to us as a book like other books, certainly not free from human passion or partisanship, certainly not from textual corruption: in fact, we could almost say that anything that can go wrong with a book has gone wrong with the Bible at some point or other. "It is difficult," says Milton, "to conjecture the purpose of Providence in committing the writings of the New Testament to such uncertain and variable guardianship"—a statement hardly less true of the Old Testament.

On this level of meaning the organizing principle is the one that we may call the Feuerbach principle: that man creates his gods in his own image. This is the principle that religions apply to one another: all that an adherent of any particular religion can say is that all the *other* religions are human constructs. Thus T. S. Eliot's *The Rock* speaks of man as having invented the higher religions, though the context of *The Rock*, a pageant written for a church fund-raising drive, makes it clear that some such saving clause as "present company excepted" has to be understood. The structure of secular knowledge, so far as it bears on the Bible, is not only a rooting of the Bible in its human context, but a manifesting of the human struggle to unify its world. The need to unify, we suggested, is an indication of the finiteness of the human mind, unity and the finite being aspects of the same thing.

The next turn of the dialectic brings us back to what we have been calling the royal metaphor, and which it is now perhaps time to think of also as something more like a real universal, the sense of the individuals of every class, including man, as forming one body, which is less a concept than an axiom of behavior. Whether we think it *is* true or not matters little, in actual life: there, it is the determination to make it true, to live *as though* individual and class were an identity, that is important.

The relating of one's "literal" understanding of the Bible as a book to the rest of one's knowledge, more particularly of the Bible's "background" in history and culture, thus creates a synthesis that soon begins to move from the level of knowledge and understanding to an existential level, from Dante's "allegorical" to his "tropological" meaning, from Kierkegaard's "either" or his "or." Such an intensification, whether it has anything to do with the Bible or not, takes us from knowledge to principles of action, from the aesthetic pleasure of studying a world of interesting objects and facts to what Kierkegaard calls ethical freedom. This shift of perspective brings us to the word "faith."

Two considerations arise about this word. First (a point to which I have often reverted), there seem to be two levels of faith, the level of professed faith—what we say we believe, think we believe, believe we believe—and the level of what our actions show that we believe. Professed belief is essentially a statement of loyalty or adherence to a specific community. To profess a faith identifies us as Unitarians or Trotskyists or Taoists or Shiite Muslims or whatever. Beyond this is the principle that all one's positive acts express one's real beliefs. In very highly integrated people the professed and the actual belief would be much the same thing, and the fact that they are usually not quite the same thing is not necessarily a sign of hypocrisy, merely of human weakness or the inadequacy of theory. Even Paul says that his actions do not always accord with his own precepts.

Second, professed belief in itself is instinctively aggressive. I have given the example elsewhere of a Spaniard and a Turk facing one another at the battle of Lepanto. Neither knows the first thing about the other man's religion, but each is convinced that it is utterly and damnably wrong, and would be ready to fight and die for that conviction. We may consider this only an example of Swift's remark that men have just enough religion to hate each other but not enough for love. But even on a high level of integrity, where theory and practice coincide, faith is still militant, still something to be symbolized, as Paul does, by armor and weapons. Its central axiom is Luther's "Hier stehe ich," an affirmation of a certain position in time and space, held in the face of death.

A militant faith of this kind strives to become free of doubt, just as a soldier in battle abolishes from his mind all question of the justice of his country's cause. Structures of faith are normally structures of unity and integration, and hence reflect back to us the finiteness of the human mind. A human theological system that assigns an unconscionable number of people to hell merely to keep God's actions logically consistent can hardly deal with a God who can remind Jonah, with a delicate irony, that sometimes inconsistency may be a better principle:

And should not I spare Nineveh, that great city, wherein are more than sixscore thousand persons that cannot discern between their right hand and their left hand; and also much cattle? (Jonah 4:11)

We are back here to the contrast between the Tower of Babel, the building of which was accompanied by a confusion of tongues, and the "pure speech" (Zephaniah 3:9) or gift of tongues (Acts 2:4) promised for the new age. There comes a point at which a structure of faith seems to become a part of the Tower of Babel, one of a number of competing and mutually unintelligible assertions with a vague factual basis. This is true whether the structure is founded on belief or a repudiation of all assertive structures as concerned with the unknowable or the morbid. The mind seems to want to expand, to move from the closed fortresses of believer and skeptic to the community of vision.

At this point we realize that faith has its dialectical opposite as well, and must somehow combine with it. Doubt then ceases to be the enemy of faith and becomes its complement, and we see that the real enemy of faith is not doubt, but merely the mental insensitivity that does not see what all the fuss is about. The bedrock of doubt is the total nothingness of death. Death is a leveler, not because everybody dies, but because nobody understands what death means. Hence to move into the final anagogic level of meaning we have to meet the question: What speaks to us across death? We cannot give the simple cultural answer: everything in our cultural heritage produced by people now dead, because that is an answer on the second level only. On the third or existential level, the question becomes: What speaks to us across our own death?

All such questions are usually presented simply as extensions of belief, and in such forms as What comes after? or What lies beyond? These are metaphors from time and space respectively: language still clutches its accustomed metaphors, even when they seem clearly not to apply. What speaks across death, in this perspective, is usually the promise or threat of an afterlife in heaven or hell, where something like the ego survives in something like unending time, and in something like a place. After all the centuries of sacramental processing, this whole subject seems to be as much up for grabs as it ever was: I am concerned here only with the share that a student of the human imagination may reasonably claim.

Paul speaks of a moment of enlightenment (II Corinthians 12) in which two things are remarkable. First, the sense of a solid ego dissolved so completely that he can hardly say whether the experience happened to him or to someone else—"je est un autre," as Rimbaud says. He even apologizes for "boasting" in speaking about his experience as though it were his own. Second, he is not sure whether he was "in" or "out of" his body, or whether such distinctions really applied at all. He feels a certain reluctance in stressing the experience, mainly, no doubt, because of his strong revolutionary slant: he wants the world as a whole to wake up, and individual enlightenment is useful chiefly because it may be contagious, which it cannot be if it is incommunicable. He heard, according to the AV, "unspeakable words" (*arreta rhemata*), "not lawful for a man to utter." The experience, however, seems to be of a new language, which he heard and to some extent understood, but cannot translate into the categories of ordinary language. The emphasis seems to fall on his inability to make it intelligible, rather than on his being forbidden to do so.

Yet one may dimly glimpse something of the conditions under which such a language might be spoken, and we conclude with two suggestions about it. In the first place, although the "Word of God" is described in the New Testament as a two-edged sword that cuts and divides (Hebrews 4:12 and elsewhere), this can hardly mean in such a context a Hegelian dialectic like the one we have been dealing with, in which every statement implies its own opposite. What it ultimately divides is rather the world of life and the world of death, and this can be accomplished only by a language that escapes from argument and refutation. The language used in the Bible is, in short, the language of love, which, as Paul reminds us in a passage even more luminous than the one quoted above (I Corinthians 13:8), is likely to outlast most forms of communication.

Wherever we have love we have the possibility of sexual symbolism. The *kerygma*, or proclaiming rhetoric, of the Bible is a welcoming and approaching rhetoric, addressed by a symbolically male God to a symbolically female body of readers. Coming the other way is the body of human imaginative response, as we have it in literature and the arts, where the language is purely imaginative and hence hypothetical. Here the imaginative product seems to be symbolically female, the daughter of a Muse. Yet perhaps it is only through the study of works of human imagination that we can make any real contact with the level of vision beyond faith. For such vision is, among other things, the quality in all serious religions that enables them to be associated with human products of culture and imagination, where the limit is the conceivable and not the actual.

Secondly, we are here approaching once again the boundary of what we have been calling the legal perspective, with its antithesis between divine and human, creator and creature. As soon as we begin to wonder whether, to use Nietzsche's phrase again, the limit we see there really is a limit, we find ourselves stumbling over the traditional Christian doctrine of "original sin." This doctrine holds that since the fall of Adam human life has been cursed with a built-in inertia that will forever prevent man from fulfilling his destiny without divine help, and that such help can be described only in terms of the external and the objective. From our present vantage point we can characterize this conception of original sin more precisely as man's fear of freedom and his resentment of the discipline and responsibility that freedom brings.

Thus in Milton, whom we have cited so frequently because he is one of the most rewarding examples in Western history of the combination of Biblical and secular cultures, liberty is the chief thing that the gospel has to bring to man. But man for Milton does not and cannot "naturally" want freedom: he gets it only because God wants him to have it. What man naturally wants is to collapse back into the master-slave duality, of which the creature-creator duality is perhaps a projection. *Paradise Lost* tells again the story of the fall of Adam to explain, among other things, the failure of the Puritan Revolution as Milton saw it. Many other revolutions have failed since then in precisely the same way, and there seems to be a good deal of historical evidence in favor of Milton's view. But perhaps the history of the Bible's influence in Western culture may tell us more than any other subject about where the real failure of nerve begins.

Man is constantly building anxiety-structures, like geodesic domes, around his social and religious institutions. If Milton's view of the Bible as a manifesto of human freedom has anything to be said for it, one would expect it to be written in a language that would smash these structures beyond repair, and let some genuine air and light in. But of course anxiety is very skillful at distorting languages. There is a sardonic Old English riddle (at least, I doubt if its progression of imagery is pure accident) that begins:

An enemy deprived me of life, took away my strength, then soaked me in water, then took me out again and put me in the sun, where I soon lost all my hair.

The answer is "book," specifically a Bible codex. The riddle obliquely describes the method of preparing a codex in the writer's day, and seems to be referring also to the shearing of Samson in Judges 16:17-22. The normal human reaction to a great cultural achievement like the Bible is to do with it what the Philistines did to Samson: reduce it to impotence, then lock it in a mill to grind our aggressions and prejudices. But perhaps its hair, like Samson's, could grow again even there.

Notes

p. xiii, line 12   "Claude Bernard." The phrase from Europe's *The Mirror of Art*, loosely transl... after science, is quoted in the introduction by Arthur D. Enter to his translation of Bernard's *The Rhetoric of the Triumphant Beast* (1964), 46. Professor Jean Bruneau has pointed out to me an echo from Horace, *Epistle* I, 1, 32.

CHAPTER ONE

p. 3, line 16   See *Aeschylus and Poetic Syntax* of the original text, Tr. H. Canter (19??), II, 90 ff. (Hymn...

INTRODUCTION

p. xii, line 12   "Blake's line." From the introduction to the *Songs of Experience*. There are more than seven, but the really important ones are Genesis 2:7, Isaiah 21:12, Jeremiah 22:29, Song of Songs 6:13, and John 1:5. The Genesis verse says that God formed Adam from the "dust of the ground," "ground" being the feminine noun *adamah*. The "lapsed Soul" who is urged to return in Blake's poem is the original union of a symbolically male humanity with a symbolically female nature. See below, chapter six.

p. xii, line 39   "*ta biblia.*" So in I Maccabees 1:56 and elsewhere.

p. xv, line 25   "*ainoi.*" This word occurs in the New Testament (e.g. Luke 18:43), but only in its later sense of "praise."

p. xv, line 37   "Eliot's phrase." From "Tradition and the Individual Talent," *Selected Essays* (1932), 21.

p. xvi, line 12   "Kierkegaard." See *The Present Age*, tr. Alexander Dru (1940). The essay "On the Difference Between an Apostle and a Genius" forms the second half of this book.

p. xvi, line 20   "Blake." The phrase is from Blake's annotations surrounding his engraving of the Laocoön (*Poetry and Prose*, ed. Erdman and Bloom [1965], 271).

p. xvii, line 13   "little use." These ungrateful comments are getting steadily more obsolete, but I feel they are still true enough to be recorded.

p. xviii, line 1   "Claudel." I make this statement about Claudel with some diffidence, but the influence of Hugh of St.-Victor on his work seems to me to deserve more emphasis than it has had.

p. xix, line 23   "Coleridge's brilliant insights." See Elinor Shaffer, "*Kubla Khan*" *and the Fall of Jerusalem* (1975).

p. xix, line 35   "three in particular." See especially Hans-Georg Gadamer, *Truth and Method* (Eng. tr. 1975); Paul Ricoeur, *The Conflict of Interpretations* (Eng. tr. 1974); Walter Ong, *The Presence of the Word* (1967).

p. xxi, line 8   "essay on Blake." *Selected Essays*, 317 ff. For Lévi-Strauss's term see *The Savage Mind* (Eng. tr. 1966).

p. xxi, line 37   "Kenneth Burke." See his *The Rhetoric of Religion* (1961).

p. xxii, line 6   "Derrida." See Jacques Derrida, *Of Grammatology*, tr. G. C. Spivak (1976), esp. 10 ff.

CHAPTER ONE

when He was already engaged in the act of creation" (*Philo*, tr. F. H. Colson and G. H. Whitaker, Loeb Library ed. [1929], I, 21).

p. 18, line 20   "Erasmus." See Roland H. Bainton, *Erasmus of Christendom* (1969), chap. 6.

p. 18, line 30   "Goethe's Faust." *Faust*, pt. I, 1224 ff.

p. 19, line 12   "Homer." *Odyssey*, xi, 601.

p. 20, line 21   "Dante." *Inferno*, x, 10 ff.

p. 21, line 6   "Blake." "There is No Natural Religion (b)," *Poetry and Prose*, 2.

p. 22, line 27   "Elizabethan critics." See especially the extract from Harington and Chapman in *Elizabethan Critical Essay*, ed. Gregory Smith, vol. II (1904). See also Millar MacLure, *George Chapman* (1966), chap. 2.

p. 22, line 34   "critics of the god Thoth." Plato, *Phaedrus*, 274 ff.

p. 25, line 39   "Wallace Stevens." "Connoisseur of Chaos," *Collected Poems* (1954), 215.

p. 26, line 17   "Karl Barth." *Church Dogmatics*, vol. I, *The Doctrine of the Word of God* (Eng. tr. 1975), pt. I, xiii.

p. 27, line 40   "Aristotle." *Rhetoric*, bk. i, 1354.

p. 28, line 33   "Hegel." From the preface to *The Phenomenology of Spirit*, tr. Miller and Findlay (1977), 6. Hegel's term (*erbaulich*) was doubtless a negative inspiration for Kierkegaard's *Edifying Discourses*.

p. 30, line 1   "Bultmann." See particularly the symposium *Kerygma and Myth*, ed. H. W. Bartsch (1953). I think it unfortunate that the term "demythologizing" has been associated with Rudolf Bultmann, whose conception of the New Testament is not really a "demythologizing" one at all. See below, chapter two.

CHAPTER TWO

p. 35, line 39   "local flood." J. G. Frazer, *Folklore in the Old Testament* (1918), I, 332 ff.

p. 36, line 24   "deluge myths.' Geza Roheim, *The Gates of the Dream* (Eng. tr. 1952), VIII, iii. I am not of course belittling the importance of such work in its own area, merely resisting the reductive tendency to account for one group of phenomena in terms of another. Roheim himself does not do this without qualification.

p. 37, line 40   "Hazlitt's phrase." "Why the Arts Are Not Progressive," *Selected Essays*, ed. Keynes (1938), 603.

p. 38, line 10   "Frazer again." From the introduction to his translation and edition of Apollodorus's *The Library* (Loeb Library ed., 1921), xxvii.

238 *Notes*

|---|---|
p. 41, line 7	"abstract painting." For the cultural connection between abstraction (and other forms of stylizing) in painting and mythopoeia in literature, see my *Anatomy of Criticism* (1957), 131 ff.
p. 41, line 21	"Renan." *Vie de Jésus* (1863), chap. 1, "Jésus naquit à Nazareth."
p. 42, line 12	"major historical figure." This phrase is important, because even if, for example, the passage on Jesus in Josephus (*Jewish Antiquities*, XVIII, iii) were genuine (a large concession), it would hardly amount to making him that.
p. 42, line 38	"Greenland and Eirik sagas." These are conveniently grouped together in *The Vinland Sagas* (Penguin Books, Eng. tr. 1965).
p. 44, line 10	"Immanuel Velikovsky." *Worlds in Collision* (1950).
p. 44, line 17	"seventeenth century." See Don Cameron Allen, *The Legend of Noah* (1949), chap. 5.
p. 48, line 19	"more idiosyncratic use." It should however be added that in one very unlikely place (*Civilization in Transition* [Eng. tr. 1964], par. 847), Jung does characterize an archetype as I should do: "The myths and fairy tales of world literature contain definite motifs which crop up everywhere."
p. 48, line 26	"Mircea Eliade." See *Cosmos and History: The Myth of the Eternal Return* (1954), esp. chap. 2. The phrase *in illo tempore* (162, below) occurs in several of Eliade's books, including this one.
p. 49, line 15	"Byron." *Vision of Judgment*, st. lxxxvii.
p. 50, line 39	"Wallace Stevens." "Description Without Place," *Collected Poems*, 339.

CHAPTER THREE

|---|---|
p. 54, line 18	"metaphors." On the theory of metaphor, I am particularly indebted to Paul Ricoeur, *The Rule of Metaphor* (Eng. tr. 1977); Max Black, *Models and Metaphors* (1962); Philip Wheelwright, *Metaphor and Reality*; and Christine Brooke-Rose, *A Grammar of Metaphor* (1958).
p. 55, line 10	"Gospel of Thomas." See Robert M. Grant et al., *The Secret Sayings of Jesus* (1960), 120.
p. 56, line 23	"Ezra Pound." See Ernest Fenollosa, "The Chinese Written Character as Medium for Poetry," ed. Ezra Pound (1936).
p. 57, line 6	"other books." See, for example, the distinction between "sense" (*Sinn*) and "reference" (*Bedeutung*) in Gottlob Frege, *Philosophical Writings*, tr. P. Geach and M. Black (1960).
p. 59, line 15	"Wittgenstein's *Philosophical Investigations*." Tr. Elizabeth Anscombe, 3rd ed. (1968), par. 70. I am aware that the issue involved is more complex than the use I am making of it.
p. 60, line 22	"Gershom Scholem." *Major Trends in Jewish Mysticism* (1961), 51.

p. 67, line 7   "Book of Enoch." I Enoch 78 (Charles, *APOT*, II, 243 ff.)

p. 68, line 4   "poets." The Dylan Thomas poem has the line quoted for its title; the Wordsworth reference is to *The Prelude*, I, 398 (1850 version); the Baudelaire quotation is from "Correspondances" in *Les Fleurs du Mal*.

p. 70, line 6   "primitive belief." See Mircea Eliade, *Patterns in Comparative Religion* (1958), chap. 2.

p. 70, line 28   "fertility goddess." On goddess-figures in, and in the background of, the Old Testament, see Raphael Patai, *The Hebrew Goddess* (1967).

p. 71, line 23   "Augustine." *Confessions*, bk. xii.

p. 72, line 24   *"ver perpetuum."* Perpetual spring was an attribute of the earthly Paradise and of most versions of the literary commonplace of the *locus amoenus*, or pleasant place. See E. R. Curtius, *European Literature and the Latin Middle Ages* (1953), 195 ff.

p. 74, line 3   "friend of mine." The friend was the late Marshall McLuhan: I do not know if he has published the remark anywhere.

p. 74, line 5   "Apocalypse of Peter." See *The Apocryphal New Testament*, ed. M. R. James (1924), 505 ff.

p. 74, line 37   "Jung." See C. G. Jung and W. Pauli, *The Interpretation of Nature and the Psyche* (1955).

p. 76, line 30   "Eliot." "Burnt Norton" (*Four Quartets*), 89.

CHAPTER FOUR

p. 79, line 26   "traditionally given." See Quaestionum S. Augustini in Heptateuchum, in Migne, *Patrologia*, XXXIV, 623: "quanquam et in Vetere Novum lateat, et in Novo Vetus pateat." For the historical background see Beryl Smalley, *The Study of the Bible in the Middle Ages* (1952).

p. 79, line 33   "'figure.'" See Erich Auerbach, "Figura," in *Scenes from the Drama of European Literature* (1959).

p. 81, line 15   "Whitehead." A. N. Whitehead, *Science and the Modern World* (1925), chap. 1.

p. 85, line 18   "Newman." In John Henry Newman, *Apologia pro Vita Sua*, pt. III.

p. 85, line 41   "Milton." *Complete Prose Works* (Yale ed.), I: 727-78, 755.

p. 88, line 9   "Melville." Quoted in the introduction to Walter E. Bezanson's edition of *Clarel* (1960), xvii.

p. 88, line 17   "cultural trauma." See Sigmund Freud, *Moses and Monotheism* (Eng. tr. 1939), III, i, 3.

p. 88, line 38   "priestly functions." See Aubrey R. Johnson, "The Role of the King in the Jerusalem Cultus," in *The Labyrinth*, ed. S. H. Hooke (1935), 73 ff.

p. 90, line 20   "Nebuchadnezzar." See Henri Frankfort, *Kingship and the Gods* (1948; rev. ed. 1978), 313 ff.

p. 90, line 36   "hymn." First isolated, perhaps, as a problem in Emil Bala, *Das Ich der Psalmen* (1912), but any standard commentary on the Psalms will discuss the point.

p. 92, line 6   "Wallace Stevens." "Description Without Place," *Collected Poems*, 341.

p. 95, line 7   "Marcus Aurelius." *Meditations*, bk. xi; however, many scholars translate the word differently and in any case regard the reference to Christianity as an interpolation.

p. 96, line 17   "Augustine's attack." *City of God*, XII, xii.

p. 97, line 1   "Stoical world view." See Franz Cumont, *Astrology and Religion among the Greeks and Romans* (Eng. tr. 1912).

p. 97, line 30   "future metamorphosis." Not only of nature: the verb *metamorphoo* is used in the New Testament to describe both what is usually called the Transfiguration and its counterpart in the individual Christian life (Mark 9:2; Romans 12:2; II Corinthians 3:18). Compare what is said about the term *metanoia* in chapter five, below. A corollary of this conception of upward metamorphosis is that "spirit" may be thought of as an antitype of "soul" (see chapter one, above). Thus Augustine (*City of God*, XIII, xxiv) takes John 20:22 (Jesus' "breathing" the Holy Spirit on his disciples) as an antitype of Genesis 2:7.

p. 98, line 14   "Felix . . ." "Happy is he who has been able to understand the causes of things" (Virgil, *Georgics*, ii, 490). The word *causas*, however, covers a good deal more than the conception of causality. For a modern counterpart of the Christ-Caesar dichotomy, compare what Victor Hugo says of an admirer of Napoleon: "Napoleon became for him the man-people as Jesus Christ is the Man-God" (*Les Misérables*, III, iii, 6).

p. 100, line 30   "Simone Weil." See *The Simone Weil Reader*, ed. George A. Panichas (1977), 24.

CHAPTER FIVE

p. 107, line 27   *"Paradise Lost."* See my essay "The Revelation to Eve," in *The Stubborn Structure* (1970), 135 ff.

p. 108, line 6   *"golem."* See Chayim Bloch, *The Golem* (1919; Eng. tr. 1972).

p. 108, line 30   "Heraclitus." See Philip Wheelwright, *Heraclitus* (1959), 19. This aphorism is one of the two that form the epigraphs to Eliot's *Four Quartets*.

p. 111, line 26   "not causally associated." See Allen Upward, *The Divine Mystery* (1909), chap. 6.

p. 112, line 4   "gigantic illusion." The view of creation as being a phase of revelation, and hence more a vision of awakening consciousness than of the beginning of the natural order, appears to be a Kabbalistic conception: see Gershom Scholem, *On the Kabbalah and its Symbolism* (1965), chap. 2.

p. 112, line 15   "Wallace Stevens." "So-and-So Reclining on Her Couch," *Collected Poems*, 206

p. 112, line 33   "Plotinus." "Against the Gnostics," *Ennead* II, 9. I have used the MacKenna translation. See also Hans Jonas, *The Gnostic Religion* (1958).

p. 115, line 3   "Japan." See G. B. Sansom, *Japan: A Short Cultural History* (1931), chap. 4.

p. 116, line 5   "editorial anxiety." The fact that one of the commonest words for God in the Old Testament is *Elohim*, an intensive plural, enables some translators to substitute "angels" (i.e., the true "gods") in some passages. The AV has done this in Psalm 8:5.

p. 116, line 21   "ancient legend." Charles, *APOT*, II, 159 ff.

p. 116, line 31   "writers of the four Gospels." This identification (Matthew with the man, Mark with the lion, Luke with the ox, and John with the eagle) is a commonplace of medieval iconography.

p. 117, line 34   "Tertullian." *De Spectaculis*, tr. R. Arbesmann, *Fathers of the Church* (1959), XL, 47.

p. 117, line 40   "counteracting the neuroses." I am treating, in Matthew Arnold fashion, "Hellenism" and "Hebraism" as a contrast, because that was what they were as a joint influence on Western culture, increasingly from the sixteenth century on. It does not follow that they were a contrast in origin: see Cyrus H. Gordon, *The Common Background of Greek and Hebrew Civilizations* (1963).

p. 118, line 27   "American life." For the role of Biblical typology in the formation of the American consciousness, see Sacvan Bercovitch, *The Puritan Origins of the American Self* (1975) and *The American Jeremiad* (1978).

p. 119, line 7   "saving remnant." For the importance of this in Biblical imagery see Karl Löwith, *Meaning in History* (Eng. tr. 1949), 182 ff.

p. 120, line 17   "Anaximander." See Philip Wheelwright, *The Presocratics* (1966), 54.

p. 121, line 8   "Sartre." See *Being and Nothingness* (Eng. tr. 1956), esp. pt. III.

p. 122, line 29   "Ahikar." See Charles, *APOT*, II, 724 ff.

p. 125, line 39   "Wen-Amon." See Pritchard, *ANET*, 25 ff.

p. 135, line 2   "nonsense." Paul's mind seems to have operated consistently on two levels, the level of *kerygma* properly speaking and the level of the tactical organizing of the Church. He sometimes speaks of being without guidance on this second level (I Corinthians 7:25), and it is here that he treats the function of women in the Church so negatively (I Corinthians 14:34-35).

CHAPTER SIX

p. 140, line 35   "Lilith." See Raphael Patai, *op. cit.*, chap. 7.

p. 144, line 20   "evidence." The evidence rests mainly on the etymological
                    link between "Hebrew" and the *apiru* referred to in Egyptian
                    inscriptions, a term which appears to mean something like
                    "bandits." The genuineness of this link is a much disputed
                    point among scholars. See Jack Finegan, *Light from the An-
                    cient Past* (1951), 56 ff.

p. 147, line 40   "'lost phallus.'" See Jacques Lacan, *Écrits: A Selection* (Eng.
                    tr. 1977), 281 ff. Lacan has made this phrase familiar, but I
                    think that what has really been lost in this context is an equal
                    balance of male and female principles, as in Blake's introduc-
                    tion to the *Songs of Experience* referred to in the first footnote.
                    See the summary of interpretations of the Song of Songs in
                    Marvin H. Pope's commentary (Anchor Bible Commen-
                    taries, 1977), esp. 153 ff.

p. 149, line 33   "Blake." The phrase "bound down upon the stems of vegeta-
                    tion" is from *Jerusalem*, pl. 60.

p. 149, line 39   "Greek pun." See Higden's *Polychronicon*, ed. Churchill
                    Babington (Rolls Series), vol. II, lib. ii, cap. 1, 183-85.
                    Trevisa's translation of Higden reads: ". . . and hatte *homo*
                    in Latyn and *antropos* in Grewe, that is as hit were a tree
                    i-torned vp so doun."

p. 150, line 33   "bull of Mithraism." See Franz Cumont, *The Mysteries of
                    Mithra* (Eng. tr. 1956).

p. 151, line 20   "Aurum . . ." This comes from a thirteenth-century poem
                    by Pierre de Corbeil, Archbishop of Sens, beginning "Orien-
                    tis partibus." The stanza quoted means "The ass's strength
                    has brought gold from Arabia and frankincense and myrrh
                    from Sheba into the church" (see Matthew 2:11).

p. 152, line 23   "mourned." For survivals of ritual laments (e.g. Micah 7:1)
                    in the text of the Old Testament see Theodor H. Gaster,
                    Thespis (1950), chap. 1.

p. 157, line 22   "Blake." *Jerusalem*, pl. 69.

p. 158, line 10   "ziggurat temple." The references are to Eliot's "Ash-
                    Wednesday," Yeat's "Blood and the Moon" (along with
                    many associated poems), and Pound's Canto 74, 1. 10.
                    Eliot's imagery is derived from Dante; Yeats's from occult
                    traditions connected with gyres and spirals; Pound's from
                    Herodotus' description in the first book of his *History* of such
                    towers in Ecbatana and Babylon. For the symbolism of the
                    ziggurat see also G. R. Levy, *The Gate of Horn* (1948).

p. 158, line 21   "keystone for the world." See Eric Burrows, "Some Cos-
                    mological Patterns in Babylonian Religion," in *The
                    Labyrinth*, ed. S. H. Hooke (1935), 45 ff.

p. 158, line 32   "Augustine." *City of God,* XV, xxvi. (See also X, xvii, for the other aspect of "ark" imagery.)

p. 159, line 11   "Caligula." See Josephus, *Jewish Antiquities,* XVIII, viii.

p. 159, line 27   "Ugaritic myth." See Pritchard, *ANET,* 129 ff., and Cyrus H. Gordon, "Canaanite Mythology," in *Mythologies of the Ancient World,* ed. S. N. Kramer (1961), 207.

p. 161, line 39   "fire of life." In some speculative literature the fire of life is associated with the temperature of warm-blooded animals. See Berkeley, *Siris,* par. 220 ff.

p. 162, line 8   "Old English poem." Translated by R. K. Gordon in *Anglo-Saxon Poetry* (1926), 265. For the link between *phoinix* as phoenix and as date-palm, see Robert Graves, *The White Goddess* (1948), chap. 11.

p. 166, line 15   "Isaac Watts." "Characters of Christ, borrowed from inanimate Things in Scripture," in *Hymns and Spiritual Songs* (1715).

p. 167, line 5   "recorded outside it." See *The Apocryphal New Testament,* ed. M. R. James (1924), 27, 35. I have quoted the second passage from a hymn based on the fragments.

p. 168, line 4   "D. T. Suzuki." See his *Essays in Zen Buddhism,* 3rd Series (1953), 78 ff.

p. 168, line 27   "Wallace Stevens." "Sunday Morning," *Collected Poems,* 70.

CHAPTER SEVEN

p. 177, line 7   "seventeenth-century England." See Christopher Hill, *The World Turned Upside Down* (1972).

p. 180, line 12   "early sketched outlines." *Works of John Milton* (Columbia ed. 1938), XVIII, 229.

p. 183, line 38   "ghost in Yeats." "All Souls' Night," *Collected Poems* (1950), 256.

p. 192, line 22   "Oannes." This was a fish-god and culture hero of Mesopotamia: see S. H. Langdon, "Semitic Mythology," *Mythology of All Races* (1931), IV, 103-5. Our only information about him comes from a late source, but scholars generally identify him with the Sumerian god Ea or Enki.

p. 198, line 7   "concern for narrative." For some parallels to the views advanced here see Hermann Hesse, "Ein Stückchen Theologie," *Gesammelte Schriften* (1957), VII, 388-402.

CHAPTER EIGHT

p. 200, line 9   "unhandy people." Josephus, *contra Apion,* bk. ii. 15.

p. 203, line 16   "variety of documents." Any of these statements about Luke may be qualified or disputed by scholars, but the one irrefutable fact, that Luke is one of three "Synoptic" Gospels, which are obviously both related to and distinct from one another, makes my point quite as fully.

p. 205, line 4   "'hermetic' literature." See Frances Yates, *Giordano Bruno and the Hermetic Tradition* (1964), chap. 1.

p. 205, line 28   "Tertullian." See James, *op. cit.*, xx, 270.

p. 211, line 4   "consistently a metrical one." See the discussion in Otto Eissfeldt, *The Old Testament: An Introduction* (Eng. tr. 1965), pt. I, sec. ii.

p. 215, line 41   "'pericope'". This word is not widely used in so inclusive a sense (apart from John 8:1-11), but "paradigm" has too many other meanings in English, and it is useful to have a general term that does not entangle us in subdivisions. I should hope that the conception of the pericope as a solution to a technical problem of narration might preserve the essential *Formgeschichte* thesis while evading some of its difficulties.

p. 216, line 4   "one scholar." Martin Dibelius, *From Tradition to Gospel* (Eng. tr. 1934), chap. 8.

p. 216, line 17   "Gurdjieff." See Kenneth Walker, *A Study of Gurdjieff's Teaching* (1957), chap. 7.

p. 220, line 37   "Dante." *Epistola* X, to Can Grande; compare a very similar passage in the *Convivio*, II, i. The verse from the Psalms that Dante quotes is employed in *Purgatorio*, ii, 46.

p. 221, line 20   "Milton." *De Doctrina Christiana*, I, xxx.

p. 226, line 32   "Blake's figure." *Jerusalem*, pl. 77.

p. 227, line 13   "recent critical study." Frederic Jameson, *The Prison-House of Language* (1972).

p. 228, line 13   "Milton." *De Doctrina Christiana*, I, xxx.

p. 232, line 33   "geodesic domes." The phrase is purely a rhetorical illustration, and implies no reflection on Mr. Buckminster Fuller's proposals for such structures.

Index

Index of Passages

OLD TESTAMENT

APOCRYPHA

NEW TESTAMENT